P9-APA-709

2nd edition

TURNSTILE JUSTICE
ISSUES IN AMERICAN CORRECTIONS

Hall

Upper Saddle River, New Jersey 07458

Library of Congress Cataloging-in-Publication Data

Turnstile Justice: issues in American corrections / edited by Rosemary L. Gido,
Ted Alleman, 2. ed.
    p. cm.
    Includes bibliographical references.
    ISBN 0-13-040952-9
    1. Corrections—United States, I. Gido, Rosemary L. II. Alleman, Ted.

HV9471.T87 2002
365'.973—dc21

00-068201

Publisher: Jeff Johnston
Executive Editor: Kim Davies
Production Editor: Linda B. Pawelchak
Production Liaison: Barbara Marttine Cappuccio
Director of Production and Manufacturing: Bruce Johnson
Managing Editor: Mary Carnis
Manufacturing Buyer: Cathleen Petersen
Cover Design Coordinator: Miguel Ortiz
Cover Image: © Tracey L. Williams / Williams Stock Images
Cover Designer: Lorraine Castellano
Marketing Manager: Ramona Sherman
Editorial Assistant: Sarah Holle
Marketing Assistant: Barbara Rosenberg
Composition: Lithokraft II
Printing and Binding: R.R. Donnelley & Sons

Prentice-Hall International (UK) Limited, *London*
Prentice-Hall of Australia Pty. Limited, *Sydney*
Prentice-Hall Canada Inc., *Toronto*
Prentice-Hall Hispanoamericana, S.A., *Mexico*
Prentice-Hall of India Private Limited, *New Delhi*
Prentice-Hall of Japan, Inc., *Tokyo*
Pearson Education Asia Pte. Ltd., *Singapore*
Editora Prentice-Hall do Brasil, Ltda., *Rio de Janeiro*

10 9 8 7 6 5 4 3 2 1
ISBN 0-13-040952-9

This book was conceptualized by Ted Alleman as part of his continuing mission to put forward quality educational materials for students of criminal justice. We had no idea that Ted's life would be so tragically shortened, as he left us on May 16, 1996. Ted's spirit and concern for the incarcerated come through the pages of his writings. May this book challenge those who read it to think critically about "turnstile justice" and the implications of imprisonment as we enter the twenty-first century.

Rosemary L. Gido

CONTENTS

5

THE INMATE SUBCULTURE IN JUVENILE CORRECTIONAL SETTINGS 57

Dorothy L. Taylor
University of Miami

Wilson R. Palacios
University of South Florida

6

HEALTH CARE FOR WOMEN OFFENDERS: CHALLENGE FOR THE NEW CENTURY 73

Phyllis Harrison Ross, M.D.
Retired, New York Medical College at Metropolitan Hospital

James E. Lawrence
New York State Commission of Correction

7

JAILED FATHERS: PATERNAL REACTIONS TO SEPARATION FROM CHILDREN 89

Jamie S. Martin
Indiana University of Pennsylvania

8

THE DEVELOPMENT AND DIVERSITY OF CORRECTIONAL BOOT CAMPS 115

Gaylene Styve Armstrong
Arizona State University West

Angela R. Gover
University of South Carolina

Doris Layton MacKenzie
University of Maryland

9

DETENTION IN INS JAILS: BUREAUCRACY, BRUTALITY, AND A BOOMING BUSINESS 131

Michael Welch
Rutgers University

10

POSTSECONDARY CORRECTIONAL EDUCATION: THE IMPRISONED UNIVERSITY 145

Jon Marc Taylor
Inmate, Missouri Department of Corrections

Richard Tewksbury
University of Louisville

11

COMMUNITY PERCEPTIONS ABOUT PRISON CONSTRUCTION: A CASE STUDY 176

Randy Martin
Indiana University of Pennsylvania

David Champion
University of Pittsburgh

Todd Gibney
Indiana University of Pennsylvania

12

BUILDING LOCAL NETWORKS: A GUIDE FOR JAIL ADMINISTRATOR LEADERSHIP 208

Dave Kalinich
Grand Valley State University

Bruce Bikle
Grand Valley State University

PREFACE

Turnstile Justice: Issues in American Corrections, second edition, provides students and practitioners in the field of corrections a set of thoughtful and critical readings on contemporary correctional issues. Designed as a free-standing text or supplement to course materials across the criminal justice/corrections spectrum, the book offers a sociology of corrections—a perspective for analyzing the social context within which current American punishment philosophy and practice take place. The author(s) of each chapter provides factual information and data on an issue or topic for the reader to examine critically for its impact on the correctional system and on society in general.

The first three chapters set the tone for the entire book by outlining a context for studying American corrections. In Chapter 1, Rosemary Gido, using the analogy of a *turnstile,* reviews the major factors that have, at the turn of the millennium, propelled the United States to become the democratic nation with the highest incarceration rate in the world. Gido illustrates the impact of the war on drugs and the politicalization of corrections behind the U.S. "incarceration binge," documenting the high percentages of drug offenders and minorities who have come through the corrections turnstile in the past 15 years. A set of fundamental questions about corrections is offered to the reader of this text as a focus for the issues covered in the remaining chapters. Linked to the race and class issues of Chapter 1, John Klofas (Chapter 2) offers an in-depth analysis of the social changes in

American cities and society and the conditions that are undermining urban community structure and vitality. Klofas thoughtfully draws out the implications of "metropolitanization" and our current "penaholic" correctional practices. Ted Alleman's Chapter 3 provides a unique, comprehensive analysis of the implications of the three predominant American correctional philosophies—utilitarian, justice, and rehabilitation—on the treatment of offenders. A practical typology matrix (page 36) summarizes features of each punishment approach.

The next two chapters take us inside the prison to understand the norms and values that form the basis of inmate subcultures today. Drawing on the rich tradition of Daniel Clemmer's *The Prison Community,* the authors focus on the violence that is endemic to adult and juvenile correctional facilities today. In Chapter 4, Victor Hassine, who writes from 19 years of imprisonment experience, provides a participant observer's insights on adult prison violence. His study documents both predictors of individual violent behavior (kindling points for violence) and prison environment variables that accelerate or retard violent behaviors and trends. Dorothy Taylor and Wilson Palacios delineate the social codes and social roles of inmates in juvenile correctional facilities in Chapter 5. Recognizing the impact of contemporary street gangs, the authors summarize the research on the war on gangs and the impact that juvenile gangs are having on juvenile correctional facilities.

Chapters 6 to 10 offer a comprehensive evaluation of five emerging correctional issues: treatment needs of women offenders, jailed fathers and their separation from their children, the variety of boot camps as alternatives for incarcerating adults and juveniles, noncitizens in U.S federal detention centers, and educational services for inmates. Phyllis Harrison Ross and James Lawrence in Chapter 6 challenge the traditional treatment regimes of women's prisons in the United States. Harrison Ross and Lawrence document the increase of poor and minority women in U.S. prisons and the impact on correctional systems of increased and intensified demand for specialized health care services. In Chapter 7, Jamie Martin summarizes her study of jailed fathers, a topic rarely researched in contemporary criminology. Martin refutes the stereotype of "the incarcerated father" and emphasizes the need to focus on the men who were involved in the lives of their children prior to incarceration. Contact visits with children, parent education, family contact programs, and inmate-family reunification programs after release are recommended. Gaylene Styve Armstrong, Angela Gover, and Doris MacKenzie offer a comprehensive report on U.S. prison and jail boot camps for adults and juveniles in Chapter 8. This chapter further clarifies differences in boot camp programming, such as treatment focus, the selection process, and eligibility requirements. Special issues for boot camp operations for female offenders and juveniles and evaluations of boot camp impact on recidivism, community supervision, and prison crowding are reported. Michael Welch assesses allegations of human rights violations in Immigration and Naturalization Service (INS) detention centers and outlines the problems inherent in INS detention practices in Chapter 9. Ongoing bureaucratic inefficiency, incidents of institutional brutality, and the increase of prison privatization are carefully documented in this chapter. Finally, Jon Marc Taylor and Richard Tewksbury examine the history and update the political developments and debates around the issue of postsecondary correctional education. Given the elimination of all state and federal inmates' eligibility for educational assistance through the Pell Grant Program since 1994 to 1995, the authors offer an in-depth review of the impact of educational programming and issues relevant to its recent demise.

The remaining two chapters in *Turnstile Justice* focus our attention on issues of key interest to practitioners and members of the community: the impact of new prison construction and the operations of the local jail. Randy Martin, David Champion, and Todd Gibney conducted a community attitude survey in a county in which the construction of a new prison had just begun. Residents were asked to indicate their expectations about the impact of the prison on their community, with a focus on safety issues, economic impact, and overall quality of life. The authors offer insights on interpreting community input and improving the prison siting process in Chapter 11. In Chapter 12, David Kalinich and Bruce Bikle address the problems of managing jails in the community. The authors challenge today's jail administrators to network with their partner agencies in the criminal justice system and take a leadership role in both improving the administration of the jail and providing an ongoing positive working environment for each agency in the network.

The following reviewers made helpful suggestions for this edition: William Kelly, Auburn University; Richard H. Martin, Elgin Community College; and Mary K. Stohr, Boise State University.

ABOUT THE CONTRIBUTORS

Ted Alleman was an instructor of sociology and criminal justice at two Pennsylvania State University campuses for 20 years. Drawing on his experience as a systems analyst, he designed a computerized jail management system used in Pennsylvania and New Jersey and authored the text *Introduction to Computing in Criminal Justice* (1996). Mr. Alleman also taught in several Pennsylvania correctional institutions.

Gaylene Styve Armstrong is visiting assistant professor in the Department of Administration of Justice at Arizona State University West. Dr. Styve Armstrong has recently completed studies examining the institutional environments in juvenile correctional facilities and the impact of these environments on juveniles' adjustment. Additionally, she has completed a national evaluation that examined the impact of privatization on the quality of juvenile correctional facilities.

Bruce Bikle is assistant professor of criminal justice at Grand Valley State University in Grand Rapids Michigan. He received his Ph.D. from Portland State University in Public Administration and Policy. Dr. Bikle has worked in both line and staff assignments in prison and jail systems and law enforcement agencies in Hawaii, Washington, Oregon, and California.

David Champion is assistant professor in the Administration of Justice Department, University of Pittsburgh—Bradford. He has a background in psychology and law enforcement. His current research focus is an examination of psychological/personality determinants of sexually aggressive behavior.

Todd Gibney is a doctoral candidate in the Department of Criminology, Indiana University of Pennsylvania. He has a background in both criminal justice and computer science. One of his main research interests at present is crime among Native Americans.

Rosemary L. Gido is associate professor in the Department of Criminology, Indiana University of Pennsylvania. The former director of research, Office of Program and Policy Analysis, New York State Commission of Correction, she directed the first national prison-based study of HIV/AIDS in the New York State prison system. A teacher at the college or university level for 30 years, her current research interest is a criminological analysis of the Molly Maguires. Dr. Gido is the editor of *The Prison Journal*.

Angela R. Gover is assistant professor in the College of Criminal Justice at the University of South Carolina. Her research interests include corrections, juvenile justice, family violence, and evaluation research.

Victor Hassine is an inmate at the Pennsylvania State Correctional Institution, Albion, Pennsylvania. He holds a B.A. degree from Dickenson College and a J.D. degree from New York School of Law. Mr. Hassine is the author of *Life Without Parole* (1996) and the play *Circles of Nod.*

Dave Kalinich is professor of criminal justice, Grand Valley State University in Grand Rapids, Michigan. He has authored and coauthored a number of books and articles in the areas of adult corrections and criminal justice administration. Dr. Kalinich has also been active in training and consulting with jails and prisons and served as a parole and probation officer for the State of Ohio for a number of years.

John M. Klofas is professor and chairperson in the Department of Criminal Justice, Rochester Institute of Technology. His research has been in the area of prisons and jails, and he is the coauthor of *Criminal Justice Organizaions: Administration and Management.* Most recently, Dr. Klofas has been focusing on issues of metropolitan development and criminal justice.

James E. Lawrence is director of operations for the New York State Commission of Correction. His 20 years' experience in the fields of prisoner mortality and correctional health care include work as a forensic medical investigator and director of the New York State Correction Medical Review

Board. He has taught various topics in correctional health care at New York Medical College School of Public Health and authored several articles on correctional health care.

Doris Layton MacKenzie is professor in the Department of Criminology and Criminal Justice at the University of Maryland. She has completed studies examining inmate adjustment to prison, the impact of intermediate sanctions on recidivism, methods of predicting prison populations, and a multisite study of boot camp prisons. Dr. MacKenzie has also directed studies examining probationers' compliance with conditions of supervision and the use of a cognitive skills program to change offenders.

Jamie S. Martin is assistant professor in the Department of Criminology at Indiana University of Pennsylvania. She has worked in the juvenile justice and mental health fields. Dr. Martin has previously published an article in the *Journal of Research in Crime and Delinquency*. Her primary research interest lies in the area of parenting issues among incarcerated fathers.

Randy Martin is professor of criminology at Indiana University of Pennsylvania. He has worked in a variety of corrections-related areas and has published articles on HIV in prison, prison riots, and risk assessment of community corrections placements. In addition, he has a long-standing interest in transpersonal and peacemaking perspectives and their application in criminology and criminal justice.

Wilson R. Palacios is assistant professor in the Department of Criminology at the University of South Florida. He holds a Ph.D. from the University of Miami, Department of Sociology. His research interests include minority risk-taking behavior, criminal justice education, and qualitative research methods.

Phyllis Harrison Ross, M.D. is a nationally recognized expert in forensic psychiatry and correctional medicine. Recently retired, Dr. Harrison Ross was professor of clinical psychiatry at New York Medical College at Metropolitan Hospital and president of the Medical Board, staff associate medical director, and director of the Department of Psychiatry and Community Mental Health Center at Metropolitan Hospital Center in New York, New York.

Dorothy L. Taylor is associate professor of sociology, University of Miami. Her research interests include delinquency theories and minorities and criminality. Dr. Taylor has published articles in *The Journal of Black Psychology, The Journal of Criminal Justice Education,* and *Juvenile and Family Court Journal*. Her current publications include *The Positive*

Influence of Bonding in Female-Headed African American Families and *Jumpstarting Your Career: An Internship Guide for Criminal Justice.*

Jon Marc Taylor is an inmate at the Jefferson City, Missouri, Correctional Center. He holds B.A. and M.A. degrees from Ball State University. The winner of both the Nation/I.F. Stone and Robert F. Kennedy Awards for student journalism, Mr. Taylor has authored scholarly articles that have appeared in the *Journal of Contemporary Criminal Justice, Journal of Correctional Education,* and *The Criminologist.*

Richard Tewksbury is professor of justice administration at the University of Louisville. His research interests include correctional education program evaluation, criminal victimization risks, sexual behavior, and gender identity management. He is the author of numerous scholarly journal articles and book chapters and editor of *Extreme Methods: Innovative Approaches to Social Science Research* (2001).

Michael Welch is associate professor in the administration of justice program, Rutgers University. He has correctional experience at the federal, state, and local level and his research interests include corrections and social control. Dr. Welch has published articles in *Justice Quarterly, Journal of Research in Crime and Delinquency,* and *Social Justice.* The author of *Punishment in America: Social Control and the Ironies of Punishment* (1999), he currently serves as coeditor of *Social Pathology: A Journal of Reviews.*

chapter 1

TURNSTILE JUSTICE
AMERICAN CORRECTIONS
IN THE NEW MILLENNIUM

ROSEMARY L. GIDO
Indiana University of Pennsylvania

INTRODUCTION

As we enter the new millennium, the U.S. corrections' turnstile has admitted almost 2 million individuals into an ever-expanding social control machine we refer to as *jails* and *prisons*. Slowly, but relentlessly, the U.S. federal and state penal systems have geared up and grown into a vast corrections-industrial complex over the last 25 years (Welch, 1999). This "machine" has tripled America's prison population since 1980, while crime rates have been flat or declining. Although criminologists are no better predictors of complex future trends than economists, the social, economic, ideological, and political forces that have fueled our current "incarceration binge" (Irwin and Austin, 1997) are not likely to decline over the next decade (Crouch, 1996). Applying the analogy of a turnstile, this chapter reviews the major factors that have propelled the United States into becoming the democratic nation with the highest incarceration rate in the world (The Sentencing Project, 1997). Based on the analysis of these

1

factors, the importance of studying emerging correctional issues is linked to a number of fundamental questions for assessing the proper role of corrections in U.S. society in the near future.

THE CORRECTIONS TURNSTILE

The standard dictionary definition of *turnstile* is "a post with bars that turn, set in an entrance or exit. The bars are turned to let one person through at a time" (*The World Book Dictionary,* 1981: 2253). Central to the incarceration debate in the United States is the notion that the corrections' turnstile is really a "revolving door." This indictment of our system was accepted by liberal scholars of the 1970s (Petersen and Thomas, 1975: 3) and "nailed to the prison door" after the release of The Martinson Report, which documented the failure of all forms of rehabilitation to prevent inmates from coming back to prison (Martinson, 1997).

Twenty-five years ago, inmates entering and re-entering the corrections' turnstile in the United States were more violent than they are today. The total violent crime victimization rate per 1,000 population in 1973 was 47.7 compared to 36.0 in 1998 ("Violent Crime Trends"). Similarly, total property crime victimizations for those comparison years were 519.9 and 217.4, respectively ("Property Crime Trends"). From the 1980s, high visibility reporting of the "crime problem" by the media, labeled "crime news entertainment" (Kappeler et al., 2000: 11), and the distortion of crime information by political office seekers produced a generalized public fear of crime. With attitudinal change came the emergence of the justice model (see Chapter 3) as the key sentencing philosophy in the United States (Irwin and Austin, 1997: 4–7). Finally, the declaration of a war on drugs starting with the Reagan administration set in place a number of forces that increased the numbers entering and returning through the corrections' turnstile:

> In the federal prison system, the number of persons serving time for drug offenses has more than doubled since 1981 and now accounts for 71 percent of the inmate population. On the state and local level. . . . Nearly 36 percent of the rise in the state prison population between 1985 and 1994 was the result of an increase in the number of inmates convicted for drug offenses. In addition, the increased emphasis on drug testing has contributed to a higher failure rate among parolees . . . . "a 284 percent increase in the number of parole violators returned to prison between 1997 and 1998." (Kappeler et al., 2000: 268)

Linked to the increase in the number and length of drug offense incarcerations, policies initiated as part of the War on Drugs have been charged with initiating racially discriminatory practices in processing drug offenders (Sampson and Lauritsen, 1997: 360). Aggressive law enforcement initiatives directed at the crack cocaine market of U.S. inner cities during the 1980s resulted in increased African American youth court referrals for drug law violations while white youth referrals to court declined (Sampson and Lauritsen, 1997: 360).

Along with criminal justice policy shifts by the police and courts, Congress passed the Sentencing Reform Act of 1984. The implementation of U.S. sentencing guidelines and the Reform Act's establishment of federal mandatory minimum sentences for drug (and other) offenses are at the heart of the sentencing disparity issue today. The 1986 mandatory minimum sentences for selling or possessing 50 grams of crack were equal to those convicted of selling 100 times these amounts of powder cocaine. A 1995 U.S. Sentencing Commission Report investigating the impact of this disparity found that more than 88.0 percent of crack cocaine–sentenced offenders were African American compared to 4.1 percent of whites (del Carmen, 2000: 93–94).

The impact on the numbers of African American men coming through the corrections turnstile has been dramatic. Of the almost 1.9 million offenders in U.S. jails and prisons on June 30, 1999, 12.3 percent were black, non-Hispanic males between the ages of 25 to 29, compared to 4.2 percent Hispanic males and about 1.5 percent white males in this age group (Bureau of Justice Statistics, 2000: 10).

The War on Drugs has also been viewed as a "war against women" (Kappeler et al., 2000: 164). Again, based on mid-year 1999 statistics, the female prison population in state and federal prisons has almost doubled since 1990—from 44,065 on December 31, 1990, to 87,199 on June 30, 1999 (Bureau of Justice Statistics, 2000: 4). Overall, drug offense– enhanced enforcement and reduced judicial discretion in sentencing have had the greatest impact on African American women. State prison commitments for drug charges rose 828 percent for black women between 1986 and 1991 (Kappeler, 2000: 164). As these women who are likely to be mothers and single heads of the household have moved steadily through the corrections turnstile, few program and policy changes have been made to assist the children they leave behind (Belknap, 1996: 263).

With little sign of reducing either the growth of prison and jail populations or the politicalization of punishment as an issue in the United States in the new millennium, students of the sociology of corrections, practitioners, scholars, and citizens can consider a number of fundamental questions as they focus on the issues covered in *Turnstile Justice: Issues in American Corrections.*

Questions Underlying Contemporary
Corrections Issues

What types of people are subject to correctional and social control? Who is being imprisoned, why, for how long, and under what conditions? Is there any evidence that citizens are being imprisoned to further political ends? Is there any evidence of biased or discriminatory treatment on the part of the correctional system?

Does the punishment fit the crime? Is the cost of punishment in line with the cost of crime? Is there any evidence that fear and emotion, rather than fairness and justice, are driving correctional policy making? Are there segments of the correctional population that are subject to levels of control beyond those required?

How effective is the criminal justice system? Are correctional agencies able to deliver on promises of less crime in exchange for more resources? Which correctional practices result in lowered rates of recidivism and which do not? In terms of doing justice and protecting society, which offender types must be imprisoned and which need not be? What are the most effective alternatives to incarceration?

What are the conditions of confinement? Are they humane and fair? Are correctional environments safe and secure or violent and dehumanizing? What effect does correctional practice have on those released from the system as well as those who find themselves working with or living next to ex-offenders?

Are correctional practices the outcome of informed and reasoned debate, or do they simply reflect unfounded fear and ignorance? On what basis is new criminal legislation proposed? Is it advanced on the basis of slick political slogans and myths, or is it an outcome of an informed public debate that combines established facts with clear policy alternatives?

What is the proper role of corrections in a democratic society? Is there evidence that the criminal justice system is treating as criminals citizens who are generally nonviolent and law abiding? Are victimless acts being defined as crimes? Are classes of innocent people being confined for political or economic reasons? To what extent are expenditures on crime and crime control diverting funds from other legitimate and needed social services? To what extent are we, as citizens, willing to trade personal liberties and freedoms for an increased police presence in our lives?

REFERENCES

Belknap, J. (1996). *The Invisible Woman: Gender, Crime and Justice.* New York: Wadsworth.

Bureau of Justice Statistics (April 2000). *Prison and Jail Inmates at Midyear 1999.* Washington DC: U.S. Department of Justice.

Crouch, B. M. (1996). "Looking Back to See the Future of Corrections." *The Prison Journal* 76(4): 486–487.

del Carmen, A. (2000). *Corrections: Blueprints.* Madison, WI: Coursewise.

Irwin, J. and Austin, J. (1997). *It's About Time: America's Imprisonment Binge* (2d ed.). New York: Wadsworth.

Kappeler, V. E., Blumberg, M., and Potter, G. W. (2000). *The Mythology of Crime and Criminal Justice.* (3d ed.). Prospect Heights, IL: Waveland.

Martinson, R. (1997). "What Works"—Questions and Answers About Prison Reform." In J. W. Marquart and J. R. Sorensen (eds.), *Correctional Contexts: Contemporary and Classical Readings.* Los Angeles, CA: Roxbury: 290–311.

Petersen, D. M., and Thomas, C. W. (eds.). (1975). *Corrections: Problems and Prospects.* Englewood Cliffs, NJ: Prentice-Hall.

"Property Crime Trends." [*www.ojp.usdoj.gov/bjs/glance/proptrd.txt*]. Bureau of Justice Statistics Web site.

Sampson, R. J. and Lauritsen, J. L. (1997). "Racial and Ethnic Disparities in Crime and Criminal Justice in the United States." In M. Tonry (ed.), *Ethnicity, Crime, and Immigration: Comparative and Cross-National Perspectives,* Vol. 21. Chicago: University of Chicago Press: 311–374.

The Sentencing Project. (1997). *Americans Behind Bars: US and International Use of Incarceration.* Washington, DC: The Sentencing Project.

"Violent Crime Trends." [*www.ojp.usdoj.gov/bjs/glance/viotrd.txt*]. Bureau of Justice Statistics Web site.

Welch, M. (1999). *Punishment in America: Social Control and the Ironies of Imprisonment.* Thousand Oaks, CA: Sage.

The World Book Dictionary (1981). "turnstile". Chicago: World Book-Childcraft International: 2253.

chapter 2

OUTSIDE IN
SOCIETAL CHANGE
AND ITS IMPACT ON CORRECTIONS

JOHN M. KLOFAS
Rochester Institute of Technology

INTRODUCTION

In criminal justice, ideas and the language used to describe them can change rapidly. With regularity, once key concepts seem to drift to the margins of academic and policy discourse. Some disappear entirely. Others are resurrected.

Once cast aside, the vocabulary of dismissed ideas inevitably sounds stunted, archaic, and—to some perhaps—even a bit loony. Think of "prison democracies," "prisoner labor unions," or even "prison furloughs." Old theories of crime and its correction are to contemporary crime policy as moon children and flower power are to today's corporate ladder climbers.

One idea whose status seems in question today is that the social conditions of American communities have important implications for criminal justice and corrections. On first glance, the truth behind that idea may seem obvious, but you would be hard pressed to find that truth reflected in many contemporary criminal justice analyses.

Even those chasing law enforcement's "holy grail," community policing, would have to admit that the objective conditions of communities—their racial, ethnic, and economic makeup, for example—have not figured prominently in their work (Buerger, 1994: 270–273). The justification for this seems to be the belief that good policing can overcome the influence of other community forces such as poverty, poor housing stock, and racial and economic segregation (Kelling, 1998). In that way, community policing denies rather than affirms the power of community conditions.

Not long ago, community occupied a much different place in the hearts and minds of many criminologists. Interest in community conditions was central to virtually all major governmental task forces and commissions on crime and justice. Most prominent among those was The Report of the President's Commission on Law Enforcement and Administration of Justice in 1967.

CORRECTIONS THEN AND NOW

In 1967, The President's Commission contrasted the "old model" in which criminal justice was regarded as a contest between the police and the criminal with a "new model" in which there emerged the broad role of maintaining order in communities. The Commission focused on urban environments and identified social conditions in communities as a primary ingredient defining the role of criminal justice.

The Commission wrote the following:

> It is in the cities that the conditions of life are the worst, that social tensions are the most acute, that riots occur, that crime rates are the highest, that the fear of crime and the demand for effective action against it are the strongest (1967: 91).

For the Commission, crime and delinquency were symptoms of failures and disorganization of the community as well as of individual offenders (Task Force on Corrections, 1967: 7).

The logic of this view of communities permeated the task force reports of the President's Commission. In corrections, the argument justified a new and radically different goal: offender reintegration (1967: 7). The Commission wrote:

> The task of corrections . . . includes building or rebuilding ties between the offender and community, integrating or reintegrating the offender into community life—restoring family ties, obtaining employment and education, securing in the larger sense a place for the offender in the routine functioning of society. This requires not

only efforts directed toward changing the individual offender, which has been almost the exclusive focus of rehabilitation, but also mobilization and change of the community and its institutions. (Task Force on Corrections, 1967: 7)

The concept and language of reintegration may seem alien at a time when incapacitation, deterrence, and punishment dominate the discourse of corrections. But in 1967, the President's Commission seemed willing and even anxious to understand the social conditions that seemed to be effecting American society. By contrast, social conditions, especially concentrated poverty and racial isolation, have today become the "elephant in the living room"—obvious, omnipresent—but often unacknowledged.

FROM URBAN TO METROPOLITAN COMMUNITIES

The 1992 presidential election was a milestone in electoral politics. It was the first such election in which a majority of the votes came from suburban communities rather than from cities and rural areas (Schneider, 1992). It was an important landmark in the movement of the population of the nation from a primarily urban to a primarily metropolitan population. This signals a sea change in American society similar to the country's movement from a rural and agrarian nation to an urban one a hundred years ago (Jackson, 1985). And just as those early changes had broad implications for communities, so does the metropolitanization of much of American society.

At least six trends characterize this shift in American society. In many ways, the trends are universal, affecting all American communities, although their strongest effects may be in older cities. In this case, the trends can be illustrated by examining the cities of upstate New York. These industrial northeast cities provide a good demonstration of these national trends.

Shrinking Cities—Expanding Suburbs

Many small and medium-size cities, particularly those in the Northeast, have seen dramatic population shifts. For example, peak population levels for upstate New York cities were reached with the 1950 census. Over the next 40 years, the populations of Buffalo, Rochester, Syracuse, Utica, and Albany declined by between 25 percent and 43 percent. The largest loser was Buffalo. Its population fell from 580,000 to 328,000 during this period. In Rochester, the population fell by more than 100,000.

While city populations fell, their suburbs grew, spurred on by highway construction and favorable financing and tax policies (Jackson, 1985).

Buffalo's suburbs grew by 100 percent between the 1950 and 1990 censuses. As the City of Rochester lost nearly one-third of its population, its suburbs grew by more than 200 percent. In 1950, two thirds of all Rochester area residents lived in the city. By 1990, that situation had reversed and two-thirds of area residents lived in Rochester's suburbs. As the cities shrank and their suburbs expanded, other changes also occurred.

Increased Racial Segregation

The movement to the suburbs has not been uniform across demographic groups. Whites fled the cities at fairly uniform rates during the past 40 years. In Buffalo, 1.0 out of every 1.6 whites left the city. In Rochester, 1.0 of every 1.8 whites left. As whites left the cities, the nonwhite population increased as a proportion of the total city population and in real numbers.

A nonwhite migration into the cities by blacks and later by Latinos has been masked by the overall decline in city populations. As late as 1950, nonwhites composed only 3 percent of the population of the City of Rochester. That rate was 40 percent in the 1990 census. From 1950 to 1990, the nonwhite population grew by more than 200 percent in Buffalo and by more than 350 percent in Albany.

As the proportion of nonwhite residents of the cities grew rapidly, the suburbs remained almost exclusively white. The upstate suburban towns and villages have generally stayed below a nonwhite level of 5 percent.

Increasing Concentration of Poverty in Cities

As overall city populations decreased and their minority populations increased, cities also experienced dramatic increases in their rates of poverty (Wilson, 1987). Between 1970 and 1990, poverty levels increased by two to three times across the four New York cities. More than one-quarter of Buffalo's population fell below the poverty level in 1990. The other cities all experienced poverty levels of around 20 percent.

In Rochester, half of all census tracts are now classified as "high-poverty" tracts in which 20 percent or more of the population lives below the federal poverty level. The metropolitan region's extreme poverty tracts, with poverty levels of 40 percent or more, are all located in the City of Rochester.

Along with the racial gap between cities and suburbs, the poverty gap is increasing. Suburban poverty levels have changed only slightly as urban poverty has increased. Only Utica's suburbs reached a poverty level as high as 8 percent. The other metro-area suburbs had poverty rates of 4 or 5 percent for the 1990 census.

Strain on Urban Institutions

A fourth trend associated with the metropolitanization of communities involves the strain this places on urban institutions. Institutions that functioned for an urban society may not serve their new metropolitan communities as well. The best example may be public education; many urban school systems appear to be failing because they are overwhelmed by the concentrated poverty of the urban core (M. Orfield, 1997).

The Rochester school system provides an illustration. Although city poverty levels are at the 25 percent mark, the figure is much higher for children. According to census figures, 38 percent of Rochester's children fall below the poverty line. That figure is still much higher when the public school system is considered. As late as 1980, 22 percent of Rochester school district children were from families who met income requirements to participate in the free and reduced cost lunch program. In 1998, the figure had risen to 90 percent.

Those high poverty levels have also been tied to falling student performance. When comparing educational outcomes, city schools do not compare well with their suburban counterparts. In the Rochester metro area, 85 of 100 suburban students entering high school can be expected to graduate in four years. In the city school district, however, that number is just 27. And only 5 percent of city students as compared with 50 percent of suburban students will earn Regents diplomas—the highest standard in New York and the standard currently being phased in as a general graduation requirement for all students.

The situation in Rochester is not unique. According to Gary Orfield (1997), urban education across the country suffers similar problems. Although some classrooms and even schools do fair better, no school district as a whole has made significant progress in the face of such high poverty levels.

Spread of Effects to Inner Ring. Movement to the suburbs actually began in the 1930s but escalated dramatically after World War II. The early suburbs, which grew on the outskirts of cities, were the first expanding bands of development that reached out many miles around most cities. Now those early inner ring suburbs are experiencing many problems once regarded as limited to cities. Increasingly, those suburban inner rings are being plagued by decaying infrastructures, faltering local economies, and growing pockets of poverty.

A pattern being repeated around the country shows a decline of many inner ring suburbs as wealth and resources move ever outward, often clustered in one direction, which has been referred to as a community's "golden crescent" (M. Orfield, 1997). In these crescents, executive homes, office parks, and upscale retailing thrive while drawing resources from the central city and now the inner suburbs as well. But those inner suburbs lack even the strength of the city's business district or the concentration of social services found in cities, and so they may decline further and faster than even the urban core (Rusk, 1995).

This trend is illustrated by the condition of Rochester's inner ring of suburbs. The oldest suburbs are experiencing population declines and very slow rates of economic growth. In the inner ring of suburbs, tax base growth has averaged 32 percent over the past 20 years while it has been 132 percent in the fastest-growing "golden crescent" suburbs.

What was once regarded as differences between cities and their suburbs is now surfacing in the form of disparities across suburbs. The tax base of the City of Rochester has not grown in more than 20 years and is beginning to show significant declines. Total assessed value fell by 13 percent in the most recent year of available data.

Sprawl to Outer Ring and Rural Areas

The final trend, which can be recognized as part of the metropolitanization of communities, is the continued sprawl of suburban development. Since 1970, the population of Greater Rochester has increased by a mere 30 percent but the overall urbanized land use has increased by more than 100 percent. Similar patterns are found for other cities across the country. Communities continue to use land at a pace far faster than their population increases.

THE SOCIAL MEANING OF METROPOLITANIZATION

In the nineteenth century, as the nation raced from its agrarian roots toward urbanization, the reform of social institutions and the development of new ones was inevitable. Public health, housing reform, and improved public education are only a few of the reforms that occurred with burgeoning cities. In criminal justice, institutional treatment of offenders and later the juvenile court and alternative sanctions such as probation and parole were all tied to the great change in American society.

In the midst of this tumultuous change, however, not everyone embraced the new urban America. In the late nineteenth century, the Populist Party emerged as a reactionary force in American politics. Populists pushed an agenda of economic and social reform that was meant to support threatened agrarian and rural interests. By the turn of the century, the Populist Party had all but disappeared, overwhelmed by the forces of industrialization and urbanization.

Today, a clear reform agenda addressing metropolitanization is only beginning to emerge (Rusk, 1999). As yet, no consistent national policy has developed, and states and localities are struggling sporadically with initiatives such as Smart Growth, a planning movement intended to address urban sprawl (Bollier, 1998). Like the Populists of the last century, many city and suburban interests resist such an agenda and desire a return to an earlier era.

Despite the modern populists, the social implications of this demographic shift are substantial. Left unchecked, many are also quite harmful.

The movement of people from city to suburbs has enabled them to experience home ownership, fine schools, and rising property values. Many have gone to the suburbs in search of the American dream. And many, both whites and minorities, have found it there. At a time when technology is making the world smaller and bringing cultures together, however, this pattern of development also threatens to divide us.

With the growth of metropolitan areas there has also been a growth in the distance, both physical and social, between our nation's poor and her middle and upper classes. As Wilson (1987) has pointed out, it is a distance with significant economic and cultural consequences. As it widens, a burgeoning underclass falls further from social mainstream.

The isolation by class and by race can also be exacerbated as opportunities for success through education, for example, are closed or remain closed to succeeding generations of poor children. Conditions in poor neighborhoods are also likely to grow worse as local municipal budgets are strained.

The decline of the urban core and the population spread to older suburbs cannot occur without even wider social consequences. The great question for the near future will be whether we can build communities without building barriers. Fear can strengthen psychological barriers and engender hostility and conflict in older suburbs. It can spawn gated communities in the developing outer ring, and it can push aside the bucolic isolation of rural America as we sprawl ever outward.

METROPOLITANIZATION AND CORRECTIONS

The world of corrections cannot long remain insulated from the changing social world around it. The President's Commission in 1967 first acknowledged the broad community influences on the components of criminal justice. Each office, agency, and institution is tied to the others in the criminal justice system, influenced by them and by the world beyond them.

The logic of such influences suggests ways in which metropolitanization may be important to corrections.

Preeminence of the Police

As urban areas continue to experience the growing concentration of poverty, concern with its effects is certain to rise. That concern will ensure that policing and its current efforts to address problems of order and perceived disorder will dominate the criminal justice system including corrections.

Community policing, in all of its various forms from problem solving to concentrating on quality of life offenses, has come to emphasize the goal of restoring order in urban neighborhoods (Kelling and Coles, 1996: 21). Until recently, corrections, even at the local level, have had a little role in these efforts. Instead corrections reformers have pursued policies intended to reduce the level of short-term incarceration, to control jail crowding, and to establish alternatives to pretrial detention. Appearance tickets, release on recognizance and other bail alternatives, and night and weekend arraignment courts are only a few of the policy directions pursued with the goal of reducing pretrial incarceration (Hall et al., 1985; Klofas, 1990). Underlying such policies was a philosophical position advocating minimizing the use of incarceration, which was viewed as unnecessary or even harmful to the individual.

Neither those philosophical underpinnings of local corrections nor the policies that flow from them can expect to find broad support in a climate in which order maintenance takes precedence. Instead, police, politicians, and citizens are likely to look to local corrections to support the mission of aggressive order maintenance. Limiting the use of jail incarceration is likely to find little support.

The assertion of community rights under an order maintenance approach relies heavily on police discretion to arrest and to detain (Kelling and Coles, 1996). Although confinement following arrest on minor changes may be for only short periods of time, confinement none the less may be seen as contributing to order maintenance efforts. In addition, there are few checks on police use of short-term detention. As Kelling and Coles (1996: 176) point out, neither the courts nor legislatures can effectively control police behavior when it comes to enforcing laws and ordinances against low-level serious offenses.

In the early 1990s, considerable research and policy were directed at reducing local jail populations. It was a policy pursued on financial as well as humanitarian grounds. Already those interests seem to have been supplanted by concerns for order. Local corrections policy and research appear to be increasingly directed by those interests and by the way the police implemented them.

The Convergence of Corrections and Policing

The National Advisory Commission on Criminal Justice Standards and Goals (1973) defined *corrections* as the communities' official response to the convicted offender. The Commission noted the lack of a stated purpose for corrections but defended the definition because it allowed for many specific purposes depending on the agency and the type of offender.

Surveillance has always been among the objectives pursued in corrections. Among the services provided by probation and parole officers was crime control through observing offenders in the community and revoking their freedom when necessary.

Community corrections also meant much more, however. Corrections workers provided counseling and other services and were expected to broker education, job training and placement, substance abuse, and other services. Those services seem increasingly rare today. Instead, assisted by technological developments such as drug testing and electronic monitoring, surveillance has come to dominate community corrections. The distinction between policing and corrections seems largely organizational and no longer based on significantly different missions.

Greater Isolation and Marginalization of the Corrections Population

The pattern of metropolitan growth, which has concentrated poverty in urban neighborhoods and surrounded it by middle class and wealthy suburbs, also helps define the population of corrections programs. That population will increasingly be drawn from the margins of U.S. society, the urban underclass.

Extensive evidence suggests that concentrated poverty is associated with serious crime (Hagan, 1994: 76). Thus, correctional programs deal disproportionately with offenders from such communities. Beyond this, however, support is growing for the proposition that concentrated poverty also affects criminal processing (Miller, 1998). Thus, inhabitants of high-poverty neighborhoods are not only more likely to be involved in crime but also are more likely to experience aggressive police tactics, to be arrested, to be prosecuted, and to be sanctioned.

Hagan (1994:150) has examined the geography of policing and argues that police regard some areas as "offensible space," that is, space in which high crime rates justify concentrating police resources. Risk of arrests are elevated there as are the rates of detention, prosecution, and conviction. Furthermore, criminal records compound the risk as each arrest raises the likelihood of further processing by the criminal justice system. It is estimated that as many as 90 percent of nonwhite males in cities will be arrested and jailed at least briefly (Miller, 1998: 6).

As a result of both involvement in crime and differences in processing in the criminal justice system, the population of corrections programs increasingly reflects the urban underclass. Corrections programs thus contend with an identifiable class of offenders who share not just a record of conviction but also poverty, minority status, and increasingly tenuous attachments to the American mainstream.

Growth of the Culture of Corrections

Separation from the mainstream is an increasingly significant problem with which corrections must contend. Prisons and jails themselves contribute to the separation through the social systems and culture they produce as well as by reinforcing the criminal subculture carried in from the street. Deprivation and importation perspectives have long found support as theories for understanding the prison environment. What is new and frightening for many, however, is the extent of interconnection between the culture of penal institutions and that of the outside communities from which many prisoners are drawn.

Ethnographic studies have demonstrated the interplay among these cultures. Studies of gangs, for example, have shown strong links between prison and community branches of these organizations. Upon release from prison, offenders are often pressured to continue gang affiliations that began behind bars (Hagedorn, 1988). For others, links to a street gang may ease their initiation into prison.

Other researchers have described cultural themes in poor urban neighborhoods in terms similar to those once thought unique to prisons. Anderson (1990) has described an "oppositional culture" found in inner cities. There violence can be regarded as a legitimate response to being "dissed" or treated with insufficient respect. John Hagan (1994: 94) has described the problem of "criminal imbededness" in which ties to delinquent groups and criminal organizations have replaced attachments in the labor force in many poor communities.

It is a sad statistical truth that incarceration has become an experience too commonly shared among poor minority males in urban areas. Among the unintended consequences of that shared experience appears to be a cultural exchange that has brought the prison culture and the culture of the ghetto closer together.

Metropolitan Life and the New Penology

Today the report of the President's Crime Commission of 1967 can seem like "an archaic reminder of softer, sentimental times" (Clear, 1998: 142). Clearly, crime policy has moved in directions often antithetical to the Commission's views.

Nowhere is that clearer than in corrections. Far from reducing the use of incarceration, we have become a "penaholic" society with nearly 1.5 million people incarcerated in the year 2000. We also have adopted an agenda for corrections that bears little resemblance to goals set forth by the Commission.

Instead of charting a course designed to change individuals and improve communities, corrections has embraced a philosophy of risk management. As Feeley and Simon (1992) have pointed out, the "new penology" is concerned with managerial efficiency. Incarceration is based on actuarial models and probabilities rather than on prospects for change.

This new penology is well represented in a study of maximum security prison by Fleisher (1989). In *Warehousing Violence,* he argues that many maximum security prisoners are serious repeat offenders who are incapable of succeeding on the street. He advocates a regime of long-term warehousing of these offenders in environments in which they are free from victimization and occupied by work. In the new penology, this is described as a progressive and humane approach to incarceration.

To some, warehousing human beings would seem to deny the basic humanity of those people. In contemporary penology, it can pass as a humanitarian reform. The new penology seems not only less hopeful but also less interesting than its earlier incarnations.

The history of corrections is a history of optimism about the prospects for individual and social change. That optimism has found expression in religious reformation, rehabilitation, and, most recently, reintegration. Some will argue that the new penology has grown out of the failures of those past ideas. But the powerful forces of metropolitanization with its growing concentrations of poverty and developing underclass have also helped usher in this new era.

For the President's Commission in 1967, questions of race and class were central to the field of criminal justice. Although many of the conditions cited by the Commission have deteriorated, those conditions are all but ignored within criminal justice today. Outside the field, however, a growing body of scholarship is concerned with the social consequences of metropolitan patterns of development. Scholars and policy makers have used this framework to examine a broad range of issues including education (G. Orfield, 1997), fiscal policy (M. Orfield, 1997), employment (Wilson, 1996), politics (Rusk, 1995), land use (Porter, 1997), and environmental justice (Bullard, 1994).

Perhaps the interest in the metropolitan community in other academic and policy areas will spill over into the field of criminal justice. In the other fields, scholars are examining the impact of metropolitan social structures and are developing programs and policies designed to change both individuals and their communities. Those arguments sound vaguely reminiscent of the 1967 President's Commission and they raise the possibility, if not the hope, that the ideas of more than 30 years ago may once again be considered in this field.

REFERENCES

Anderson, E. (1990). *Streetwise: Race, Class and Change in an Urban Community*. Chicago: University of Chicago Press.

Bollier, D. (1998). *How Smart Growth Can Stop Sprawl*. Washington DC: Essential Books.

Buerger, M.E. (1994). *The Limits of Community*. In D.P. Rosenbaum (ed.), *The Challenge of Community Policing*. Thousand Oaks, CA: Sage: 270–273.

Bullard, R.D. (1994). *Dumping in Dixie: Race, Class and Environmental Quality*. New York: Westview.

Clear, T. (1998). "Societal Responses to the President's Commission: A Thirty Year Retrospective." In Office of Justice Programs (ed.), *The Challenge of Crime in a Free Society: Looking Back Looking Forward*. Washington, DC: U.S. Department of Justice.

Feeley, M.M. and Simon, J. (1992). "The New Penology: Notes on the Emerging Strategy of Corrections and Its Implications." *Criminology, 30(4): 449–474.*

Fleisher, M.S. (1989). *Warehousing Violence*. Newbury Park, CA: Sage.

Hagan, J. (1994). *Crime and Disrepute*. Thousand Oaks, CA: Pine Forge.

Hagedorn, J. (1988). *People and Folks: Gangs, Crime and the Underclass in a Rustbelt City*. Chicago: Lakeview.

Hall, A., Henry, D., Perlstein, J., and Smith, W.F. (1985). *Alleviating Jail Crowding: A Systems Perspective*. Washington, DC: National Institute of Justice.

Jackson, K. T. (1985). *Crabgrass Frontier: The Suburbanization of the United States*. New York: Oxford.

Kelling, G. L. (1998). "Crime Control, the Police and Culture Wars: Broken Windows and Cultural Pluralism." In National Institute of Justice (ed.), *Perspectives on Crime and Justice: 1997–1998 Lecture Series*. Washington, DC: U.S. Department of Justice.

Kelling, G. L. and Coles, C.M. (1996). *Fixing Broken Windows: Restoring Order and Reducing Crime in Our Communities*. New York: Touchstone.

Klofas, J. (1990). "The Jail and the Community." *Justice Quarterly, 7(1): 69–102.*

Miller, J.G. (1998). *Search and Destroy: African American Males in the Criminal Justice System*. New York: Cambridge.

National Advisory Commission on Criminal Justice Standards and Goals. (1973). *Corrections*. Washington, DC: Government Printing Office.

Orfield, G. (1997) *Dismantling Desegregation: The Quiet Reversal of* Brown v. Board of Education. New York: New Press.

Orfield, M. (1997). *Metropolitics: A Regional Agenda for Community and Stability*. Washington DC: Brookings.

Porter, D. R. (1997). Managing Growth in America's Communities. Washington, DC: Island Press.

President's Commission on Law Enforcement and Administration of Justice. (1967). *The Challenge of Crime in a Free Society: A Report*. Washington, DC: U.S. Government Printing Office.

Rusk, D. (1995). *Cities Without Suburbs*. Washington, DC: Woodrow Wilson Center.

Rusk, D. (1999). *Inside Game/Outside Game: Winning Strategies for Saving Urban America*. Washington: Brookings.

Schneider, W. (1992). "The Suburban Century Begins." *Atlantic Monthly,* 240(1):33–44.

Task Force on Corrections. (1967). "President's Commission on Law Enforcement and Administration of Justice." *Task Force Report: Corrections*. Washington, DC: U.S. Government Printing Office.

Wilson, W.J. (1987). *The Truly Disadvantaged: The Inner City, the Underclass and Public Policy*. Chicago: University of Chicago Press.

Wilson, W. J. (1996). *When Work Disappears: The World of the New Urban Poor*. New York: Vintage Press.

chapter 3

CORRECTIONAL PHILOSOPHIES
VARYING IDEOLOGIES OF PUNISHMENT

TED ALLEMAN
Late, The Pennsylvania State University

INTRODUCTION

This chapter discusses the implications of the rehabilitation, justice, and utilitarian punishment approaches to the treatment of offenders. As will be apparent, each philosophy has a different focus. Rehabilitation is most concerned with reforming the criminal, justice emphasizes fairness and restitution, while utilitarian punishment seeks swift and certain retaliation. Each of these philosophies holds a different view as to who criminals are and how they should be treated. Each philosophy, through its implementation, has a direct impact on the focus and actions of the criminal justice system.

Crime and punishment go hand in hand. Defending oneself by striking back is a predictable human response. From this perspective, punishment serves the purpose of stopping or thwarting an attack. Who among us would not raise a hand to defend ourselves or our loved ones from injury or harm? Taking an "eye for an eye" is an age-old dictum. Getting even is basic to what many mean when they use the terms *fairness* and *justice*. In a fundamental way, correctional philosophies are grounded in personal experience.

Correctional philosophies are broad-based and relatively cohesive sets of ideas that serve to guide and justify the treatment of offenders. The kinds and levels of sanctions imposed on criminal defendants are reflective of the general values and beliefs that are held concerning what kinds of people commit crimes and what should be done with them. Different philosophies imply different approaches to crime control. In American criminal justice, the philosophies of rehabilitation, justice, and utilitarian punishment represent three varying perspectives as to the proper treatment of criminal offenders.

To a significant degree, many public issues and debates hinge on which of these three philosophies is assumed to be the best strategy for dealing with crime. In addition to understanding the basis of many public debates concerning crime and punishment, a knowledge of the varying correctional philosophies that are predominant today is important for understanding how specific criminal justice programs and practices come to be adopted. Rather than taking sides as to which philosophy is personally most appealing, the following discussion encourages an objective analysis of the pros and cons associated with each of these varying approaches to corrections.

THE PHILOSOPHY OF UTILITARIAN PUNISHMENT

The utilitarian punishment model is not difficult to understand. Utilitarian punishment is based on the premise that those who commit criminal acts do so with full knowledge of what they are doing and that when they are caught and prosecuted, they deserve levels of punishment commensurate with the harm or damage they have done. In addition to being "just deserts" for criminal offenders, the imposition of punishment is believed to deter others from committing offenses and, by keeping habitual offenders in prison, to incapacitate offenders from committing further criminal acts. Retribution, deterrence, and incapacitation are three of the principal rationales behind the utilitarian punishment approach.

Applying the utilitarian punishment philosophy to criminal justice is akin to "being tough on crime." Because of the fear associated with crime, the general public is responsive to the language of utilitarian punishment. Commonsense notions stemming from child rearing support the argument that problem behaviors can result when parents fail to provide and enforce clear definitions of right and wrong. When applied to criminal justice, popular conceptions of criminal offenders think them to be deceptive, malicious, and/or dangerous persons who need to have a sense of responsibility and respect for authority instilled in them. A conservative philosophy of child rearing is compatible with the "grab them by the neck and show them who is boss" orientation of utilitarian punishment. Additionally, politicians, judges, and criminal prosecutors have found that spouting the rhetoric of utilitarian punishment can be an effective political strategy for getting elected to public office. Elements of traditional Christian dogma that teach "an eye for an eye, and a tooth for a tooth" as a proper response to social transgression further add to the general appeal of the utilitarian punishment approach to criminal justice.

Utilitarian punishment is the oldest and most commonly accepted approach to criminal justice. The history of criminal justice is to a great extent a history of the imposition of different forms of punishment. It is clear that utilitarian punishment is and will continue to be a primary rationale for dealing with crime. An objective of correctional research is to clarify the true effects of utilitarian punishment and to identify when and under what conditions punishment serves as an appropriate response and an effective deterrent to crime.

History of Utilitarian Punishment

As a response to nonconformity and social transgression, punishment is as old as human history. The notion that punishment serves a general utilitarian purpose in society is of a more recent origin and can be dated from the writings of Cesare Beccaria and Jeremy Bentham in the eighteenth century.

Adding a utilitarian component to the punishment model implies that punishment results in a general social good. The social good associated with the imposition of punishment stems from the belief that penalties that have been preassigned to unlawful behavior provide a clear definition of right and wrong as well as a warning to those who might contemplate the commission of a criminal act of the consequences they will suffer as the result of their actions. Arguments that support utilitarian punishment as a general approach to crime control, therefore, assert that utilitarian punishment prevents as well as punishes criminal acts. When confronted by critics who view utilitarian punishment as simply a vengeful, vindictive, barbaric, and repressive response to the crime problem, proponents of utilitarian punishment point to the social good that punishment serves for the prevention of crime.

Cesare Beccaria, an influential social critic of his time, is commonly identified as the founder of the modern utilitarian punishment philosophy. This is ironic since Beccaria's classic work, *On Crimes and Punishment* (1764), was primarily reformist in nature and was intended to provide a social remedy to the rampant use of harsh and brutal punishments by the criminal justice system of his day. Another social philosopher, Jeremy

Bentham, who was influenced by Beccaria, further refined the utilitarian punishment perspective by emphasizing his belief that people, in general, pursue that which is pleasurable and avoid that which is painful. In his book, *A Fragment on Government and an Introduction to the Principles of Morals and Legislation* (1789), Bentham expanded on Beccaria's idea that crime could be prevented through law and stressed that the imposition of sure and immediate penalties was central to the control of criminal behavior. Thus, the works of both Beccaria and Bentham established the idea that the law (and the penalties to be imposed when the law was violated) was just in terms of punishing criminals as well as effective in keeping others who might contemplate committing criminal acts from doing so.

The term *calculus* is commonly applied to the mental weighing of the pros and cons of committing a criminal act that supposedly goes through a person's mind prior to the commission of a crime. According to the classical school of criminology established by Beccaria, punishment should fit the crime and should be severe enough to outweigh any advantage or gain that might result from the commission of the criminal act. In this way, punishment (the imposition of specific sanctions on those who commit specific unlawful acts) performs a social good by acting as a deterrent to the commission of crime. Whether or not criminal sanctions have such a deterrent effect, of course, depends on the knowledge that persons have of the law and to what extent they believe that they will be caught and punished for their actions.

Utilitarian Punishment in Practice

A number of current policies and practices that stem from the application of utilitarian punishment can be identified. In summary form, the utilitarian punishment philosophy supports

> *A hard-line policy toward serious juvenile offenders.* Juvenile offenders are perceived to be dangerous and a by-product of a permissive society. Juvenile offenders must be taught that "crime does not pay." Serious juvenile offenders, especially violent offenders, should be sent to reform schools and, when appropriate, subjected to adult court proceedings.
>
> *Greater use of determinate and mandatory sentences.* Crime prevention requires stiff and sure penalties. Discretion should be taken out of the hands of judges and parole boards. Imprisonment is relied on as the primary response to serious crime.
>
> *Development of a more effective court system.* To impose sure and certain penalties, criminal prosecution should not be delayed. Upon conviction, court-mandated punishments (including application of the death penalty) should be administered as soon as possible. For

criminal justice to serve as an effective deterrent to crime, criminals must face a swift and decisive sanctioning process. The courts should be more concerned with imposing justice than catering to the presumed rights of criminal defendants.

Get tough policy with drug offenders. Advocates of utilitarian punishment see drug use as pervasive and representing a clear and present danger to the moral fiber of the nation. Drugs are seen as undermining the motivation and morals of American citizens and must be dealt with in a stern and uncompromising fashion. Maximum penalties for drug pushers and the death penalty for drug "kingpins" are advocated. Drug use is not viewed as an excuse for crime nor is it looked on as a disease or an illness.

Expanded use of boot camps. Military style boot camps are seen as the ideal setting for resocializing misguided youths who think they are able to break the law and get away with it. A primary benefit of the boot-camp approach is the opportunity to instill respect for authority while giving new offenders one last chance to avoid imprisonment.

Use of the death penalty. The death penalty is the ultimate punishment for those offenders who have taken a life or have engaged in egregious behavior that does substantial social harm (such as distributing dangerous drugs). For those who believe in the efficacy of utilitarian punishment, capital punishment is necessary to demonstrate to incorrigible felons that serious crime will not be tolerated.

In general, the utilitarian punishment philosophy relies on imprisonment as the primary means for dealing with crime. Utilitarian punishment advocates the need to protect society by removing serious juvenile and adult offenders from the community. Utilitarian punishment also advocates a clear definition of the law and the punishment that will be imposed on those who choose to break the law. Any competing philosophy or practice that impedes or lessens the impact of the efficient delivery of punishment to convicted felons is viewed as undermining the function as well as the effectiveness of the criminal justice system.

Advantages of Utilitarian Punishment

Advocates of utilitarian punishment justify this approach in terms of retribution, deterrence, and incapacitation. Therefore, to judge its efficacy, we must look at each of these functions of the utilitarian punishment approach to crime control.

Retribution. Retribution means getting even. The retributive function of criminal justice implies inflicting at least as much pain on the offender as the offender has inflicted on his or her victim. Fines, the imposition of a negative social stigma, the maintenance of criminal records, restriction of certain kinds of employment, withholding the right to hold public office, denying the right to vote in public elections, the loss of liberty through incarceration, or the loss of life through execution are examples of criminal sanctions. There is little doubt that criminal sanctions serve a retributive function. There is some argument that sanctions can always "even the score," especially when long-term trauma, physical maladies, or loss of life results from criminal acts.

Deterrence. Deterrence can be divided into two types: (1) general deterrence and (2) specific deterrence. General deterrence takes the form of laws that define the penalties that will be imposed upon violation of the law. Specific deterrence refers to the imposition of penalties on a particular person who has broken the law and is made aware of "specific" penalties that will result if subsequent violations of the law, or of conditions of probation or parole, occur. Strict penalties, whether in the form of tough laws or strict rules governing the behavior of convicted felons, are seen as essential if deterrence (prevention) of crime is to take place.

It is not clear how effective general deterrence is in terms of dissuading criminal activity. What is evident is that many people who commit crimes are aware that their behavior is illegal, but they may not know the exact nature of the penalties associated with particular crimes. When evaluating the deterrent effect of criminal sanctions, it is also important to take into consideration the fact that punishment has a subjective dimension, in that people vary as to whether or not they consider treatment by the criminal justice system as punishment. In some social circles, for example, being picked up and charged by the police may actually enhance status. In general, laws most affect those who are law-abiding. In other words, it is those people who have the greatest stake in society who have the most to lose from the imposition of criminal sanctions. Therefore, the threat of punishment often serves to keep those who are generally law-abiding anyway from committing criminal offenses.

Incapacitation. Incapacitation means that during the period of time in which an offender is institutionalized, the offender is unable to commit further criminal acts. There is no question that this dimension of utilitarian punishment works. To the extent that the criminal justice system is able to identify and incarcerate habitual offenders, the goal of preventing particular offenders from committing crimes is achieved. The problem with this approach is that it is very difficult to identify which offenders would be committing additional crimes if on the street. This approach also has many legal ramifications, since sanctions cannot be imposed for behavior that has not yet taken place.

Disadvantages of Utilitarian Punishment

In many ways utilitarian punishment is an oversimplified solution to a complex problem. There is little argument that prison is an important and necessary component of the criminal justice system. The problem associated with the utilitarian punishment approach is that prison is relied on almost exclusively as a method of crime control. Incarcerating a person for a number of years is a very expensive proposition. It is also clear that prison makes people worse, not better. Today's prisons are filled with non-violent offenders who might be more effectively treated by alternative methods. To improve the effectiveness of the criminal justice system, we need to see prison as only one of many treatment alternatives.

It is also important to take into consideration the full effect of punishment-based policies and programs. Punishment, as a form of social control, has many drawbacks. The imposition of punishment promotes avoidance behavior. For those persons who have frequent contact with the criminal justice system, authority figures can come to be viewed as the enemy. Punishment can result in alienating youthful offenders even further from the mainstream of society. Criminal subcultures to some extent owe their existence to a commonly held antagonism toward legitimate authority. Punishment, therefore, can have unanticipated social consequences.

Punishment can also create aggression in those who are punished. When we put people in prison, we run the risk of making them more angry, frustrated, or hateful than before (Jeffery, 1990). Punishment can cause people to strike out in an increasingly destructive fashion. Of course, offenders must be punished for their criminal acts, but, in order to serve as an effective deterrent, punishment must be used wisely and judiciously. The indiscriminate use of punishment can have a criminogenic effect. We must be sure that punishment does not serve to increase rates of crime among those who are processed by the criminal justice system.

To be effective, punishment must be applied as quickly and decisively as possible. But this is not how the criminal justice system works. In many cases, months and sometimes even years pass before formal sanctions are imposed by the courts. If the association between the criminal act and punishment is not clear, punishment can be essentially ineffective as an agent of change. And, if punishment is perceived to be undeserved or unwarranted, punishment can again serve to escalate destructive and antisocial patterns of behavior.

Punishment is most effective when it is only part of a correctional strategy. Punishment does get people's attention and does serve to inhibit behavior when it is applied at the right time and under appropriate conditions. But, unless revenge or hate are primary intentions, punishment by itself is generally ineffective as a correctional strategy. To make punishment effective, the offender must be provided with alternative means for reinforcement. This implies that correctional strategies must combine programs that serve to block illegal opportunities while at the same time providing behavioral programs that create legitimate opportunities (Jeffery, 1990). Punishment, therefore, proves most effective when it is used wisely and judicially as only one element in a coordinated program for change.

As a response to crime, punishment holds much personal appeal. Striking out at those who have done harm or damage is a perfectly natural reaction. It makes us feel better. But, as a correctional strategy, the limitations of relying solely on punishment must be acknowledged. If used indiscriminately and without purpose, repressive measures can clearly lay the groundwork for continued and increasingly destructive criminal behavior among inmate populations who are released from prison even more bitter and alienated than when they first entered the system.

THE REHABILITATIVE PHILOSOPHY

When someone says that rehabilitation cannot work, they are really saying that people cannot change. We all know that people do change. Some people, in fact, go through dramatic, life-altering changes. In this regard, rehabilitation can be defined as the systematic attempt to change criminal offenders so that deviant propensities, especially those that are damaging or destructive to others, are reduced or eliminated from their lives.

In terms of rehabilitative change, there are three major areas of focus. For some classes of offenders, an objective is to change the way in which they respond to cues in their environment. Another is to change the motivations of criminal offenders. And, as a third objective, it is necessary to strive to alter or reduce problem behaviors and/or change deviant lifestyles. Each of these objectives involves the creation of programs through which significant and lasting personal change takes place.

The first objective aims to change the ways in which offenders habitually perceive, interpret, and/or react to the world around them. Eliminating the tendency to see their world in a threatening, fearful, domineering, acquisitive, or egocentric manner is therefore a major rehabilitative goal. The goal of changing criminal motivations involves eliminating the desire, pleasure, excitement, or reward associated with criminal activity. The last objective, changing an offender's habitual patterns of behavior or lifestyle, is most difficult because these patterns often reflect a person's self-concept. Creating programs in which such fundamental kinds of personal change take place is not an easy task.

Methods of Rehabilitative Change

In the case of the vast majority of offenders, criminal behavior is learned. Criminality, especially in terms of offenders who demonstrate regularity and progression in their criminal careers, often involves an extended period of socialization in which criminal motivations, techniques, attitudes, and lifestyles are learned. Teaching offenders to disassociate themselves from these aspects of socialization is a difficult but not impossible task.

Socializing offenders into alternative, noncriminal social roles is a general rehabilitative strategy. In one way or another, the rewards of noncriminal social roles must come to outweigh the rewards of criminal roles. And, concurrently, the social costs of criminal pursuits must become greater than their inherent or perceived rewards. Although difficult to engineer, treatment programs must somehow guide offenders away from behavior or pursuits that are likely to result in arrest. Everyday incentives and inducements for ex-offenders must be weighted in the direction of legitimate, noncriminal careers and lifestyles. More to the point, criminal offenders, if they are to extricate themselves from further processing by the criminal justice system, must prove successful in gaining a personal overriding stake in conventional society.

The specific methods used for instituting rehabilitative change in offenders vary from one general class of offender to another. An essential element of rehabilitative strategy is the application of the most effective treatment alternatives to those classes of offenders who demonstrate rehabilitative success through reduced rates of recidivism. Identifying which strategies are most successful with which classes of offenders is a major objective of correctional research.

History of Rehabilitative Methods

Implicitly, theories of rehabilitation view criminals as people who need to be fixed. Rehabilitation starts with the premise that offenders have something wrong with them.

When put into practice, rehabilitation tends toward a model that puts offenders into some form of dependency relationship. This occurs because prisoners are seen as people who are lacking in one way or another. Correctional educators provide the schooling they are lacking, counselors provide the emotional stability they are lacking, and pastors provide the moral standards they are lacking, all with the belief that their instruction will in some way "cure" or "transform" the offender. A good part of the history of rehabilitation can be summarized by identifying the roles into which rehabilitative approaches have placed prisoners. Historically, depending on whether a religious, medical, or counseling approach to rehabilitation was taken, prisoners have been treated as sinners, patients, and/or clients.

To some extent, rehabilitative methods require the cooperation of prisoners. Programs are most successful when prisoners themselves actively seek help or assistance and are willing participants in their own resocialization. As students, they must want to learn; as sinners, they must want to be saved; and as clients or patients, they must want to be remedied or cured. Unlike justice or utilitarian punishment approaches, which do something *to* prisoners, rehabilitative methods seek to work *with* prisoners. As such, rehabilitation programs often include incentives for participation and sanctions for noninvolvement. Rehabilitation is essentially a "carrot and stick" approach to correctional treatment.

An underlying premise of rehabilitative programming is the elimination of the causes (pushes, forces, conditions, etc.) that have resulted in the commission of criminal acts. The logic of rehabilitation includes the assumption that people will not commit criminal acts if the source of their discontent, frustration, or adverse conditioning is reduced or eliminated from their lives. The true proof of rehabilitative success, therefore, lies in lowered rates of recidivism.

A General Approach to Rehabilitation

In very general terms, contemporary rehabilitative methods include the following steps (Figure 3.1):

1. Identify the conditions and/or circumstances that led or contributed to the commission of the criminal act.
2. Solicit the cooperation of the client and discuss the nature of the problem and a program for change.
3. Identify the specific behavioral goals of the program and how the program will be carried out.
4. Provide a conditioning environment conducive and supportive of the actualization of program goals.
5. Provide frequent, accurate feedback to the participant that includes a personally meaningful system of positive reinforcement.
6. Perform follow-up evaluations and reinforcement sessions after specific programs have been completed.
7. Have one program flow into another in terms of arranging a long-term rehabilitative strategy designed to address all aspects of the participant's individualized needs.

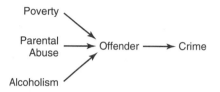

FIGURE 3.1
Depiction of general rehabilitative strategy.
Remove the causes of crime and crime itself
will be eliminated.

Rehabilitation is a scientific approach to changing offenders. Criminality, like all other forms of social behavior, is seen as a byproduct of
social and/or personal factors and conditioning. To a great extent, criminals are viewed as social actors who have been unduly exposed to and
influenced by adverse social conditions. Remove or eliminate the cause, so
say rehabilitative practitioners, and the consequences (criminal behavior)
will be eliminated. The rehabilitative philosophy adds an aura of exactness
and definitiveness to the dynamic, bizarre, and many times unpredictable
world of criminality.

By viewing criminality in terms of cause and effect, rehabilitation
programs process offenders according to plan and design. Rehabilitative
strategies place a great emphasis on technique and method. Because of the
scientific nature of rehabilitative approaches to corrections, the mistaken
assumption can be engendered that programs work simply because they
are well designed or properly administered. The truth is that defining and
"programming out" undesirable personal traits or behaviors is a difficult,
complicated, and less than certain process. The success of instituting pro-
grammed change in a prison environment is subject to the following factors and considerations.

Realities of Instituting Prison-Based Rehabilitative Programs

- All prisoners are not responsive to rehabilitative programs. Some
  prisoners do consciously choose criminality as a life course.
- If effective treatment programs are not offered, prisoners generally
  come out of prison worse off than when they went in.
- Many programs instituted in prison are ineffective. They do not
  address individual needs and are simply "window dressing" that
  allows the administration to claim that programs are being offered.
- Many offenders fail to face up to the actual harm that has resulted
  from their criminal actions. Directly confronting prisoners on this
  issue generally does not work. Although difficult, rehabilitative programming should include subtle, indirect, but effective means of overcoming prisoners' attempts to deny and avoid responsibility for their
  actions. Offenders who do not come to have a degree of empathy for
  their victims will have difficulty consciously altering their behavior
  upon release.

- Incarceration in maximum security warehoused institutions is expensive and generally ineffective as a rehabilitative strategy for the majority of offenders. Valuable prison space, especially in maximum security institutions, should be reserved for the most violent and habitual types of offenders.
- Rehabilitation and treatment philosophies have come and gone, but the realities of prisons, along with their primary orientation toward the security, custody, and control of prisoners, have changed little over their two-hundred-year history. Prisons have a built-in resistance to programs and policies that treat prisoners as positive, potentially productive human beings.
- Effective treatment options exist but they will not be used extensively (system wide) unless they seem to fit in with an overriding political or economic rationale.
- Prisoners, as a group or class of people, are politically impotent. Unfortunately, the only avenue by which the majority of prisoners can bring attention to unfair or inhumane prison conditions is through some form of collective violence or protest.
- The history of enlightened wardens and superintendents is a history of their objectives and programs being undermined by incompetent bureaucrats and lower-echelon staff. Rehabilitative programs that are not understood, supported, and participated in by all levels of the prison bureaucracy will eventually fail.
- Out of all the criminal justice agencies, prisons represent a significant opportunity for the change and reform of prisoners. It is only when felons are incarcerated that the system potentially has complete control over their behavior and social environment. Ways in which incentives and programs for change can be effectively implemented in prison environments are often overlooked by administrative staff who are simply interested in maintaining custody and control over the prison population.
- The rehabilitative, justice, and punishment models are not necessarily competing treatment alternatives. Offenders vary significantly from one another and respond differently to the way in which they are treated by the system. To be successful at reducing crime, the criminal justice system must become more sophisticated and diverse in terms of its treatment options.

Advantages of Rehabilitation

Prisoners, like all people, are capable of changing for the better. Therefore, the continual development and identification of successful programs is a worthy objective of corrections. It is true that some rehabilitative programs have failed. But this does not mean that rehabilitation as a general correctional strategy is a failure. Many individual rehabilitative programs have failed because

1. Offender types have not been appropriately matched with specific programs.
2. Custodial staff typically are not educated or included in rehabilitative programming; therefore, they often work to undermine methods with which they do not agree or do not understand.
3. Most treatment programs have not been designed to carry over into the community.
4. Follow-up and objective evaluation generally have not been used to identify good programs and eliminate poor ones.

Rehabilitation is a positive, constructive way of dealing with criminal offenders. Our prisons and jails are filled with offenders who respond well to rehabilitative programs and would jump at the chance to work their way out of prison and out of trouble with the law. Treatment programs that are clear, objective, and not subject to manipulation, by prisoners or staff, have good histories of success. Successful programs that result in reduced rates of recidivism should be expanded and made generally available to inmate populations.

Disadvantages of Rehabilitation

Some programs can lead to abuse. Prisoners should not be forced or coerced into participation in rehabilitative programs. Prisoners who decide that they do not wish to participate in programs should not be threatened with additional years of imprisonment. Like all correctional philosophies, rehabilitation can become dogmatic and authoritarian in its application.

It is very difficult to reverse years of antisocial conditioning by administering a few programs of short duration to prisoners. Because rehabilitative programs are offered does not mean that rehabilitation is actually taking place. Programs that are improperly administered or designed can be a total waste of time, money, and effort.

It is also difficult to punish and rehabilitate at the same time. The punitive nature of prison can outweigh any potential benefits associated with rehabilitative programming. It is difficult to successfully implement rehabilitative change in punitively oriented prison environments.

It is simply not true that all prisoners commit crimes because of some personal or social defect. Like all correctional strategies, rehabilitation applies to some but not all offenders. Effective rehabilitation programs successfully recognize and meet the needs of particular types of prisoners. Otherwise, rehabilitation as an exclusive approach to corrections is inherently no better or worse than its justice or utilitarian punishment counterparts.

THE JUSTICE MODEL

The justice model, as an approach to the treatment of criminal offenders, lies conceptually somewhere between the rehabilitation and the utilitarian punishment philosophies. The justice approach to treatment contains elements of both philosophies and is currently a popular approach to corrections. The model was first elaborated by David Fogel in *We Are the Living Proof,* published in 1979. Since then, the rationale of the justice model has been used by administrators nationwide to implement a wide variety of correctional strategies. By recognizing the need for rehabilitative programs (but downplaying their importance) and by sharing with the philosophy of utilitarian punishment, the desire for sure and determinate sentencing, the justice model fits the mood of the times in terms of being tough on crime in a purportedly humane and constitutional fashion.

The justice model incorporates two of the fundamental tenets of present-day corrections—those of punishment and treatment. The model, by insisting on consistent, determinant sentences, validates an emphasis on punishment. But far from being simply a "lock them up and throw away the key" type of approach, the justice model also emphasizes that an obligation of the system is to provide educational, counseling, and treatment programs to all prisoners who voluntarily request them. Pragmatically, the justice model allows jails and prisons to continue to be run with a predominant "security, custody, and control" focus while concurrently providing a role for the treatment infrastructure that is an established fixture in most correctional institutions.

Although the justice model clearly recognizes the rights of prisoners and advocates a number of measures designed to address inmate concerns, the justice model, to some extent, has been co-opted by utilitarian punishment proponents who find it expedient to justify the implementation of their custody-oriented strategies by speaking the language of justice. Because the justice model takes a passive approach to treatment, the warehousing of prisoners has evolved over the past two decades as a predominant administrative strategy. In many instances, the adoption of the justice model has resulted in an ever-increasing flow of prisoners into large, warehoused facilities. Ironically, such consequences were never envisioned nor intended by those who initially formulated the justice approach to corrections.

Elements of the Justice Approach to Corrections

The justice model is intended to be a fair and equitable approach to corrections. To its credit, the justice model takes into consideration all of those who are affected by crime: offenders (those charged with crimes and are forcibly processed as criminals), correctional personnel (those hired to see that punitive mandates are carried out), and victims (those who experience personal loss or suffering as the result of crime). Even though the implementation of the justice model has not yielded all that it promises, it is a viable approach to correctional treatment that addresses many of the problems inherent in the imposition of punishment in a democratic society.

Coming from a rehabilitation background, "revisionists" such as David Fogel have maintained a positive regard for prisoner's rights as well as a general distrust of the power of the state (Bartollas, 1985). Admittedly, the destructive prison riots of the 1970s played a role in the development of this new approach to correctional treatment (Fogel, 1979). It is clear that in prison, custody and control practices generally override concerns for prisoners' rights. As such, if pushed too far, justice practitioners are well aware that contempt and rage can breed and fester among prisoners sometimes to the point of riot. Instituting administrative controls such as establishing prisoner grievance processes and using outside ombudsmen to settle prisoner/staff disputes is seen as important for preventing prison violence. Treating prisoners as responsible persons who deserve a say in the affairs of the prison is also advocated as part of the justice approach, but, in practice, this is often successfully resisted by correctional staff who maintain traditional custody and control perspectives.

The justice model advances a number of specific revisions to the correctional system. Some have been adopted, and some have not. In outline form, the following can be identified as being central elements of the justice model:

> *Retribution rather than deterrence or reformation.* As a primary goal of the correctional system, the justice model justifies a level of punishment proportionate to the harm resulting from criminal acts. Punishment is viewed as a legitimate goal of the justice system. Offenders deserve to be punished but only to the extent that they have inflicted harm on others. Unlike the rehabilitative philosophy, reforming the criminal is not a legitimate goal of the system. And, unlike the utilitarian punishment approach, punishment is not seen as an appropriate means of attempting to prevent crime. In simple terms, those who violate the law deserve to be punished. No additional rationale for state-imposed punishment is needed or, in terms of the justice model, justified.

Criminal offenders have full knowledge of their criminal acts and must be held responsible for their actions. Unlike a rehabilitative approach, those who break the law are not seen as acting out of need or want or ignorance. Offenders in large part are viewed as people who, after a conscious weighing of the consequences, have decided to commit a criminal act. The justice model provides no excuses for criminal behavior. Without question, criminal behavior is defined as wrong and punishable by law. The justice model, like utilitarian punishment, holds offenders personally responsible for their criminal actions.

Offenders should be required to make restitution to the victims of their crimes. An idea that clearly differentiates the justice model from both rehabilitation and utilitarian punishment is an emphasis on victim restitution. The justice model, whenever possible, advocates that offenders be made to repay the victims of their crimes. The justice model makes the victim a central element in judicial and correctional decision making. Justice practitioners attempt to restore victims to their precrime condition. The presentence investigation report, for example, is used to document the damage to persons and/or property that resulted from the defendant's actions and then applied in the form of court-mandated restitution plans (Bartollas, 1985). Sanctions such as deducting prisoner wages from direct monetary payments to victims and/or requiring some form of community service as part of an offender's sentence are examples of practices that grew out of the justice model.

Discretionary justice should be eliminated. In order to do justice, sentences should be fair and exact. Determinate sentencing is a hallmark of the justice approach. Justice practitioners want judges to follow sentencing guidelines so that the punishment fits the crime, not the defendant or the circumstance. According to the justice model, defendants who commit similar crimes should be given similar punishments. This is seen as the only fair way of dispensing justice. To make justice exact, the justice model requires convicted felons to serve the full term of their sentence. Practices such as sentencing felons to a variable term (five to seven years, for example) or releasing prisoners early to parole are eliminated from systems employing the justice model. In terms of reform, the justice model seeks to eliminate indeterminate sentencing and abolish parole altogether. According to the justice approach, convicted felons should know upon sentencing the date of their release from prison. The only exception to this is the reduction of time served by allowing prisoners to earn "good time" credits in exchange for good behavior in prison.

Advantages of the Justice Model

The justice model is a pragmatic approach to corrections. By emphasizing "justice" and "fairness" as centerpieces of its operational mandate, the justice model champions a correctional system that recognizes the rights and responsibilities of all the parties involved: victims, offenders, and correctional staff. The justice model accepts the reality of crime and, unlike rehabilitation or utilitarian punishment, it has no illusions about being able to stop or prevent crime. Given the fact that crime exists, the justice model reacts by meting out punishment proportionate to the harm that has been done, creates a system that treats felons humanely, and does all that is possible to restore victims to their precrime condition.

Disadvantages of the Justice Model

As a philosophical approach to corrections, the justice model is sound in its orientation. In practice, however, the justice model contains elements that weaken it as an overall correctional strategy.

By insisting that rehabilitative programs be totally voluntary, some prisoners with identifiable problems may never be treated. Such a passive approach to treatment demands nothing of prisoners. As a result, the primary goal of many prisoners becomes that of simply sitting back and doing their time. This means that upon release, if their crimes were in fact the consequence of personal or social problems, recidivism is likely.

Prisons that employ the justice model tend to be warehoused facilities. The warehousing of prisoners results when large numbers of compliant prisoners are herded in large groups, day in and day out, from one activity to the next. Prisoners who do their time in warehoused facilities basically eat, sleep, and recreate their way through the correctional system. A basic flaw of the justice model of corrections is that "correction" is missing from its operational definition.

In addition, over the past decade, the language of corrections has been used to justify a punitive orientation toward the treatment of offenders. Utilitarian punishment practitioners readily adopt the determinate sentencing and retribution emphasis of the justice model while forgetting justice's emphasis on prisoner rights and humane treatment. Additionally, punitive-oriented practitioners actively support the abolition of parole while ignoring justice's demands for reduced sentences and less of a reliance on prison as the primary means of crime control. To some extent, the massive overcrowding of America's prisons can be attributed to utilitarian punishment practices that have been implemented under the rubric of justice and fairness for all.

CONTEMPORARY CORRECTIONAL PHILOSOPHY—
AN INTEGRATIVE PERSPECTIVE

Utilitarian punishment, justice, and rehabilitation are three competing philosophies of correctional treatment. Throughout the history of corrections, each of these philosophies has, at one time or another, come into prominence and has dominated correctional practice. Upon assessing the advantages and disadvantages of each approach, which is best? Which of these philosophies most effectively reduces crime, reforms criminals, and protects society? The correct answer is none of them.

For too long we have accepted as legitimate arguments that portray criminals as being all of one type and correctional strategies that are successful with everyone. The truth is that utilitarian punishment works with some offenders and fails with others, justice works with some offenders but fails with others, and rehabilitation works for some offenders and fails with others. Each philosophy works well with certain classes of offenders and fails miserably when used as a sole approach to correctional treatment. Successful strategies for dealing with criminal offenders, therefore, hinge on our knowledge of the full range of correctional options available to us and our willingness to match specific offender types with adequate and effective treatment strategies.

Table 3.1 provides an overview of each of the major correctional philosophies. By identifying the major elements of each philosophy, this typology can be used to compare and contrast traditional responses to crime and the treatment of convicted felons.

Major issues in contemporary corrections stem from the predominately punitive approach to crime that has been undertaken over the past 25 years. Associated with the use of imprisonment as the principal mode of correctional practice has been an escalating rate of incarceration (at the same time that the rates of many types of crimes have remained steady or have dropped), the growth of large numbers of dangerously overcrowded prisons (filled in many instances with nonviolent offenders), and skyrocketing public expenditures on correctional facilities (that now directly rival education, medical care, and other public services for funding). Although these present-day concerns are a direct outgrowth of the predominant use of utilitarian punishment and justice practices, and even though present imprisonment practices clearly cannot continue without generating enormous social and economic costs, it would be a mistake to argue now for a complete switch to rehabilitative strategies.

A large and diverse array of people make up America's prison populations. Some offenders are addicted to drugs, some are violent and dangerous, some suffer from a range of personal or social problems, many

Table 3.1 Typology of Correctional Philosophies

	UTILITARIAN PUNISHMENT	JUSTICE	REHABILITATION
Image of the Criminal	Deliberate, calculating, habitual, and, at times, vicious in their criminality	Citizens who happen to break the law	People who, no matter what they may have done in the past, can be changed for the better
Principle Orientation Sentencing	Swift and certain retaliation Determinate, maximum penalties	Fairness and restitution Determinate penalties commensurate with harm or damage done	Reformation of criminals Indeterminate sentences that motivate offenders to participate in their own rehabilitation
Criminal Motivation	Criminals rationally decide to take advantage of their victims	Criminals are aware of their crimes and are also aware of the consequences if caught	Criminals are not fully aware of the reasons for their actions
Purpose of Punishment	Inflict pain on criminals, prevent further victimizations, and deter those who might consider engaging in crime	In terms of fairness, punish criminals to the same degree that they have harmed their victims	Use punishment to make criminals realize the harm they have done and want to participate in their own reformation into law-abiding citizens
Primary Treatment	Incarceration in prison	A least restrictive approach that imposes punishments commensurate with crimes	A variety of settings (from prison to half-way houses) designed to resocialize offenders and, prior to release, prepare them for integration back into the community
Apt Offender Types	Hardened, habitual, violent criminals who have little regard for their victims	Citizens who commit crimes and must pay the consequences of their actions	Disadvantaged persons who would not commit crime if they had other alternatives available to them
Distinctive Characteristics	Hard-line approach that assumes prison to be a central element of crime control	Accepts crime as a fact of life, treats offenders as citizens who have debts to repay, and attempts to return victims to their precrime condition	Institutes programs that reform criminals and release from custody persons who are less likely to commit further criminal acts

are poor and undereducated, while still others have simply made bad decisions. Choosing one approach for dealing with this diverse array of criminal offenders is as silly as trying to fit everyone into the same size suit of clothes—it just won't work.

So, what is the answer? Do solutions exist? For correctional treatment to advance, it is necessary to move beyond emotional and one-sided arguments for the strict use of one approach or another. Crime is a complex, multidimensional phenomenon reflecting the actions of diverse populations of people responding to a wide range of social, personal, and situational events. Therefore, in order to be effective, the reality of crime requires that crime control measures become equally diverse and sophisticated. By learning to incorporate the relative strengths and weaknesses of each of the major philosophical approaches to crime control, correctional practices of the future need not suffer from the narrow and often dogmatic practices of the past.

REFERENCES

Bartollas, C. (1985). *Correctional Treatment: Theory and Practice.* Englewood Cliffs, NJ: Prentice Hall.

Beccaria, C. (1764). *On Crimes and Punishment.* Reprint, Indianapolis: Bobbs Merrill, 1963.

Bentham, J. (1789). *A Fragment on Government and an Introduction to the Principles of Morals and Legislation.* W. Harrison (ed.). Oxford, England: Basil Blackwell, 1967.

Fogel, D. (1979). *We Are the Living Proof: The Justice Model for Corrections.* Cincinnati, OH: Anderson.

Jeffery, C.R. (1990). *Criminology: An Interdisciplinary Approach.* Englewood Cliffs, NJ: Prentice Hall.

chapter **4**

PRISON VIOLENCE
FROM WHERE I STAND

VICTOR HASSINE
Inmate, Pennsylvania Department of Corrections

INTRODUCTION

Prisons have become metaphors for violence. When people hear the word *prison,* what is conjured up in their minds are images of rape, violence, and brutality. For those living and working in prisons at the beginning of the new millennium, those free-world images of prison are as real as the bricks and mortar of the place they now call their home.

For convicts and prison guards alike, prison violence is never an abstract discussion on whether the violence is imported, home grown, the product of mental disorder, or a genetic predisposition. For those living and working in prisons today, such theoretical distinctions serve only to distract from the business of identifying patterns of prison violence as part of their daily efforts to predict its occurrence so that it might be avoided or prevented.

As a convict, I eat prison violence for breakfast, lunch, and dinner. It is with me when I wake in the morning and when I go to sleep at night. It stalks me during the day, and, steel-eyed, it glares at me throughout the night. It is the lead actor in my dreams and the villain during my conscious hours. I have learned the markings, scents, footprints, and the ways of violence, and, like a tracker, I hunt it down before it has an opportunity to do the same to me. In my endless efforts to elude prison violence, I have been forced to press against it, flesh to flesh, and have become intimate with it. Through my forced contact with prison violence, I have been able to develop a sixth sense, enabling me to feel its approach before it makes its arrival and to sense its presence before it has made a sound.

What follows is an account of my acquired knowledge of the day-to-day workings of prison violence. It is a sharing of the intelligence I have gathered after nineteen years of incarceration and survival in some of the most violent state prisons in the nation. It is the documentation of a process I have refined to assist me in predicting the whos, whens, and wheres of prison violence so that I may be better able to avoid that beast. I do not pretend to offer any explanations for the origins of or the underlying reasons for prison violence, nor do I claim to know the reasons that violence in prisons behaves in the way I describe. My purpose is to describe *what is* and to offer my opinion/perspective as to why I believe what is, is. Therefore, while my disclosures may not contribute to a greater academic or philosophic understanding of prison violence, they do reveal how prison staff members and residents alike deal with the growing threat of violence in contemporary prisons.

Please take what I present only for what it is worth. With that understanding, allow me to introduce to you my constant companion, *prison violence.*

WHO IS VIOLENT?

It never takes long for even the greenest convict to realize that given the right conditions and circumstances, everyone has the potential to become violent. Some convicts have the good fortune to possess this valuable knowledge before ever coming to prison, having learned the hard way (in county jail, juvenile detention, or maybe on the streets) never to underestimate someone's potential for violence. If anyone ever decides to formulate universal precautions for the prevention of violence in prisons, certainly, the first protocol would be, *Consider Everyone to Be Capable of Extreme Violence.*

THE KINDLING POINT FOR VIOLENCE

Once I had become convinced that anyone could become violent, I went about the business of refining my understanding of prison violence by developing a process for evaluating individuals' thresholds of intolerance to determine under what circumstances, conditions, and/or environment an individual can be expected to react in a violent manner. I soon discovered that, in the same way, different substances have specific kindling points (the temperature at which an object will begin to burn), individuals seem to have something akin to a point of combustion in the form of a kindling point for violence (KPV).

I began the process of determining individuals' KPV by first identifying what I considered to be the extremes in violent and nonviolent behavior. These extremes are violent—physical—responses to name calling (people falling into this category I consider to have the lowest KPV) and passivity during a physical assault (people falling into this category I consider to have the highest KPV). Between these two extremes, I draw a continuum.

Routinely, I go about observing individuals' reactions to everyday conditions and circumstances within the prison. Based on these observations, I have been able to make reasoned conclusions as to where on the continuum particular patterns of behavior fall. These points on the continuum indicate an individual's KPV.

Once I have rated and marked the KPV of most, if not all, of the people around me, I calculate whether their collective KPV ratings fall closer to the lowest or highest extreme of the continuum. If a clear majority of KPV ratings favor the high end of the continuum, I can conclude that my surroundings have less potential for violence than the norm. If the collective KPV ratings greatly favor the lower half of the continuum, I can conclude that my surroundings have a greater potential for violence than the norm. A bell-shaped distribution of KPV ratings, peaking at the center of the continuum, would suggest an average potential for violence.

Despite how it appears, maintaining KPV ratings and extrapolating from their clustering between extremes is not an overly cumbersome or complicated process. Over time, it becomes second nature and, in truth, most convicts and prison guards employ some method for determining individuals' KPV ratings from which to draw reasoned conclusions about a prison population's potential for violence. Actually, the most difficult aspect of the process is that of intelligence gathering since most people try to mask their violent tendencies.

Prison Life When the Kindling Point of Violence Is Unknown

After having adjusted to their surroundings, prison residents are usually extremely reluctant to move from one cell block to another or from one prison to another, no matter how violent or unpleasant their living conditions. One reason for this is that such moves render their years of observations, intelligence gathering, and assessments worthless and force them to begin anew the tedious and sometimes dangerous process of assessing individuals' KPV rates. The process may take years to complete and, until then, even the most seasoned convict feels vulnerable and unsafe. Staying safe in prison means knowing what to expect from your neighbors.

Not surprisingly, prisons that have a high turnover rate in its resident population (50 percent or higher) within a short period of time (less than one year) are more likely to have a relatively high rate of violence. A reason for this is that most of the residents in these institutions do not remain long enough to permit adequate opportunities to assess the KPVs of their neighbors. Without sufficient intelligence, accurate information regarding residents' potentials for violence cannot be gathered or shared, leaving the painful experience of prison violence as the primary method of learning who is violent. Then, once residents have remained long enough to accumulate adequate and accurate information regarding individuals' KPVs, they will be released to the community or transferred to another institution where this once valuable information will be of little use.

Institutions with high and quick turnovers in general population are usually county jails (which generally release or transfer commitments within two years) and state inmate classification centers (which generally transfer their commitments to other prisons within less than a year). Understandably, most state classification centers/units permit very limited and controlled resident movement in order to offset the heightened potential for violence. In contrast, most county jails do not have the resources needed to prevent the increased violence generated by high and quick turnovers in resident population and, predictably, it has been my experience that county jails are often the most violent facilities within a state's adult corrections system.

The Kindling Point of Violence of Groups

Since the KPV is based on subjective factors, it is therefore unique to each individual. However, there are ranges of KPV ratings within which large groups of people displaying similar behaviors or characteristics can be expected to fall. If a prison population is overrepresented by a class of individuals who can be expected to have KPV ratings that fall within a range at the higher end of the KPV continuum, this prison population is likely to be less violent than one consisting of a class of individuals who can be expected to possess KPV ratings that fall within a range at the lower end of the KPV continuum.

For example, assume the following:

1. People 25 years old and younger tend to have a much lower KPV than do people 30 and older.

2. Convicts who have been incarcerated five or more years tend to have a much higher KPV than do those who have been incarcerated less than five years.
3. People with sentences of 10 or more years tend to have a higher KPV than do those with a sentence of five years or less.

It is likely that a prison population consisting exclusively of long-term inmates (serving 10 or more years), who have all served at least 5 years and who are over 30 years of age, will experience less violence than one equal in size consisting exclusively of residents under 25 years of age, who are serving less than 5 years and who are new arrivals to the prison.

Changes in the Kindling Point of Violence

An individual's KPV can shift either higher or lower as a result of changes in conditions or circumstances that have the ability to affect the potential for violence. For example, a person who would normally walk away from a fight even after he has been physically attacked might respond violently to only slight provocation when he is drunk. In this case, the effects of the alcohol act as an *accelerant to violence* (AV). In contrast, a person who is normally quick to throw a punch might become much more passive and tolerant when under the influence of heroin. In this case, the effects of the heroin acts as a *retardant to violence* (RV).

It is very important to the process of predicting the occurrence of violence within a prison to identify the most influential AVs and RVs affecting the members of the resident population. That is to say, if you know (1) that a person has a very low kindling point of violence and (2) that at a given time and place, that person will be acted upon by an AV, you can reasonably conclude that violence is likely to occur at that particular time and place when the individual encounters the AV.

Prisons are large, complicated, and elaborate facilities of completely contrived social and physical environments within which bricks, bars, guards, bells, whistles, sounds, and walkways are utilized in a manner meant to maximize conformity, control, and submission. Within these fabricated social and physical environments, almost every action, sound, and structure can in some way act as either an RV or an AV. Therefore, within every prison community there is the constant play of AVs and RVs that continually modifies individuals' and group attitudes and behaviors (including the attitudes and behaviors of prison employees).

Knowing the difference between RVs and AVs and how they might interact to influence members of a prison population can provide important information about the potential for violence within that population. Unfortunately, most prison managers do not measure the effects of changes that prison policies, conditions, and physical design may have in terms of their likelihood to lower or elevate individuals' potential for violence. The main concerns of prison-o-crats are fiscal and, consequently, the cost effectiveness of security measures are considered before the possibility of secondary impacts on the potential for violence. As a result, the rate of violence within a given prison population can depend upon the random dominance of either AVs or RVs.

Applications of Retardants to Violence and Accelerants to Violence

Often a multiple of differing RVs or AVs acts upon an individual or group at the same time. Generally, the higher the number of RVs acting upon an individual or group, the greater the retardant effects on that individual's or group's potential for violence. Similarly, the higher the number of AVs acting upon an individual or group, the greater the accelerant effects on that individual's or group's potential for violence. As a consequence, the more RVs there are acting upon an individual or group, the greater the upward migration of the individual's or group's KPV. The more AVs there are acting upon an individual or group, the greater the downward migration of the individual's or group's KPV.

When three RVs act upon an individual or group with no AVs to balance or offset their effects, the result is expressed as an increase in the individual's or group's KPV by three RVs. When three AVs act upon an individual or group with no RVs to balance or offset their effects, the result is expressed as a drop in the individual's or group's KPV by three AVs.

No two AVs or RVs are equal. At any given time, each will exert a lesser or greater influence upon an individual or group. For example, *single celling* (having only one resident in a single cell) is a much greater RV than is television in dayrooms, and good and plentiful food is a much greater RV than central air conditioning in the housing units. Therefore, in these cases, the RVs of single cells and good and plentiful food can be expected to result in a greater upward shift in the KPV than the RVs of televisions in dayrooms or central air conditioning in the housing units. Similarly, prison overcrowding is a much greater AV than poor lighting, and unappetizing and insufficient food is a much greater AV than hot weather.

Therefore, the AVs of overcrowding or unappetizing and insufficient food can be expected to result in a greater downward shift in the KPV than the AVs of poor lighting and hot weather.

The different weights of RVs and AVs, in terms of their varying degrees of influence on the behavior of individuals or groups, should always be taken into account when measuring their effects on the KPV. For the sake of simplification, when ranking the KPV of large groups or whole resident populations, all RVs and AVs should be considered equal because large collections of RVs and AVs will usually produce a balanced averaging of their differences in influence.

Accordingly, an equal number of AVs and RVs acting at the same time, upon the same group, can be said to cancel each other out, thereby causing no change in the KPV. But if a group is acted upon, at the same time, by three RVs and only two AVs, the result will be a net increase in the KPV of one RV.

For example, if inmates are given single cells in an overcrowded prison, the retardant effects of the single cell will be deemed fully offset by the accelerant effects of the overcrowding, and resulting in no shift in the KPV. If inmates in an overcrowded prison are given single cells and permitted televisions in their cells, there will be a net increase in the KPV of one RV. Thus, by first adding all of the influential AVs and then all of the influential RVs that are acting upon a group and then subtracting the lesser total from the greater, a quick determination can be made as to how much higher or lower a group's KPV will shift.

Retardants to Violence and Accelerants to Violence in Groups and Subgroups

AVs and RVs not only affect individuals but also can affect the conduct or behavior of a group of individuals. For example, prison facilities with poorly prepared and/or insufficient food can bring about a decrease of the KPV in all the residents of the institution, while tasty and plentiful meals can bring about an increase of the KPV in all the residents of the institution. Meanwhile, conditions in a particular housing unit might be unique to that particular unit and therefore affect the KPV of only individuals living in that unit. It is always important to discern which AVs and RVs assert their influences both locally and prisonwide.

In accessing the collective tendencies for violence of individuals within a particular prison housing unit, localized AVs and RVs should be considered as more influential than general AVs and RVs. When assessing the collective potential for violence of all the residents of a prison population, localized AVs and RVs should not be considered at all; only prisonwide AVs and RVs should be counted. This is so because separate housing units and other discrete areas within a prison often operate independently and, therefore, differently from each other, thereby forming subgroups within the larger group of a prison's general population. Some of these subgroups can experience much more or much less violence than is experienced within the general population as a whole. Thus, a resident living in a safe institution may find himself housed in a particularly violent housing unit. If the resident knows this, a simple move to another cell block will bring about an immediate increase in safety. On the other hand, a resident may find himself in a housing unit that has a much higher KPV than that of the overall prison population. Knowledge of this might cause aresident to think twice about moving to another housing unit.

Properties of Accelerants to Violence

Some AVs merely facilitate violence while others actually elicit a violent response. For example, a security blind spot in a housing unit (a place routinely unobservable by prison guards) can facilitate violence by providing predators a place to victimize in relative secrecy. So a security blind spot can be considered a facilitating AV that will affect the KPV of only those individuals who are already predisposed to violence.

In contrast, some AVs actually incite violence in people who normally would not act violently. For example, drugs, such as cocaine and methamphetamine, can, and often do, trigger violent responses. These AVs can be considered triggering AVs. Triggering AVs can affect the KPV of everyone exposed to them.

At first glance, it would seem that facilitating AVs, since they tend to act only on those already predisposed to violence, should not pose as great a concern as do triggering AVs, which can turn whole populations from nonviolent to violent. It is this mistaken belief that makes facilitating AVs so dangerous.

Chronic and abundant facilitating AVs can stimulate many collateral triggering AVs. For example, an abundance of security blind spots in a housing unit or prison will greatly increase the incidents of predatory violence. This, in turn, will increase the levels of fear and concern over personal safety throughout the prison population. These widespread feelings of fear and danger are, in fact, triggering AVs that may cause otherwise peaceful residents to overreact and respond violently to minor incidents.

One of the most obvious examples of the collateral triggering effects of a facilitating AV is the routine practice of housing two residents in a cell designed for one (double celling). Widespread double celling greatly facilitates predatory attacks by allowing potential victims to be locked in unsupervised cells with predators. While double celling does not create predators, its prisonwide practice can create a great deal of anxiety and worry within the resident population over eventually being forced to double cell with a predator. This worry and anxiety can quickly turn into prisonwide fear and panic once word of victimization begins to spread. Such feelings are very influential in triggering AVs, which can quickly and greatly decrease the KPV in even the safest of prison environments.

PATTERNS OF PRISON VIOLENCE

Certain conditions/events/circumstances occur within institutions that will always increase tendencies for violence. These consistent patterns of violence are commonly known to prison staff and residents and occur in all prison populations. The following lists some common patterns of violence that have existed in every facility in which I have been housed:

- When a prison population is locked down for a long period of time (more than 24 hours of total confinement in a cell), there will be a dramatic increase in aggressive behavior and a potential for violence throughout the prison during the hours immediately following the release of residents from their cells. This may be a result of the sudden shock of spatial expansion.

- Generally, prison residents have the highest potential for violence (1) during the months immediately following incarceration and (2) during the months immediately preceding release from a prison. The tendency for violent behavior that effects most people immediately following incarceration might be a by-product of the initial resistance to institutionalization (similar to a wild horse resisting being saddled) as one moves from relative freedom to a state of captivity. The violence preceding release from institutionalization might be the product of anxiety and concerns over the ability to survive outside an institutional setting. Conventional prison wisdom states that the fear and anxiety experienced when a person is first confined in a prison are exceeded only by the fear and anxiety that precedes release. Prisons have absolutely no programs to help a person through the transition from years of institutionalized dependence to self-sufficiency and to meet the demands of a competitive society.

- In Pennsylvania prisons, every year at about the time of the vernal equinox (spring), an extra two hours of yard activity–known as *Night Yard*—is permitted every day from about 6 P.M. to 8 P.M. At about the autumnal equinox (fall), Night Yard is discontinued, and evening recreation activities are, for the most part, restricted to the dayrooms in the various housing units.

Thus, every spring, prison residents across Pennsylvania greatly increase their outdoor recreation through participation in Night Yard activity. Then every autumn, prison residents throughout the state have their outdoor recreation significantly restricted with the termination of Night Yard.

Interestingly enough, there is always an expected increase in the incidents of violence and in the number of rule infractions during the first few weeks immediately following the commencement and the termination of Night Yard. This spiking of violence may be caused by *seasonal affective disorder* (SAD), the shock of sudden spatial contraction and expansion, or some combination of the two.

Influential Retardants to Violence

Alcohol. Alcohol is a depressant and as such can retard violence; however, alcohol also lowers inhibitions and can therefore be considered an AV, depending on the individual's reaction to the drug.

Heroin and Other Opiates. These drugs are powerful depressants, and most people under their influence will spend hours in a relaxed and peaceful state of euphoria. However, for collateral reasons, heroin and other opiates often initiate many influential triggering AVs.

Prescription Anti-depressants and Physiatric Drugs. These drugs were specifically designed to calm and tranquilize people. Under the influence of these drugs, most people are not inclined toward violent behavior. Since these drugs are prescribed by prison doctors and distributed at no cost to the resident, they are extremely effective RVs.

Good and Plentiful Meals. After eating a tasty and hearty meal, the last thing on a person's mind is fighting or violence. More likely, the individual will want to nap.

Cold Temperatures. During the coldest part of winter, violence in a prison is greatly reduced. During a prison riot—one I had the misfortune of getting caught in—the only reason there were no killings was that the temperature was −14° F and most people were concentrating their efforts on trying to stay warm.

Air Conditioning. Cool temperatures maintained within the comfort zone in a cell block, work area, and common area provide an excellent RV. One reason for this is that people tend to sleep better when the temperature around them is kept within the comfort zone. In turn, people who get a good night's sleep tend to behave less irritably when awake and therefore are less inclined toward violence.

Keeping this in mind, the solitary confinement units in many prisons with air conditioning routinely maintain the temperature in these units well below the comfort zone in an effort to reduce violent outbursts against prison staff working in the units. Unfortunately, the temperatures in these units are so cold that the residents do not sleep well for the duration of their stay and, therefore, suffer the effects of sleep deprivation once they are released into the general population. This tends to increase the prison population's potential for violence.

Good Lighting. Prisons with good lighting provide its residents a sense of safety the same way brightly lit streets at night provide communities a sense of safety.

Visits and Access to Telephones. Contact with family and community members is extremely important to institutionalized individuals. Having such contact gives a person some sense of belonging and identity. The more contact people have with their families and friends, the calmer and less aggressive they become. Also, because visits and the use of phones are so important to maintaining contact with friends and family, institutionalized people who wish to maintain these ties are reluctant to do anything that might jeopardize these privileges. The threat of losing visiting and phone privileges serves as an excellent RV, especially if these privileges are liberal and well established.

Showers. There is nothing more invigorating, refreshing, and calming than a shower, especially on a hot day or during times of stress. Liberal access to showers along with adequate shower facilities are excellent RVs, in addition to being good for community hygiene.

Rainy Days. Rainy, overcast days tend to serve as an RV. I believe this is so because many people respond to this kind of weather by remaining indoors, thereby reducing interaction with others. Less interaction translates into fewer opportunities for violence to erupt.

Television in the Cell. Television viewing has an almost narcotic effect on people. When a television is made available, many people will spend hours watching it. If televisions are allowed in the cells, many people will spend hours in their cell watching TV programs without ever complaining too much about being locked up. While TVs in common areas can act as RVs, if an adequate number of televisions is not available to meet all of the residents' preferences, fights and arguments will erupt over channel selection. Therefore, the most effective use of television as an RV is when it is allowed in the cells.

Privileges and Possessions. The more privileges a prison extends to its residents and the more private possessions they are allowed to retain, the greater is the deterrent of the threat of losing these privileges and possessions. There is no greater instigator of violence than to ensure that the members of a prison population have nothing to lose.

Adequate Recreation Facilities. Adequate recreation facilities, including adequate space, equipment, and staffing, is an excellent RV because many people will exhaust themselves by engaging in recreational activities. Consequently, these people will not have the energy to act out violently. It is worth noting that being physically fit does not in any way trigger violence.

Employment. Having meaningful full-time jobs is an extremely effective RV because it keeps people busy and provides them with feelings of self-worth. After a day's work, people are also usually too tired to consider acting out violently.

Hobbies. Hobbies provide a productive means for occupying idle time and for maintaining a sense of achievement and self-worth. The most common hobbies in prison are drawing, painting, reading, and arts and crafts. People tend to focus much of their attention on their hobbies, leaving them with little time or interest to engage in violent conduct.

Feelings. People's moods and feelings have an important impact on their likelihood to act out violently. The more successful a prison administration is at encouraging peaceful feelings such as the following within the resident population, the less violence that prison will experience:

- Safety
- Contentment
- Hopefulness
- Spaciousness
- Purpose
- Self-worth
- Healthiness
- Fair treatment
- Fullness (not hungry)

General Populations of Under 1,000 and Housing Units of Under 100. For prisons, fewer means safer. One reason for this is that in small populations, it is easier for people to identify and to get to know all of the people around them, which provides residents with a tremendous feeling of comfort because they will know whom they must guard against.

Single Cells. Single cells represent one of the most effective RVs. They provide people a place to retreat where they can feel safe and apart from the prison madness. A great deal of general population discomfort and anxiety can be overcome by providing single cells.

Radios. Radios are considered "the poor convict's television." They work as an RV in the same way televisions do except that radios are not as mesmerizing. With a radio, however, residents can be expected to spend more time in their cells.

Good Rapport Among Residents and Staff. It has been my experience that institutions with the least amount of social distance between residents and staff are the least likely to be violent. The reason for this is that

to maintain a good rapport, staff must operate as more than mere discipli-
narians and must demonstrate actual concern for the safety and well-
being of residents. When a good rapport exists, staff will be motivated not
to let conditions become too unpleasant or dangerous. This in turn will
lead to less violence.

Large Prision Populations of Individuals Over Forty Years of Age. Forty
seems to be the magic age when the likelihood of an adult committing
crimes or recidivating sharply decline. Likewise, in prisons, people over
40 years of age are notably more calm and less resistant to institutionalization than are younger people. This could be a sign of either maturity
or fatigue. Whatever the reason, it means less interest in engaging in
violence.

Large General Populations of People Serving More Than Ten Years.
There is definitely a relationship between the length of time being served
and the tendency to respond violently. People with sentences of over 10
years know they are going to be incarcerated for a long time and so tend to
do their best to adjust to their environment (getting "dug in"). Also, people
with long sentences have the time to develop secondary adjustments to
ease some of the pressures of institutionalization.

Influential Accelerants of Violence

Alcohol, Barbiturates, and Opiates. Alcohol's tendency to reduce inhibitions can increase the likelihood of violent responses. However, to the
vast majority of people, alcohol, like barbiturates and opiates, acts as a
tranquilizer and even as an immobilizer. In a prison population, most of
the violence deriving from alcohol, barbiturate, and opiate consumption is
not related to the drugs' biochemical effects on the consumer's behavior.
Instead, violence often results collaterally from (1) the trafficking in these
highly addictive and lucrative drugs, (2) the extreme methods employed by
addicts to secure funds to purchase these drugs, and (3) their use as immo-
bilizers to facilitate predation.

Amphetamines and Cocaine. These drugs, by design, act as powerful
stimulants meant to render their users more alert, assertive, and, often,
more aggressive. These drugs are highly addictive, and their extended
abuse can lead to sleep deprivation and violent behavior associated with it.
In addition, the availability of these drugs within a prison population pro-
duces collateral violence through trafficking and disputes among dealers.

Hunger. Hunger includes the dissatisfaction with the amount and
quality of food offering. The vast majority of prison residents are completely

dependent upon staff members for providing daily meals. Most prisons feed their general population by systematically assembling hungry residents, three times a day, in groups of hundreds, and crowding them into large dining rooms where each resident is provided a tray full of various foods that must be eaten quickly. This predictable routine of crowding hundreds of hungry people into such confined and close quarters provides prison violence a convenient venue. In the environment of a crowded prison dining room, if food portions are too small, unappetizing, or ill-prepared, the hungry residents are more likely to be irritable and disgruntled when they are served their meals. These hostile feelings, repeated three times a day, greatly increase the already great potential for violence. Additionally, if portions are too small, it is very possible that violence will erupt as the "strong" take food away from the "weak." Even minor squabbles in a crowded prison dining room can lead to a full-scale riot in a matter of seconds (especially when residents have trays and utensils that can be used as weapons). Thus, the temperament of hungry prison residents crammed together in a prison dining room is an important consideration in the prison administrations' efforts to prevent planned or spontaneous prison violence and rioting.

Idleness. This term includes unemployment within a prison. (Prison employment refers to meaningful, full-time employment with adequate wage incentives). High rates of resident unemployment within a prison population generally increase the potential for violence because idle residents are likely to form gangs to facilitate theft and/or trade in contraband. The higher the percentage of unemployed residents in a prison system, the greater the potential for violence, thievery, and gang activity.

Limited Shower Use. Showers have a cooling, calming, soothing, and cleansing effect on prison residents, especially in prisons that are not climate controlled. For this reason, many members of the general population greatly value showers. If a prison limits shower use either by design or by failing to provide sufficient showering facilities, the potential for violence can increase when residents compete for use of this greatly valued allowance. Also, most prisons utilize group showering facilities that can accommodate dozens of residents at a time. Overcrowding these shower areas creates a chronic security blind spot facilitating predatory behavior and thereby increasing fear and tension within the general population.

Poor Lighting. Residents of poorly lighted prison facilities remain in a perpetual state of alarm due to poor visibility and security blind spots created by shadows. The heightened sense of worry brought about by poor lighting triggers defensive responses, often in the form of aggressiveness and irritability. Also, predators are emboldened by shadowy areas because they are not likely to be identified there by staff at a distance.

Feelings. The less able a prison administration is to prevent hostile feelings from spreading throughout a prison population, the greater the potential for violence within that prison. Similarly, the more successful a prison administration is at encouraging hostile feelings within a prison population, the greater the potential for violence within that prison. These hostile feelings includes the following:

- Depression
- Desperation
- Hopelessness
- Lack of purpose
- Fear
- Shame
- Suicide

It is important to note that the spread of suicidal behavior within a prison population creates a great potential for violence. Many suicidal people in prison express their self-destructive tendencies in the form of behavior calculated to cause others to inflict injury upon them. For example, many of these people will start fights with staff members or prison residents for the singular purpose of being injured at the hands of another. In this way, these suicidal residents manipulate others to assist them in their suicidal behavior or in their attempts to get the attention of prison staff. These instigations of violence might eventually ignite large-scale violence. In the case of nonassisted suicides and suicide attempts, their occurrence tends to foment anger toward prison staff in general (especially in cases of popular residents), who are often collectively blamed for fostering the conditions that led to the suicide or attempted suicide. This, in turn, adversely effects the rapport between staff members and residents.

Gangs. Where prison gangs are formed, violence is sure to follow. It is the nature of prison gangs to assert their power and influence through the use of force and fear. Gangs are often the collateral result of prison idleness and/or lapses in security and/or overcrowding.

Lapses in Security. These security lapses include design flaws in the building (blind spots, poor lighting, inadequate facilities, etc.), and insufficient staffing or ineffective application of security measures (having a one-to-one inmate-to-staff ratio on a housing block is of little value if the corrections officers remain in an office drinking coffee for the duration of their shifts). Predatory inmates are experts at detecting and exploiting any and all lapses in security. Prison residents will soon be made painfully aware of these lapses once predators utilize them, possibly igniting a spiraling of tension and fear throughout the prison population. As for security blind spots, basically there are two kinds: chronic and intermittent.

Chronic blind spots are the most likely to encourage violence since predators will have enough time to devise effective strategies for their exploitation. Population density can constitute a chronic blindspot whenever and wherever it predictably and routinely obstructs visibility. Excessively dense prison populations (especially when combined with other chronic blind spots such as poor lighting) can generate fear in staff members as well, which might discourage proper enforcement of rules and regulations.

Inadequate Recreational Areas/Equipment. Recreation areas and equipment can be inadequate in availability or in capacity. If a prison does not provide adequate recreational facilities and/or access to such facilities (because of prison design or policy), idleness *within the prison population* will increase, especially if there is a high rate of unemployment in the general population. If inadequate recreation occurs in the form of overutilization of recreation facilities due to prison overcrowding, an increase in the potential for violence is a by-product of the competition for access to recreational equipment and space and/or of blind spots in recreational areas due to population density.

Overcrowding. Overcrowding occurs when the number of residents housed in a prison exceeds the prison's design capacity. In addition to creating tension and frustration within the general population because of the watering down of available prison resources and services, prison overcrowding also creates population density problems. The more dense a prison population becomes, the more difficult it is to provide adequate security. Additionally, increased population density means less familiarity among residents and staff members, which fosters fear, tension, and poor rapport.

Poor Rapport Among Residents and Staff Members. There is always some social distance between staff members and prison residents, but when that social distance becomes too great, the relationship between the two groups becomes hostile, creating an "us versus them" environment. Once this occurs, staff members may become indifferent about maintaining safe and humane conditions for their charges, which, in turn, can lead to chronic lapses in security and a tolerance of resident-on-resident violence. This ultimately can create a hostile prison environment of fear and predation, which can greatly increase the potential for prison violence.

Large Percentage of Residents under 25. Prison residents under the age of 25 tend to be more aggressive and prone to violence.

Large Population of Short-Term Residents. This includes those serving less than five years, especially parole violators. People who do not have a stake in the stability of a prison population tend to be more prone to violence. It has been my experience that residents with less than a five-year sentence are not likely to consider the prison their home. Accordingly, these short-timers are more likely to disrupt prison routine and exploit other residents. This is so because these short-timers know that they will not have to deal with the long-term consequences of their behavior since they will be released soon. This is especially true of parole violators who enter prison directly from the streets and might serve only a year or two. Such short-timers with "the streets still in them" have little interest in prison stability and are more interested in exploiting prison resources and the residents.

Double Celling and Dormitory Housing. Double celling and dormitory housing increase the potential for violence by affecting mood and, therefore, facilitating violence. There is no more irritating or frustrating feeling than having to share a cell with another person or a dormitory with many other people. This irritation and frustration can quickly turn to anger and violence at the very slightest provocation. Additionally, double cells and dormitories create ideal conditions for prison predators who exploit the chronic blind spots these conditions necessarily create.

PRACTICAL APPLICATIONS

It is 2 P.M. and you enter a prison for the first time. Suddenly all of your survival instincts are heightened and stimulated as you experience the sensation of immersion into a hot and heavy alien atmosphere. All of your senses are hypersensitive, your muscles are tightly coiled, prepared for immediate action, and your mind feverishly sorts, stores, and analyzes an endless flood of new information. The distant sound of steel cell doors slamming shut and countless metal keys clanking together command your attention, while layer upon layer of angry anonymous voices endlessly reverberates all around you, keeping you on a constant vigil for impending danger of an unknown kind.

You walk, tentatively, through the prison facility toward your appointed destination, when suddenly you see the prison yard. You are overwhelmed and a little frightened by the number of people you see pressed together in the small fenced enclosure. A closer scrutiny of the men milling around in the yard reveals (1) a couple of residents casually speaking to a couple of corrections officers, (2) a group of men, all with their left pant legs rolled up to their knee, huddled together and engaged in conversation, (3) runners around a running track weaving around a dense collection of walkers, and (4) a single basketball court filled beyond capacity with players and onlookers.

Once you arrive at your housing unit, you immediately notice (1) an increase in lighting, (2) a sizable number of seated men watching a large overhead TV set, (3) small groups of men sitting at tables playing cards,

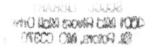

(4) three guards talking to each other around a desk at the front of the unit, and (5) two men exiting one cell to join the others watching TV.

To an untrained observer, the scenes just described would have no noteworthy significance. However, to experienced prison residents and staff members, these are important clues that reveal a great deal about the prison's relative danger or safety. For example, a crowded prison yard at mid-afternoon means that many residents are not working and are idle. It also means that the yard has many security blind spots because of the crowd density. Idleness, overcrowding, and blind spots are all influential AVs. Also, the crowded basketball court and running track indicate the AV of insufficient recreation space. The single most significant and potentially dangerous of the observations, however, is the one of the huddled group of men who all have their pant legs uniformly rolled up, indicating the influential AV of prison gang activity. In contrast, the sight of prison residents and staff talking together openly in a crowded yard is an indication of the influential RV of good staff/resident rapport.

Given that in this example there are at least five influential AVs (overcrowding, blind spots, insufficient recreation space, prison gangs, and idleness) and only one influential RV (good staff/resident rapport), it can be concluded that conditions in the yard indicate a migration of KPV toward violence.

In the housing unit, an experienced observer would notice the influential AVs of (1) inefficient security (three guards talking together instead of making their rounds) and (2) double celling. The trained observer would also notice in the dayroom the influential RVs of (1) TV, (2) adequate recreation space, and (3) good lighting. Given this mix of AVs and RVs, it can be reasonably concluded that the KPV in the housing unit is falling toward the nonviolent end of the continuum.

Based on these observations, a prison resident or staff member can reasonably conclude that, at that given time, violence is much more likely to erupt in the yard than in the housing unit. Thus, it would be wise for a resident to engage in recreation in the dayroom rather than in the yard at this time. Based on that conclusion, prison managers would be wise to in some way encourage more residents to use the dayroom for recreation during this time so that the potential for violence in the yard can be decreased by reducing resident density, without necessarily increasing the potential for violence in the housing unit.

CONCLUSION

Long before we had any real understanding of the nature or the causes of lightning, primitive peoples made it their business to watch and remember where and when lightning would strike. Certainly, some of the watchfulness was a product of curiosity and the instinctive need to know, but my guess is that most of it was simply the result of the greater instinct of survival. And so it was that people made certain to remember and to pass on the fact that storm clouds usually precede lightning while thunder follows its strike.

Eventually, enough bits and pieces of information about the whens and wheres of lightning were collected, enabling people to make reasoned predictions about the whens and wheres of future lightning strikes. It was just a matter of time until the whys of lightning were being theorized based upon existing knowledge of its habits. Finally, all of the bits and pieces of accumulated information about lightning were strung together, leading to a fuller understanding of the nature and causes of lightning.

The knowledge we possess about prison violence today is much like the primitive understanding we once had about lightning: All we know for certain about prison violence is its habits. We know very little about the actual causes and nature of prison violence. Through careful collection and analysis of the information we do have, we can at least learn how to predict and, therefore, avoid the strike of prison violence. Hopefully, someday soon we will have gathered enough information to lead us to a complete understanding of the true nature and causes of prison violence.

What we as a society may choose to do, once we have solved the mystery of prison violence, is as important as our need to understand. Will our complete understanding of prison violence be used to heal or hurt, liberate or incarcerate, build or destroy? Already every prison manager knows that overcrowded prisons breed violence, yet many prisons nationwide are still overcrowded. Every prison manager knows that unemployment and idleness encourage prison violence, yet the majority of prison residents are still kept idle and unemployed. And every prison manager knows that prison violence will ultimately lead to more violence in our society as institutionalized residents are released to their communities, yet prison violence is still tolerated in our prisons.

The storm clouds of overcrowding, hostility, idleness, and desperation are collecting and thickening above our nation's prisons, while violence strikes their residents without mercy. Even if we cannot or will not dissipate these storm clouds, there is good reason to guard, in every way possible, against the strike of prison violence, which we know is probably assailing someone, in some prison, at this very moment.

chapter 5

THE INMATE SUBCULTURE IN JUVENILE CORRECTIONAL SETTINGS

DOROTHY L. TAYLOR
University of Miami

WILSON R. PALACIOS
University of South Florida

INTRODUCTION

Two social realities coexist in juvenile correctional settings: society's official structure of rules and procedures and the less formal and more powerful inmate society. Clemmer's (1940) early research indicated that inmates eventually embrace the culture of the prison community by developing inmate social systems. Some studies have found that the inmate subculture originates because of the distress of incarceration; others have surmised that the subculture is imported from the outside. No matter how the subculture originates, empirical evidence indicates that the inmate community can profoundly influence institutional rehabilitative efforts (Clemmer, 1940; Irwin and Cressy, 1962; Larson, 1983; Sykes, 1958).

IMPACT OF CULTURAL NORMS ON VIOLENCE
IN JUVENILE CORRECTIONAL SETTINGS

Juvenile correctional institutions have existed for almost 200 years. Houses of refuge and reformatories were the first facilities created in the United States to house and rehabilitate juvenile delinquents. While attempting to transform them into worthwhile, productive citizens, these institutions encountered numerous difficulties, such as overcrowding, inadequate funding and staffing, and violence that was assumed to be caused by the increase in hard-core delinquents who were committed to them (Mennel, 1973).

Many of these difficulties still exist in juvenile correctional institutions, which include detention centers, shelters, public and private training schools, reception-diagnostic centers, work camps, and boot camps (Thornton and Voigt, 1992).

Over the years, many social scientists have questioned the professed goal of these institutions to rehabilitate (Bell, 1990; Hood, 1967; Lee and Haynes, 1980). Among the many reasons for this doubt is the impact of cultural norms on violence in juvenile correctional settings.

In discussing Turk's (1969) currently accepted conflict theory on the distinction between rule-breaking behavior and conduct defined as deviant, Thornton and Voigt (1992: 211–212) presented the following example of Turk's delineation of cultural norms (publicized norms) and social norms (actual behavior):

> Conflict and the assignment of a deviant label depend upon whether there is congruence or lack of congruence between these social norms and the cultural evaluation of the norms. For instance, when those in authority believe the use of marijuana is wrong and abstain from using it but younger members of a society believe the use of marijuana is acceptable and use it, the potential for conflict between the two groups is great. In this situation, there is a strong likelihood that those who use the drug will come to be defined as delinquent. On the other hand, if those in authority say that the use of marijuana is wrong but use the drug themselves, the conflict between the two groups is more symbolic than actual. And the assignment of deviant label is much less likely.

Turk (1969), as well as other conflict and radical theorists (Chambliss, 1984; Hagan, 1990; Platt, 1975; Quinney, 1975; Sellin, 1938; Vold, 1958), have delineated the personal and social factors that cause friction between authorities and subjects (in this case, juvenile justice practitioners and juvenile inmates). However, neither these findings nor those of subcultural theorists have been beneficial in the juvenile offender rehabilitation process.

Proponents of subcultural theories, such as Wolfgang and Ferracuti (1967) and Miller (1958), have also presented significant findings. They consider delinquency to be a concurrent response to society's cultural value system and a bond to group norms. Subcultural theorists contend that delinquency is an expression of principles advocated by one's reference group, such as other members of the subculture, and, therefore, that delinquency comprises behavior compatible with a group of norms. The issue of norms, referred to as *social codes,* will be discussed later in the chapter.

In spite of standards and guidelines set 25 years ago by the Commission on Criminal Justice Standards and Goals, most juveniles in correctional settings are just "doing time." Because of overcrowding in juvenile correctional facilities, turf wars erupt and gang violence increases (Allen and Simonsen, 1998: 338) (see Box 5.1).

The few studies that have explored the impact of cultural norms on violence in juvenile correctional settings and the consequences of inmate social systems have reported that solid and forceful inmate codes influence the behavior of both inmates and staff (Thornton and Voigt, 1992: 427).

Box 5.1   ⚖   *Juveniles and Violence*

If the criminal justice system has largely been driven by the need to protect society by punishing offenders, the hallmark of the juvenile justice system is the quite different presumption that young people who commit crimes can learn to do better if placed in the right setting and given the right care. Yet most juvenile correctional facilities in the United States are designed to hold large numbers of youths in primitive conditions. Many of these juvenile facilities are overcrowded, rely on leg shackles and handcuffs to control behavior, and "graduate" youths who often go on to commit more serious crimes as they get older. Each year about 11,000 out of the 65,000 incarcerated juveniles commit suicide acts, yet most facilities have inadequate suicide prevention programs.

In recent years, as stories of teen violence have become regular features of our newspapers and television news programs, we have lost sight of the crucial distinction between adult and juvenile facilities. Until the 1980s, the biggest threats to young people were car accidents and suicide. In that decade, according to the National Center for Health Statistics, teenage males in all racial and ethnic groups became more likely to die from a bullet than from all natural causes.

Source: Allen and Simonsen (1998): 339.

JUVENILE SOCIAL CODES

Subcultures in juvenile correctional facilities develop independently of administrators and custodians, and juveniles who enter correctional facilities observe a social world of strong inmate codes of behavior that most inmates understand. In their study of an Ohio state institution for boys, Bartollas, Miller, and Dinitz (1976) reported the emergence of a normative informal code consisting of a series of specific principles for daily living that was passed from inmate to inmate. This code had eight elements (see Box 5.2). The values of inmate social systems are embodied in this code, whose violations usually produce sanctions ranging from ostracism and avoidance to physical violence (Sykes and Messinger, 1960: 6). Although this code appears to unite inmates against the staff, Wellford (1967) found that inmates are usually not a cohesive group and typically exploit fragile and new residents.

Adult prison inmates often cope with the strict and unforgiving correctional setting by choosing certain social roles to express their individuality

---

Box 5.2 ⚖ *Juvenile Inmate Social Codes*

1. *Exploit whomever you can:* The conduct norms suggest that the powerless may be victimized in any conceivable way.
2. *Don't kiss ass:* This tenet warns inmates not to be dependent on staff and to treat youth leaders, social workers, and schoolteachers with distrust and suspicion.
3. *Don't rat on your peers:* To betray a peer is to break a very serious norm.
4. *Don't give up your ass:* Since a boy who is sexually exploited often runs the risk of becoming the cottage scapegoat, youths usually fight rather than submit to the pressure.
5. *Be cool:* This involves not "whining" when things are not going well or not running away from a fight.
6. *Don't get involved in another inmate's affairs:* This maxim promotes granting as much social distance as self-contained cottage living permits.
7. *Don't steal "squares":* Stealing cigarettes is a serious offense and youth caught doing it are often seriously assaulted.
8. *Don't buy the mind-fucking:* Here youth guard against repeated treatment attempts made by staff to modify boys' behaviors and values.

Sources: Bartollas, Miller, and Dinitz (1976): 105–128; Thornton and Voigt (1992): 428.

Box 5.3 ⚒ *Institutional Argot: The Social Roles of Juvenile Inmates*

1. *Heavy:* A leader who can maintain power by aggression or by intelligence and cooperation.
2. *Lieutenant:* The heavies' assistants.
3. *Slick:* Inmates who are highly esteemed by others for their ability to manipulate staff.
4. *Booty Bandit:* Youths who sexually exploit others.
5. *Peddler:* Generally, one inmate from a cottage who trades goods from one cottage to another.
6. *Messup:* Besides making mistakes, violating institutional rules, and creating conflict with peers.
7. *Thief:* Found in every cottage, youth who steal from other inmates; have lowly status.
8. *Queen:* Overt homosexuals.
9. *Scapegoat:* The lowest-ranking social role. A youth who becomes isolated from the group because of his amenability to exploitation, especially sexual exploitation.

Sources: Bartollas, Miller, and Dinitz (1976): 105–128; Thornton and Voigt (1992): 428; Polsky (1962).

(Irwin, 1970). These roles are also characteristic of juvenile correctional facilities, and they frequently identify the types of inmates at the top and bottom of the social system (see Box 5.3).

The staff and inmates acknowledged several roles, and the labels are incorporated into the institution's language. The formation of social roles plays an important part in the correctional setting. Whereas the institution's formal goals focus on treatment, the informal inmate roles, such as the social codes, may sabotage treatment modalities.

VIOLENCE IN JUVENILE VERSUS ADULT CORRECTIONAL SETTINGS

Increasing amounts of juvenile violence have become a national problem in schools and neighborhoods, as well as in correctional settings. Among the most critical concerns and dilemmas experienced by juvenile correctional institutions are gang activity (discussed later in the chapter) and violent assaults on staff and offenders (Willett, 1996). Because of the violence of youths in Texas correctional facilities, administrators have acknowledged the need for continuous staff development and training in the unique problems of violent youths. This training encompasses useful management tools, such as conflict resolution (Allen and Simonsen, 1998).

To address this issue, the Office of Juvenile Justice and Delinquency Prevention (OJJDP) awarded a competitive, cooperative agreement in fiscal year 1995 for a three-year project to the Illinois Institute for Dispute Resolution to develop, in concert with other established conflict resolution organizations, a national strategy for broad-based education and training in the use of conflict resolution skills. In fiscal year 1997, the project conducted additional training sessions in conjunction with conferences of national educational, justice, and youth-serving organizations (Moore and Terrett, 1999).

In their research on prison violence, Stastny and Tyrnauer (1982: 1) stated that the decade of the 1970s was "the explosive decade of prison riots." In September 1971, 43 deaths resulted from a substantial revolt at Attica prison in New York state; even after the "explosive decade," riots continued. In 1980, during a riot at the New Mexico penitentiary in Santa Fe, 33 inmates were killed, and more than 200 others were sexually assaulted as a result of revengeful prisoners out to eradicate informants. In 1987, an 11-day uprising in the Atlanta Federal Penitentiary in Georgia was caused by the discontent of Cuban inmates (Talbott, 1988).

Some researchers have found that violence occurs less frequently in female than in male correctional facilities. According to Bowker (1980: 42), "Violence seems to be used mainly to establish dominance and subordination when nonviolent means fail."

IMPACT OF GANGS ON JUVENILE CORRECTIONS

Street gangs have been part of the American social landscape for well over 200 years (Covey, Menard, and Franzese, 1992). Yet American youth gangs have been dramatically altered along many dimensions. For instance, contemporary street gangs are demographically different from their earlier counterparts (Cromwell, Taylor, and Palacios, 1992; Palacios, 1996). First, they attract and sustain both younger (under age 12) and older (over age 25) members (Hagedorn, 1988; Horowitz, 1983; Howell, 1998; Klein, 1995; Miller, 1992; Moore, 1991; Spergel, 1990; Taylor, 1990). Second, although there have been no estimates of the number of female participants in street gangs, regional surveys have estimated that 2 percent to 40 percent of the members of street gangs are female (Campbell, 1984; Klein, 1995; Miller, 1992). While traditional female auxiliary gangs (Campbell, 1984; Moore, 1991) do exist, recent surveys have suggested that there has been an increase in independent female gangs (see Curry, Ball, and Decker, 1996). Whether such recent findings indicate that young women are finally establishing themselves in the fraternity of street gangs is not certain at this time. However, prevalence and incidence data gathered in the past five years do suggest that female gang members have a higher proclivity for violence than do either nongang males or females (see Esbensen and Huizinga, 1993; Fagan, 1990; Knox, McCurrie, and Tromhanauser, 1995).

Third, individuals who seek out and join street gangs do so for a variety of reasons, ranging from prestige, identity enhancement, protection, self-esteem, racial or ethnic/cultural tensions, to status among friends at school and in the community (Decker and VanWinkle, 1996; Palacios, 1996; Toy, 1992; Vigil, 1990; Spergel, 1990). Cromwell et al. (1992: 28) added: "Under conditions of social and economic deprivation, gang membership may be seen as normal and part of the socialization process." Spergel (1990: 171) stated that "Gangs function as a residual social institution when other social institutions fail to provide a certain degree of order and solidarity for their members." Furthermore, being associated with or joining a youth gang may provide economic opportunities that are not readily available to nonmembers (Cromwell et al., 1992; Hagedorn, 1998; Pennell, Evans, Melton, and Hinson, 1994; Taylor, 1990).

Moreover, it has been argued (see Anderson, 1990; Decker and VanWinkle, 1996; Taylor, 1990) that in certain communities, street gangs have replaced traditional legal social networks that were vital in establishing legitimate work opportunities. As Maxson (1998: 9) noted, "Socioeconomic factors, such as persistent unemployment (underemployment), residential segregation, and the lack of recreational, educational, and vocational services for youth are more likely sources of gang formation or expansion." Spergel (1995: 90) added: "Gang organization, as it becomes better developed and rational, is a function of increasing criminal and decreasing legitimate sources of economic opportunity and social status."

Fourth, contemporary youth gangs also exhibit different structures. Whether the motivation for joining is economic, social, or self-preservation, the result is a gang milieu reflecting (1) looser leadership, (2) ill-defined roles, (3) intergang rivalries, (4) racial and/or ethnic diversity in membership, (4) a fluid cohesion of members, (5) criminal versatility, and (6) the predominance of gang cliques or subgroups (Klein, 1995; Spergel, 1995). Because of this dynamic social context, it is impossible to consider any one type or profile of a street gang member. Instead, according to Spergel (1995), from the perspective of understanding the structures and dynamics of gangs, especially for the purpose of controlling gangs, it is important to know the different positions and/or roles that gang members hold. In this regard, Spergel (1995: 85) outlines five types of members:

- Core members (including leaders and regulars)
- Peripheral or fringe members
- Associates
- Wannabes or recruits
- Veterans or old gangsters

Overall, the structure of a gang is based on the need for group maintenance or development (Spergel, 1990). However, the roles are not mutually
exclusive, and there may be some variance in them. These reinforcing and
competing roles serve to build the kind of group cohesiveness that is ordi-
narily tentative rather than fixed (Spergel, 1995). Furthermore, such tentative group cohesion has transformed the overall external structure of
contemporary youth gangs.

It has become common to hear the terms *vertical* and *horizontal*
(coined by the New York City Youth Board, 1960) applied to the development of contemporary youth gangs. A vertical gang structured along age
lines (age gradient), is territorial (usually bound within the originating
neighborhood), has a social history (sometimes defined by reputation and
street lore), and recruits members along generational lines (brothers,
cousins, uncles, grandfathers, and so forth). Vertical gangs are self-
contained through subsets or cliques and exist for long periods. A horizontal gang (also called a *coalition, nation,* or *supergang*) is most likely to
include members of different ages, racial and ethnic groups, and usually
exists for a shorter period.

It should be noted that both vertical and horizontal gangs have core
and fringe members (Klein, 1995). In reference to a horizontal gang, Klein
(1995: 62) stated: "This is not an organization that can readily act as a
unit. A structure like this can become far more cohesive if it perceives outside threats such as rival gangs and/or police suppression programs. This
inadvertently can bring cliques together, and force even link age-graded
subgroups into more structural hierarchical relationships." Spergel (1990:
201) noted: "For many members in this type of coalition or nation, the
prison experience only serves to further strengthen alliances, develop
structural sophistication, and increase membership."

The law enforcement community and some researchers (see Knox,
1992) commonly refer to contemporary street gangs as *supergangs* or *coalitions*. Although these supergangs have been identified as a major factor in
the rising level of drug trafficking and violence in America, the research
community is currently engaged in an open debate concerning such a connection (see Howell and Decker, 1999). Nevertheless, Knox (1992: 23)
define supergangs as "highly structured, formally organized gangs with
numerous chapters, sets, or franchises throughout the United States."
Examples of these supergangs or coalitions include the Bloods, Crips,
Latin Kings, Vice Lords, Black Guerilla Family, Aryan Brotherhood, El
Rukins, the Mexican Mafia, and People and Folk (Knox, 1992; Spergel,
1990). The primary vehicles for dealing with such groups have been legislative reform and enhanced law enforcement initiatives. However, deterrence policies (such as sentencing reform provisions; see Shichor and
Sechrest, 1996) have inadvertently contributed to the burgeoning gang
problem now confronting many correctional administrators and front-line
personnel.

RESULTS FROM THE WAR ON GANGS

A number of factors have led to the explosion of juvenile admissions to jails and prisons. These factors include higher levels of violence associated with this particular type of offender group (Curry et al., 1996; Esbensen and Huizinga, 1993; Miller, 1992; Thornberry, 1998; Thornberry, Huizinga, and Loeber, 1995), suppression tactics such as law enforcement antigang units, innovative prosecution tactics (e.g., vertical prosecution), intensive supervision (see Jackson and McBride, 1996), and legislative/prosecutorial initiatives (e.g., mandatory minimum sentences, extended jurisdiction for juveniles, blended sentencing, truth-in-sentencing statutes), three strikes and you're out, Weed and Seed programs, California's Street Terrorism Enforcement and Prevention Act, and Florida's 1990 Street Terrorism Enforcement and Prevention Act (see Austin, 1996; Gable, 1996; Klein, 1995; Spergel, 1995). In addition, recent national surveys have suggested increased gang migration and proliferation patterns (see Knox et al., 1996; Maxson, 1998; Maxson, Woods, and Klein, 1995; Moore and Terrett, 1999).

In addition, the momentum for the war on gangs has been fueled by the perception of an increase in juvenile violence, the media's increased focus on the issue, political interests, the antiquated juvenile justice system, and the assumption that the criminal justice system can do a better job (Gable, 1996). A special report issued by the National Institute of Corrections (NIC, 1995: 2) found the following among the provisions of new legislation targeting young offenders:

- Eighteen states have expanded the definitions of crimes or lowered the ages at which juveniles may be tried in adult court.
- Colorado and Wisconsin have authorized youthful offender systems to deal with serious offenders under age 18; New Mexico formally defined the categories *youthful offender* and *serious youthful offender,* both specific to offenders under age 18.
- Three states have established a separate division of the justice system to prosecute or coordinate the state's response to juvenile crime.
- Five states have authorized new housing for offenders under age 18 or defined the circumstances under which they must be separated from adult offenders.

The report continued: "Regardless of an agency's current policy on housing offenders under age 18, the effect of criminal code changes related to juvenile offenders is likely to be increased pressure on an already burdened state corrections system" (NIC, 1995: 2). For instance, according to a 1997 Bureau of Justice Statistics Report (Scalia, 1997), juveniles who were charged with acts of juvenile delinquency in U.S. district courts in 1995 were frequently charged with more serious offenses such as drug

(15 percent) or violent (32 percent) offenses. Of those juveniles who were adjudicated delinquent during 1995, 37 percent were committed to correctional facilities, 59 percent were placed on probation, and 4 percent received sentences that did not include supervision or confinement.

A recent report in the *Juvenile Justice Bulletin* (Stahl, 1999) stated that between 1987 and 1996, the total number of delinquency cases handled by juvenile courts increased 49 percent and that the increase in person offenses (criminal homicide, forcible rape, robbery, aggravated assault, simple assault, and other violent sex offenses and person offenses) was relatively steady over the same period. According to the report, the most serious offense committed by youths aged 15 or younger were property offenses (53 percent) followed by person offenses (23 percent), for youths aged 16 or older, the most serious offenses were property offenses (46 percent) and person offenses (19 percent). However, these two national surveys (Scalia, 1997; Stahl, 1999) did not provide data on the percentage of those charged with gang-related incidents or crimes. As for the use of detention, the number of delinquency cases involving such a procedure increased 38 percent between 1987 and 1996: personal offenses (97 percent), drug offenses (89 percent), and public order offenses (35 percent) (Stahl, 1999).

The war on gangs has created a special population: youthful offenders with street gang affiliations who are not necessarily supervised or managed in the same manner as other groups. This lack of supervision has inadvertently created a problem that has had social, economic, and political consequences for the overburdened, overworked, and understaffed correctional system. Roush and Dunlap (1998) contended that "transferring the problem of the most serious juvenile offenders (including street gang members) to an even more overwhelmed and less effective system makes no sense ... and that the placement of juveniles in adult prisons reflects a disregard for history, which is replete with examples of how 'get-tough' approaches fail" (pp. 15–16). However, Backstrom (1998: 14) argued that "We cannot overlook the fact that today's juvenile offenders often are sophisticated, gang-connected juveniles, committing violent crimes, and there are fewer reasons to be concerned about segregating these hard-core juvenile offenders from adults." Although the precise extent of street gang members in correctional facilities, especially juvenile correctional facilities, has been difficult to ascertain, limited national and regional surveys have attempted to fill this void.

The Presence and Impact of Juvenile Gangs in Correctional Facilities

Camp and Camp (1985) conducted the first comprehensive study on the prevalence of juvenile gangs in correctional facilities. At the time of their survey, they identified 114 gangs with a total membership of 12,634 in 33 prison systems, including the Federal Bureau of Prisons. Although their numbers are small relative to the general prison population, prison gangs are believed to be responsible for 50 percent of prison management problems (Camp and Camp, 1985), and their impact on prison order is immense (Ralph, Hunter, Marquart, Cuvelier, and Meriano, 1996: 124). In 1985, the total U.S. prisoner population was 446,244, and gang members represented fewer than 3 percent of the incarcerated population (Ralph et al., 1996). According to a 1991 survey of state prison inmates, 6 percent of inmates belonged to a gang before entering prison (Beck et al., 1993). Of those inmates who reported gang membership-affiliation, 32 percent were still members, 91 percent had served at least one previous sentence either in an institution or on probation, and 73 percent had served or were serving time for violent offenses (Beck et al., 1993).

A survey by the American Correctional Association (1993) revealed that 40 prison systems were dealing with gangs or, as they are commonly referred to in this setting, *security threat groups*. A 1990 Juvenile Correctional Institutions Survey reported that 78 percent of the responding institutions indicated a recent gang problem, 40 percent reported the involvement of female inmates in gangs, and approximately 33 percent reported one or more incidents in which violence involving gang members resulted in serious injuries (Knox, 1992). Jackson and Sharpe's (1997) descriptive analysis of gang activity in 21 eastern North Carolina prisons indicated that about 52 percent of the participants identified themselves as members of local gangs such as the Ku Klux Klan, skinheads, posse, bikers, and white pride, and about 18 percent identified themselves as members of such gang alliances as the Bloods, Crips, and Folks. Jackson and Sharpe stated that "Many urban street gang members are migrating to rural areas as they expand their gangs' recruitment efforts and activities. As we continue to implement major provisions of the crime bill, specifically becoming tougher on gang members and gang activity, there will be increases in the number of arrests and incarcerations of gang-members" (p. 6).

As for gang-related violence within juvenile correctional facilities, a survey of 300 state juvenile institutions found that 14 percent of those that participated reported that gang members have been a problem in terms of assaults on correctional staff. Twenty-eight percent reported more than one incident of aggravated assault, 33 percent indicated that these assaults on correctional staff were serious enough to warrant hospitalization, and 33 percent indicated that one or more general incidents of aggravated assaults resulted in serious injuries (Knox, 1992). Furthermore, 9 percent thought there was a link between the fear of violence from gang members within correctional facilities and staff turnover. Fifty-three percent indicated that juvenile gang members were responsible for vandalism and other types of property damage in juvenile facilities.

How did the juvenile facilities deal with gang members? The survey (Knox, 1992) found that juvenile correctional institutions primarily handled this situation on a case-by-case basis (25 percent), followed by isolating leaders (13 percent), transferring members to other institutions (12 percent), interrupting communications (11 percent), segregation (9 percent), and imposing institutional lockdowns (8 percent) as control measures. In addition to these methods, state systems such as the New York City Department of Corrections use advanced technology in their attempts to control and manage gang members. As of 1996, the New York City Department of Corrections had identified 1,153 inmates as members of 32 gangs and gang-like organizations, both large, well-organized gangs with national reputations and smaller groups (Gaston, 1996). One component of the New York City Department of Corrections Gang Control Program is a database containing an inmate's gang affiliations, status within the organization, arrest history for gang-related incidents, and other institutional information. Another component is a digitized imaging program that allows intake and classification officers to take the complete histories and personal data of gang members, including distinguishing tattoos and other marks. The system is portable and allows for multiple searches on the basis of any data in this file. As Gaston (1996: 9) noted, "Every registered person in the entire gang network who fit a description would be displayed on the screen in a photo array—constituting a virtual computerized line-up."

Correctional administrators and front-line personnel have been faced with the realities of a new type of inmate in their facilities. Along these same lines, the prison industrial complex has given way to a new prison culture that many correctional officers, managers, and staff personnel must maneuver and negotiate on a daily basis. Initially, prison officials adopted a working-with philosophy when they encountered prison gangs, but such an approach led only to quasi-control and stability in many of these institutions (Spergel, 1990). Gido (1991) identified several key issues (such as jail architecture and operations, litigation strategies, lawsuit-prevention programs, and information systems and comparative analyses of populations across jails) pertaining to the establishment of a relevant jail research agenda. The contemporary youth (street) gang member (younger as well as older, with a higher proclivity for violence, female as well as male, and racially and ethnically diverse) presents a new type of jail-prison population. Since get-tough-on-crime mandates show no sign of abatement, correctional professionals are faced with finding new and innovative operational practices and inmate management strategies.

SUMMARY

Juvenile inmate subcultures evolve independently of the objectives of correctional administrators, and juveniles who enter correctional institutions find a social reality of concerns, values, roles, and jargon already in place that they must accept or be exposed to threatening rejection.

Proponents of delinquency theories have been attempting for almost 200 years to determine the impact of cultural norms on violence in juvenile correctional settings. Although some theorists have reported on personal and social factors related to friction between inmates and administrators, the findings have not been useful in the juvenile rehabilitation process.

Violence and other problems that exist in the larger society also exist in correctional communities. Gang activity is an escalating problem for juvenile corrections and has detrimental consequences for rehabilitation.

In the past 10 years, American correctional facilities and juvenile detention centers have experienced a dramatic increase in inmates with gang affiliations, specifically with ties to street gangs. Contemporary deterrence provisions have inadvertently contributed to this burgeoning institutional gang problem. Many political opponents of the juvenile justice system have been responsible for enacting legislative provisions that have increased the total number of "youthful" offenders now being warehoused in these facilities. The war on gangs has created a special population, youthful offenders, who are not necessarily supervised or managed in the same manner as are other inmate groups. This get-tough-on-crime initiative has created a volatile working environment for correctional administrators and front-line personnel, who find themselves engaged in a delicate balancing act: finding new and innovative operational practices in inmate management strategies while delivering programs that show promise of breaking the cycle of gang violence.

REFERENCES

Allen, H. E., and Simonsen, C. E. (1998). *Corrections in America: An Introduction.* Upper Saddle River, NJ: Prentice Hall.

American Correctional Association. (1993). *Gangs in Correctional Facilities: A National Assessment.* Washington DC: U.S. Department of Justice, Office of Justice Programs, National Institute of Justice.

Anderson, E. (1990). *Streetwise: Race, Class, and Change in an Urban Community.* Chicago: University of Chicago Press.

Austin, J. (1996). "The Effect of Three Strikes and You're Out on Corrections." In D. Shichor and D. K. Sechrest (eds.), *Three Strikes and You're Out: Vengeance as Public Policy.* Thousand Oaks, CA: Sage: 155–176.

Backstrom, J. C. (1998). "Housing Juveniles in Adult Facilities: A Common-Sense Approach." In *Point Counterpoint: Correctional Issues.* Lanham, MD: American Correctional Association: 13–14.

Bartollas, C., Miller, S.J., and Dinitz, S. (1976). *Juvenile Victimization: The Institutional Paradox.* New York: Wiley.

Beck, A., Gilliard, D., Greenfield, L., Harlow, C., Hester, T., Jankowski, L, Snell, T., Stephen, J., and Morton, D. (1993). "Survey of State Prison Inmates, 1991." *Bureau of Justice Statistics.* Washington, DC: U.S. Department of Justice, Office of Justice Programs.

Bell, J. (1990, April). "Advocates Persevere in Jail Removal Efforts." *Youth Law News:* 10–26.

Bowker, L. H. (1980). *Prison Subcultures.* Lexington, MA: Lexington Books.

Camp, G. and Camp, C. (1985). *Prison Gangs: Their Extent, Nature, and Impact on Prisons.* Washington, DC: U.S. Department of Justice.

Campbell, A. (1984). *The Girls in the Gang.* New York: Basil Blackwell.

Chambliss, W. J. (1984). *Criminal Law in Action.* (2d ed.). NewYork: John Wiley.

Clemmer, D. (1940). *The Prison Community.* Boston: Christopher.

Covey, H. C., Menard, S. and Franzese, R. (1992). *Juvenile Gangs.* Springfield, IL: Charles C. Thomas.

Cromwell, P., Taylor, D., and Palacios, W. (1992). "Youth Gangs: A 1990s Perspective." *Juvenile and Family Court Journal,* 43: 25–31.

Curry, G. D., Ball, R. A., and Decker, S. H. (1996). *Estimating the National Scope of Gang Crime from Law Enforcement Data, Research in Brief.* Washington, DC: U.S. Department of Justice, Office of Justice Programs, National Institute of Justice.

Decker, S. H. and VanWinkle, B. (1996). *Life in the Gang: Family, Friends, and Violence.* Cambridge, England: Cambridge University Press.

Esbensen, F. and Huizinga, D. (1993). "Gangs, Drugs, and Delinquency in a Survey of Youth." *Criminology,* 31: 565–589.

Fagan, J. E. (1990). "Social Process of Delinquency and Drug Use Among Urban Gangs." In C. R. Huff (ed.), *Gangs in America.* Newbury Park, CA: Sage: 182–218.

Gable, R. (1996). *The Juvenile in Adult Jails: Emerging Trends and Concerns.* Longmont, CO: National Institute of Corrections Information Center, Jail Division.

Gaston, A. (1996). "Controlling Gangs through Teamwork and Technology." *Large Jail Network Bulletin.* Washington, DC: U.S. Department of Justice, National Institute of Corrections.

Gido, R. (1991). "A Jail Research Agenda for the 1990s." *Setting the Jail Research Agenda for the 1990s.* Washington, DC: U.S. Department of Justice, National Institute of Corrections.

Hagadorn, J. M. (1988). *People and Folks: Gangs, Crime, and the Underclass in a Rustbelt City.* Chicago: Lakeview Press.

Hagan, J. (1990). *Modern Criminology: Crime, Criminal Behavior, and Its Control.* New York: McGraw-Hill.

Hood, R. B. (1967). "Research in the Effectiveness of Punishments and Treatments." In *Collected Studies in Criminological Research,* Vol. 1. Strasburg, France: Council of Europe.

Horowitz, R. (1983). *Honor and the American Dream: Culture and Identity in a Chicano Community.* New Brunswick, NJ: Rutgers University Press.

Howell, J. C. (1998). *Youth Gangs: An Overview.* Washington, DC: U.S. Department of Justice, Office of Justice Programs, Office of Juvenile Programs, Office of Juvenile Justice and Delinquency Prevention.

Howell, J. C. and Decker, S. H. (1999). *The Gangs, Drugs, and Violence Connection.* Washington, DC: U.S. Department of Justice, Office of Justice Programs, Office of Juvenile Programs, Office of Juvenile Justice and Delinquency Prevention.

Irwin, J. (1970). *The Felon.* Englewood Cliffs, NJ: Prentice Hall.

Irwin, J., and Cressy, U. (1962). "Thieves, Convicts, and Inmate Culture." *Social Problems,* 10: 142–155.

Jackson, M. S. and Sharp, E. G. (1997). "Prison Gang Research: Preliminary Findings in Eastern North Carolina." *Journal of Gang Research,* 5: 1–8.

Jackson, R. K., and McBride, W. D. (1996). *Understanding Street Gangs.* Placerville, CA: Cooperhouse.

Klein, M. (1995). *The American Street Gang: Its Nature, Prevalence, and Control.* New York: Oxford University Press.

Knox, G. (1992). *An Introduction to Gangs.* Bristol, IN: Wyndham Hall Press.

Knox, G., Houston, J. G., Tromanhanquer, E. D., McCurrie, T. F., and Laskey, J. (1996). "Addressing and Testing the Gang Migration Issue." In S. M. Miller and J. P. Rush (eds.), *Gangs: A Criminal Justice Approach.* Cincinnati: Anderson: 71–83.

Knox, G., McCurrie, T. F., and Tromanhanauser, E. D. (1995). "Findings on African American Female Gang Members Using a Matched-Pair Design: A Research Note." *Journal of Gang Research,* 2: 61–72.

Larson, J. (1983, February). "Rural Female Delinquents' Adaptation to Institutional Life." *Juvenile and Family Court Journal:* 83–92.

Lee, R. and Haynes, N. M. (1980). "Project CREST and the Dual-Treatment Approach to Delinquency: Methods and Research Summarized." In R. R. Ross and P. Gendreah (eds.), *Effective Correctional Treatment.* Toronto: Butterworth: 497–503.

Maxson, C. (1998). *Gang Members on the Move.* Washington, DC: U.S. Department of Justice, Office of Justice Programs, Office of Juvenile Justice and Delinquency Prevention.

Maxson, C., Woods, K. J., and Klein, M. W. (1995). *Street Gang Migration: How Big a Threat?* Washington, DC: U.S. Department of Justice, Office of Justice Programs, National Institute of Justice.

Mennel, R. M. (1973) *Thorns and Thistles: Juvenile Delinquents in the United States, 1825–1949.* Hanover, NH: University Press of New England.

Miller, W. B. (1958). "Lower Class Culture as a Generating Milieu of Gang Delinquency." *Journal of Social Issues,* 15: 5–19.

Miller, W. B. (1992). *Crime by Youth Gangs and Groups in the United States.* Washington, DC: U.S. Department of Justice, Office of Justice Programs, Office of Juvenile Justice and Delinquency Prevention.

Moore, J. W. (1991). *Going Down to the Barrio: Homeboys and Homegirls in Charge.* Philadelphia: Temple University Press.

Moore, J. W. and Terrett, C. P. (1999). *Highlights of the 1997 National Youth Gang Survey.* Washington, DC: U.S. Department of Justice, Office of Justice Programs, Office of Juvenile Justice and Delinquency Prevention.

National Institute of Corrections, U.S. Department of Justice. (1995). *Offenders Under Age 18 in State Adult Correctional Systems: A National Picture.* Longmont, CO: National Institute of Corrections Information Center.

New York City Youth Board. (1960). *Reaching the Fighting Gang.* New York: Office of Juvenile Justice and Delinquency Prevention.

Palacios, W. R. (1996). "Side by Side: An Ethnographic Study of a Miami Gang." *Journal of Gang Research,* 4: 27–38.

Pennell, S., Evans, E., Melton, R., and Hinson, S. (1994). *Down for the Set: Describing and Defining Gangs in San Diego.* San Diego, CA: Criminal Justice Research Division, Association of Governments.

Platt, A. M. (1975). "Prospects for a Radical Criminology in the U.S." In I. Taylor, P. Walton, and J. Young (eds.), *Critical Criminology.* London: Routledge and Keagan Paul: 38–46.

Quinney, R. A. (1975). *Criminology: An Analysis and Critique of Crime in America.* Boston: Little, Brown.

Ralph, P., Hunter, R. J., Marquart, J. W., Cuvelier, S. J., and Meriano, D. (1996). "Exploring the Differences Between Gang and Nongang Prisoners." In C. R. Huff, (ed.), *Gangs in America.* Thousand Oaks, CA: Sage: 123–138.

Roush, D., and Dunlap, E. L. (1998). "Juveniles in Adult Prisons: A Very Bad Idea." In *Point Counterpoint: Correctional Issues.* Lanham, MD: American Correctional Association: 15–16.

Scalia, J. (1997). "Juvenile Delinquents in the Federal Criminal Justice System." *Bureau of Justice Statistics Report.* Washington, DC: U.S. Department of Justice, Office of Justice Programs.

Sellin, T. (1938). *Culture Conflict and Crime.* New York: Social Science Research Council.

Shichor, D. and Sechrest, D. K. (1996). *Three Strikes and You're Out: Vengeance as Public Policy.* Thousand Oaks, CA: Sage.

Spergel, I. A. (1990). "Youth Gangs: Continuity and Change." In M. Tonry and N. Morris (eds.), *Crime and Justice: A Review of Research.* Chicago: The University of Chicago Press: 171–275.

Spergel, I. A. (1995). *The Youth Gang Problem: A Community Approach.* New York: Oxford University Press.

Stahl, A. (1999). "Offenders in Juvenile Court, 1996." *Juvenile Justice Bulletin.* Washington, DC: U.S. Department of Justice, Office of Justice Programs, Office of Juvenile Justice and Delinquency Prevention.

Stastny, C. and Tyrnauer, G. (1982). *Who Rules the Joint? The Changing Political Culture of Maximum-Security Prisons in America.* Lexington, MA: Lexington Books.

Sykes, G. M. (1958). *The Society of Captives: A Study of a Maximum Security Prison.* Princeton, NJ: Princeton University Press.

Sykes, G. M. and Messinger, S. L. (1960). "The Inmate Social System." In Richard A. Cloward et al. (eds.), *Theoretical Studies in Social Organization of the Prison.* New York: Social Science Research Council: 5–19.

Talbott, F. (1988, February) "Reporting from Behind the Walls: Do It Before the Siren Wails." *The Quill:* 16–21.

Taylor, C. S. (1990). *Dangerous Society.* East Lansing: Michigan State University Press.

Thornberry, T. P. (1998). "Membership in Youth Gangs and Involvement in Serious and Violent Offending." In R. Loeber and D.P. Farrington (eds.), *Serious and Violent Offenders: Risk Factors and Successful Interventions.* Thousand Oaks, CA: Sage: 147–166.

Thornberry, T. P., Huisinga, D. and Loeber, R. (1995). "The Prevention of Serious Delinquency and Violence: Implications from the Program of Research on the Causes and Correlates of Delinquency." In J. C. Howell, B. Krisber, J.D. Hawkins, and J. J. Wilson (eds.), *A Sourcebook: Serious, Violent, and Chronic Juvenile Offenders.* Thousand Oaks, CA: Sage: 213–237.

Thornton, W. E. and Voigt, L. (1992). *Delinquency and Justice.* New York: McGraw Hill.

Toy, C. (1992). "Coming Out to Play: Reasons to Join and Participate in Asian Gangs." *Journal of Gang Research*, 1:13–29.

Turk, A.T. (1969). *Criminality and the Legal Order.* Chicago: Rand McNally.

Vardalis, J. A. (1997). *Florida's Criminal Justice System.* Incline Village, NV: Copperhouse.

Vigil, D. (1990). "Cholos and Gangs: Culture Change and Street Youths in Los Angeles." In C. R. Huff (ed.), *Gangs in America.* Newbury Park, CA: Sage: 45–62.

Vold, G. B. (1958). *Theoretical Criminology.* New York: Oxford University Press.

Wellford, C. (1967). "Factors Associated with the Adoption of the Inmate Code: A Study of Normative Assimilation." *Journal of Criminal Law, Criminology and Police Science,* 56: 197–203.

Willett, J. (1996). "Programs and Services." In H. E. Allen and C. E. Simonsen (eds.), *Corrections in America: An Introduction.* Upper Saddle River, NJ: Prentice Hall.

Wolfgang, M. E., and Ferracuti, F. (1967). *The Subculture of Violence: Toward an Integrated Theory of Criminology.* London: Tavistock.

chapter 6

HEALTH CARE FOR WOMEN OFFENDERS
CHALLENGE FOR THE NEW CENTURY

PHYLLIS HARRISON ROSS, M.D.
New York Medical College at Metropolitan Hospital

JAMES E. LAWRENCE
New York State Commission of Correction

INTRODUCTION

Based on the unprecedented increase in the number of incarcerated women, particularly poor and minority women, in the last 15 years, this chapter addresses the specific health care needs of women in U.S. prisons. Prisons have been notorious for their neglect of women and their treatment needs, and the influx of women who have abused drugs has created critical care needs for HIV/AIDS, tuberculosis, and related respiratory and reproductive tract diseases. A model of improved care to address this new prison crisis is presented.

The population of incarcerated women underwent profound change in the 1980s, as did the impact of women offenders on jail and prison systems. Some of this is related to the fact that U.S. jail and prison populations became the world's largest during the past decade (Butterfield, 1992). However, the real change in focus on women is associated with the impact on correctional systems of increasing and intensified demand for specialized health care services hitherto not delivered on a large scale in prisons and jails. The combined effect of high rates of incarceration employed as the social sanction of choice and the increased involvement of poor and minority women in behaviors regarded as criminal has been to concentrate unprecedented numbers of women with serious medical problems in state and local correctional institutions. The forces driving this change are unlikely to abate in this new century.

The largest U.S. prison and jail systems, such as those in New York and California, have not traditionally been called on to respond to the special health care needs of large populations of women or even to provide basic parity of the quality and availability of primary care afforded men. Jail and prison health care systems have largely been defined and operated by men for a nearly exclusive male clientele. In New York, for example, 18 county jails (35 percent) had no services for women in 1990; in fact, they were even unable to detain them. Women were boarded out to the relatively few facilities that would accept them, leaving incarcerated women far from home, family supports, and legal counsel (New York State Commission of Correction, 1993). The closed and punitive nature of prison life amplifies impediments to primary care access widely experienced by poor women in the community at large, as does the episodic, discontinuous approach to ambulatory health care encounters within prison and jail settings.

The medical problems of urban women of color who most often find themselves incarcerated are usually more severe and intractable than those of their male counterparts. Often these needs have been ignored or given low priority outside of prison in favor of meeting the needs of male domestic partners and children. Including the unique reproductive health problems of women, 28 percent of women admitted to state prison in New York in 1993 had medical problems requiring immediate and ongoing intervention (New York State Department of Correctional Services, 1994). In most large correctional systems, women offenders, particularly women of color, have the highest rates of HIV infection and associated tuberculosis, far exceeding rates for male offenders. In New York, mortality among incarcerated women remains more than twice that of women in the same age group in the community (New York State Executive Chamber, 1994). High-risk pregnancies that come to term or premature delivery can be expected to increase annually with the growth in offender census. The growing population of incarcerated women has also evidenced high rates of mental health problems. A California study found more than 40 percent of incarcerated women with a *DSM-III-R* (IV) diagnosis (Fogel and Martin, 1992). Anxiety disorders predominated among incarcerated mothers and grew proportionately over time. Among both mothers and nonmothers, a high prevalence of depression was found (Fogel and Martin, 1992).

As both the volume and intensity of demand for services rise in coming years, prison and jail administrators will be required to critically examine their traditional male-centered health care delivery models and refocus on the needs of women. An emphasis on managed primary care, on planning parity of services for women into new systems, and on changing attitudes and beliefs antithetical to quality care for women must come about as women offenders become a larger part of the criminal justice clientele.

In this chapter we examine the changing demographics of women offenders that drive health care service demand, the scope and prevalence of women's health problems, and the current impediments to adequate services. Some recommendations for positive change are discussed.

WOMEN IN CUSTODY

The last half of the 1980s saw a dramatic increase in the number of women committed to local jails. Nationally, the census of women in jail increased an average 6.5 percent annually between 1990 and 1997, a rate nearly two thirds greater than that of men over the same period (U.S. Department of Justice, 1998) (Figure 6.1).

In New York, the second largest American jail system, women represented 5 percent of jail admissions in 1984. By 1998, 10 percent of the jail census were women (Figure 6.2). Moreover, women no longer went to jail for criminal court processing and expedited release; they remained as detainees and local sentence servers. In upstate New York and Long Island in 1984, 13,000 women were sent to jail, but the average daily census was only 550. In 1992, there were 24,432 total admissions of women and a daily census of 1,595, a proportional increase of 63 percent.

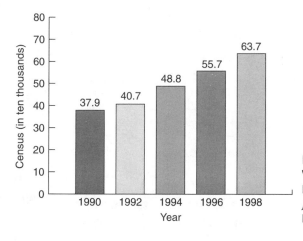

FIGURE 6.1
Women in U.S. jails: 1990–1998. (*Source:* Bureau of Justice Statistics, *Women in U.S. Jails 1999*. Washington, DC: Government Printing Office, 1999.)

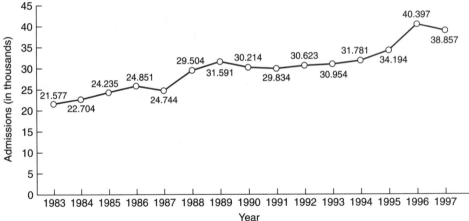

FIGURE 6.2 Admissions of women to jail in New York: 1983–1997.
(*Source:* 1994 Crime and Justice Annual Report.)

Women were sent to state prisons at a rate that increased faster than jail admissions. In 1984, New York's prison system incarcerated about 1000 women on an average day in only two facilities.

By 1997, New York's average daily prison census of women was 3,600 in eight facilities. The mean annual increase in New York's population of imprisoned women was 14 percent over that period compared to an annual growth of the male prisoner population of 8 percent. In 1994, this growth leveled off at 10.6 percent, a figure still higher than the increase in male

FIGURE 6.3 New York prisons—women in custody: 1981–1997.
(*Source:* 1997 Crime and Justice Annual Report.)

inmates (8.5 percent). Much of this extraordinary change is a function of the war on drugs plus the involvement of women in the substance-use culture. Between 1980 and 1984, admissions to New York jails for drug-related charges increased at an annual rate of 13 percent. Beginning in 1985, the annual rate of increase tripled to 39 percent; commitments of women for these charges increased accordingly. In 1984, only 640 women were admitted to jail for drug possession or sale. By 1996, 5,060 women were charged with drug crimes and sent to jails in upstate New York and Long Island (Figure 6.3).

MORTALITY AMONG WOMEN OFFENDERS

Figure 6.4 illustrates mortality among women offenders in New York and in the five other largest correctional jurisdictions in the nation, compared with women ages 15 to 54 in the nation's general population. While mortality rates for young women in the community have remained static, rates for women in large penal systems around the country now exceed those of the general population. New York's mortality rate for incarcerated women was more than twice that of the population-at-large in 1991, a reflection in part of the disproportionate prevalence of HIV/AIDS in New York and the

FIGURE **6.4** Mortality—women in prison (with U.S. general rates): 1986–1996. (*Source:* NYS Commission of Correction, National Center On Health Statistics, Bureau of Justice Statistics.)

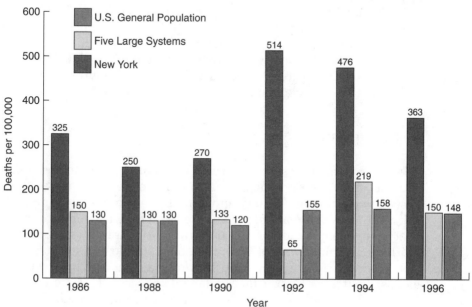

increasing concentrations of HIV-infected women in that state's correctional system. It is evident that incarcerated women experience higher morbidity and mortality than young American women generally and may be considered less healthy as a group, HIV notwithstanding.

It is clear that women have changed the demographics of prison and jail populations in the United States and with it the picture of prisoner morbidity and health care delivery imperatives.

HEALTH CARE NEEDS OF WOMEN OFFENDERS

The social histories of women prisoners are instructive in exploring their health problems as a group. The vast majority of women prisoners are poor people of color with substandard housing, legitimate incomes of less than $500 per month, and dependent children. Thirty-two percent head broken homes, 53 percent come from broken homes, and 41 percent report a history of sexual or physical abuse (U.S. Department of Justice, 1998). These women have limited access to the community-based health care system and limited experience in negotiating its complexities. To an increasing extent, women as a group are immersed in the illicit drug culture as alcoholics, addicts, or the domestic partners of alcoholics or addicts. Recent studies of syphilis reveal that its incidence follows that of cocaine use in a manner that suggests an increasing prevalence of sex-for-drugs exchange not explained by prostitution alone (Farley, Hadler, and Gunn, 1990; Forney, Inciardi, and Lockwood, 1991).

The medical problems of women are associated with these conditions and behaviors. They most often include asthma; diabetes; HIV/AIDS; tuberculosis; hypertension; unintended, interrupted, or lost pregnancy; dysmenorrhea; chlamydia infection; papillomavirus (HPV) infection; herpes simplex II infection; cystic and myomatic conditions; chronic pelvic inflammatory disease; anxiety neurosis; and depression.

Mental Disorder

Wherever women prisoners have been available in numbers sufficient for reliable study, their mental health service needs have been shown to exceed those of men. Anxiety and depression are the most important mental health problems among women prisoners, with some recent evidence that many women suffer from posttraumatic stress disorder while in jail. Mothers and nonmothers typically show similarly high levels of depression. The mean depression level shown by a sample of incarcerated women assessed with the Center for Epidemiologic Studies' Perceived Depression Scale was more than twice that found in general population samples of women using the same instrument. Moreover, these patterns did not abate over the period of incarceration, as might be expected if they were purely situational (Forney, Inciardi, and Lockwood, 1991). There is also a growing suspicion that manic and depressive states in women are underdiagnosed in prison populations (Good, 1978). Maternal incarceration was most responsible for high prevalence rates of anxiety among incarcerated women (Sobel, 1980). At the North Carolina Correctional Center for Women, 51 percent of mothers had high anxiety levels when first studied, and 54 percent of the same group had high anxiety levels six months later (Fogel and Martin, 1992). Among the 41 percent of women inmates who report histories of physical and sexual abuse, the phenomenon of being locked up in a small space by intimidating male authority figures can be a potent stressor. A woman's first symptoms of posttraumatic stress syndrome may be encountered in prison, something not considered for either sex until recently, and then mistakenly thought to be confined to combat veterans. Women victims of abuse and other crimes may become floridly ill when subjected to confinement, separation from children, strip searches, and other stressors reminiscent of abuse (Dvoskin, 1990). Abused women inmates often exhibit histories of long duration involving multiple episodes at the hands of fathers, husbands, boyfriends, and strangers, and this abuse is often directly linked to the offense for which they find themselves in jail (Browne, 1987).

In Great Britain, a study of 638 women in prison revealed that 20 percent of the women detained for trial were mentally ill, as were 15 percent of the sentenced offenders and 16 percent of those in prison only for failure to pay a fine. Similar proportions of the same group reported a history of psychiatric hospitalization. An average 25 percent of detainees and sentenced women reported past suicide attempts (Gibbens, 1975).

It is also increasingly apparent that deinstitutionalization has begun to show its effects in populations of women offenders, effects long seen only among men. Mentally ill women who, before deinstitutionalization, would have been lifetime residents of psychiatric institutions now find themselves in jail. A California study explored the nearly systematic diversion of women from psychiatric institutions to jails through a failure to address problems such as homelessness, prostitution, violent acting-out behaviors, inability to care for children, and impediments to access to psychiatric treatment (Lamb and Grant, 1983; Bachrach, 1984).

Figure 6.5 is based on medical problems elicited from a random sample of 5 percent of the women offenders entering New York's prison system in 1993–1994. It is immediately apparent that 29 percent of women who were admitted to prison in New York had health problems requiring intervention. What is less apparent but nonetheless likely is that diagnoses of HIV and tuberculosis are less frequent than their actual incidence in the population, a grim indication that a significant pool of serious illness may escape detection at entry to prison.

FIGURE **6.5** Women's medical problems upon reception to New York state prisons: 1993–1994. (*Source:* NYSDOCS FPMS; *n* = 130.)

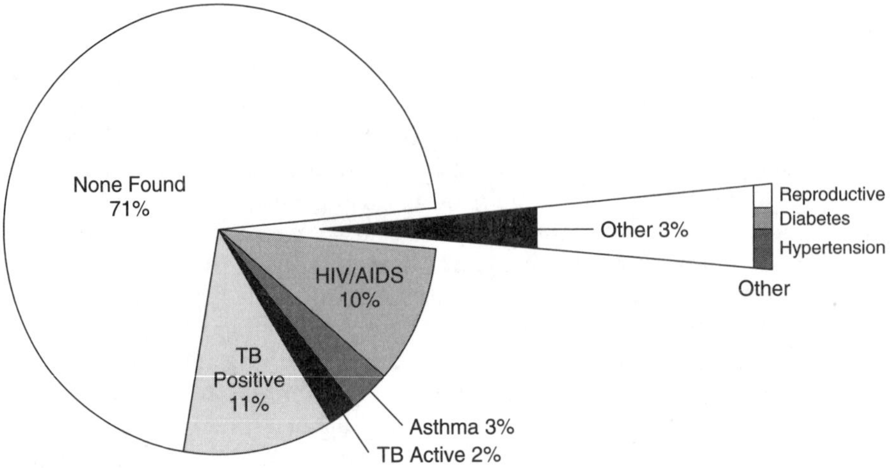

HIV/AIDS and Tuberculosis

Women, along with adolescents, have been identified as the fastest growing group of HIV-infected people in the United States (New York State Executive Chamber, 1994). The rate of HIV infection among women prison inmates now exceeds that of men in nearly every large correctional jurisdiction in the United States. AIDS was the leading cause of death for women aged 25 to 34 in New York City as long ago as 1987 (Nobles, 1987). In the Texas Department of Correction, the female HIV seroprevalence rate is 7 percent compared to 3 percent for men; in Maryland 15.5 percent of women inmates are seropositive compared to 8.7 percent of men. North Carolina found its HIV infection rate for women prisoners to be nearly twice that (6.1 percent) of men (3.1 percent) (Sutton, 1992). In New York, 20 percent of women prison entrants are HIV positive in contrast to an 11.5 percent rate for men (New York State Department of Health, 1992a), with cumulative AIDS case rates 6 percent higher than male inmates and equivalent mortality rates of 70 percent (Morse, Truman, Hanrahan et al., 1990).

The incidence of tuberculosis (TB) among women inmates is following that of HIV/AIDS. Nine percent of the sample of women admitted to New York State prisons (Figure 6.5) were PPD positive for TB and 2 percent had evidence of active disease. Contrasted with an overall reported rate of TB of 271 cases per 100,000 in 1991 for New York's prison system, it becomes apparent that occult HIV cases among women prison entrants are correlative with TB. The TB rate for men in New York prisons actually fell from 202 cases per 100,000 in 1991 to 143 in 1992 (−29 percent). Rates for women, however, increased from 200 cases per 100,000 in 1991 to 228 in 1992, an increase of 14 percent and a rate 59 percent higher than men (Greifinger, 1992). By 1997, vigorous surveillance and control efforts reduced the incidence in men to 61 per 100,000. Tuberculosis in women was also reduced but remained an estimated 34 percent higher than in men, with a rate of 82 per 100,000 (Klopf, 2000).

Asthma

Respiratory asthma has been more prevalent in the United States and Europe since the early 1970s, but its incidence among women has accelerated since 1980. Mortality from asthma increased 31 percent among all groups between 1980 and 1987, but mortality among women increased 50 percent over this period, as compared with a 23 percent increase for men. The rates are also consistently higher for blacks. The black-white ratio for mortality among females was 2.2 over this period. The greatest increase in newly detected asthma cases occurred among young women, an increase of 69 percent in this group over the period, but rates were higher for females in all age groups (Asthma–United States, 1990).

Reproductive Tract Disease

The relationship between reproductive tract disease and the general health of poor and minority women has not been thoroughly studied. Interviews and focus groups conducted with poor women and with their health care providers throughout New York in 1991 elicited a widespread complaint that the medical community discounts the importance of reproductive health to the overall wellness of women (New York State Executive Chamber, 1994). Yet many women, including physicians, argued that a particular emphasis on the reproductive tract misdirects the approach to women patients and inflates the cost of their care, particularly in view of the fact that the leading causes of morbidity and mortality among women lie outside the reproductive tract. Women's health care reform advocates point to an almost total discontinuity of clinical interest and diagnostic approach between gynecologists and other clinicians when dealing with women patients. This often forces women to act as their own primary care coordinators, evaluating and referring themselves for subspecialty care needs (New York State Executive Chamber, 1994).

With the emergence of women as a statistically relevant aspect of the HIV pandemic, interest has begun to focus on reproductive tract disease as a cofactor and/or marker in HIV/AIDS and in associated drug use behaviors (Quinn, Glasser, Cannon, and Matuszak, 1988; Forney, Inciardi, and Lockwood, 1991). A significant fraction of women in the New York study of women's health who found themselves with HIV infection reported long-standing untreated pelvic inflammatory disease, papillomavirus infection, consistently mutagenic Pap smears, and chronic dysmenorrhea (New York State Executive Chamber, 1994). Recent studies summarized in a New York State AIDS Institute paper implicated repeated and chronic sexually transmitted disease (STD), including chancroid, syphilis, and HSV II, as a co/risk factor in HIV infection (New York State Department of Health, 1992b). Vaginal candidiasis is a frequently overlooked early symptom of HIV-induced immune deficiency (Minkoff, 1987). Increasing drug abuse in women has increased their rates of STDs as well as of HIV infection and is aggravated by the phenomenon of exchange of sex for crack-cocaine by women who are not sex workers (Forney, Inciardi, and Lockwood, 1991). In the United States, 24.9 percent of women admitted to jail in 1989 were under the influence of cocaine at the time of their offense, compared to 7.4 percent in 1983. Percentages of women intoxicated with opiates or depressants decreased over the same period (U.S. Department of Justice, 1998). In the Connecticut correctional system, 7 percent of women admitted for drug offenses were infected with an STD. Women cocaine users, especially crack smokers, had the highest rate of syphilis. Interestingly, STD rates did not correlate with parenteral drug use (Farley, Hadler, and Gunn, 1990).

The most visible, growing, and problematic health care issue for incarcerated women is pregnancy and childbirth. The incidence of admission of pregnant women to Alameda County, California, jails doubled during the 1980s (Ryan and Grassano, 1992). In New York, about 7 percent of women admitted to state prison in 1991 were pregnant. This influx becomes more problematic when one considers that New York State law allows pregnant women prisoners to live with their infants at the prison for up to 18 months postpartum (New York State Correction Law, 1996). Further complicating this picture are well-founded suspicions that pregnancy can mask the symptoms of HIV disease or misdirect clinicians in cases where HIV symptoms mimic those of a high-risk or even normal pregnancy (Minkoff, 1987).

Care of newborns of HIV-infected mothers is a complex and daunting task, particularly if complicated by drug dependance in the infant. Studies of HIV seroconversion in neonates from seropositive mothers ranged from 20 percent to 50 percent and were often complicated by concomitant infection with STDs, hepatitis B or C, tuberculosis, and congenital opportunistic infection (Minkoff, 1987).

IMPEDIMENTS TO HEALTH CARE FOR WOMEN

At a series of public hearings and focus groups in New York's major metropolitan areas in 1991, women's health care providers, advocates, and patients testified that the health care problems and concerns of women, particularly poor women and those incarcerated, have been largely marginalized by the medical community. A common refrain was that health care delivery systems designed to meet the needs of men misrepresent or altogether miss female-specific manifestations of illness. Problems are trivialized as benign or functional complaints peculiar to women and are therefore thought to be of no importance. Another common perception was that physician-patient relationships are inadequate from the woman patient's point of view, characterized by poor communication, lack of insight, impatience, insensitivity, and occasional outright abuse from providers (New York State Executive Chamber, 1994). Another study points out that issues relevant to women's health receive attention only as they affect the bearing of healthy children. This has resulted in a dearth of scientific data on their health care needs. Classism, sexism, and racism have a profoundly negative impact on the health of women as a group, something not seen with men regardless of class or race (Mitchell, Tucker, Loftman et al., 1992).

These perceptions and realities are exaggerated in penal institutions where "bad women" are kept. Most health care providers adhere to a middle-class ethic regardless of ethnicity, so their judgment may come down hardest on women offenders. Women attempting to access care in correctional facilities are often regarded as a complicating nuisance, and those who displease authority figure providers by demanding attention will, more often than not, see their care suffer (Mitchell, 1988).

There has been a traditional reluctance to invest in the services and support mechanisms necessary to adequately address the primary care needs of women prisoners that is only now being addressed in large prison systems. At New York's largest prison exclusively for women, a court-appointed physician found in 1988 that women were treated by five per diem physicians who never saw each other and never consulted. These physicians did not record diagnoses or plan for necessary diagnostic tests. The diagnostic studies and subspecialty consultations that were done were rarely reviewed or followed up at the facility. Tuberculosis incidence had been rising at an alarming rate since 1986, yet no surveillance program had been contemplated (Rundle, 1988). The appointment of a full-time medical director in 1989 resulted in significantly improved continuity of care and coordination of support services at this facility designated expressly for management of women offenders, which has been under a federal court order to improve health care for women since 1978 (*Todaro* v. *Ward,* 1977). Support for health care providers, most notably in-service training in detection, diagnosis, and management of HIV, has improved dramatically.

Jails in large jurisdictions have not fared as well. In 1990, the New York State Commission of Correction evaluated the care of a young woman who died several days after childbirth. She had received no antepartum care in jail and no postpartum evaluation, and she died from complications of undiagnosed and untreated sepsis with sickle cell crisis in the most sophisticated contracted jail health care delivery system in the United States (New York State Commission of Correction Medical Review Board, 1991). In upstate New York in the same year, a woman inmate delivered an infant at 26 weeks gestation two hours after transfer from jail, never having seen an obstetrician during two separate incarcerations and despite three days of complaints of pain, spotting, and amniotic leakage (New York State Commission of Correction, 1991).

Reproductive health care access notwithstanding, the systematic denial to women of parity of services readily and routinely available to incarcerated men is the most widespread and invidious impediment to adequate health care for women offenders. Alternate levels of care, such as skilled nursing care, chronic and rehabilitative care for the physically disabled, services for geriatric inmates, sheltered communities for the retarded and developmentally disabled, renal dialysis, reconstructive surgery, investigational therapies, and cardiovascular surgery are all routinely available to men in federal and large state correctional systems. They are generally unavailable, restricted, or provided on an ad hoc basis to women (Resnick and Shaw, 1980; Pennsylvania Prison Society, 1983; Anno, 1991).

The available research characterizes mental health treatment for women offenders as "conspicuous by its absence," almost entirely focused on the needs of men (Moss, 1986). Current widely accepted standards for prison health care proceed on the assumption that when standards are met, women have the same access to quality primary and specialty care as men, in addition to the services unique to them as women (Moss, 1986). This assumption is by no means validated by experience. This issue will likely become a central theme supporting a tide of equal protection litigation that will seek to compel rapid and comprehensive improvements in many jurisdictions, something Eighth Amendment litigation has hitherto been unable to accomplish for women (Dale, 1990; Rafter, 1990).

A MODEL OF IMPROVED CARE

Although the reflex defense mechanisms of state and local governments when confronted with prison reform litigation often become impediments to improved care, the courts have prodded some jurisdictions into developing and implementing improved women's services. In California, Santa Rita County officials implemented a consent decree in 1989 in settlement of *Jones* v. *Dyer* that established a comprehensive OB/GYN and prenatal service for incarcerated women (Ryan and Grassano, 1992). It features a new $174 million facility that is staffed according to a specially tailored $21 million provider contract. The discrete OB/GYN unit is staffed by a multidisciplinary medical team composed of a perinatal case manager, a nurse practitioner, a physician, and a nursing staff. All women admitted to the facility are afforded a comprehensive reception health appraisal and are screened for pregnancy. Pregnant substance users are immediately sent to the outpatient OB service of the hospital, evaluated, and enrolled in a substance abuse treatment program.

All pregnant women receive relevant prenatal laboratory studies, ruling out diabetes, HIV, Hepatitis (B) (C-D), tuberculosis, herpes simplex virus, and so on. A Pap smear and STD serologies are obtained, and therapeutic abortion is available on request. Counseling with credentialed mental health professionals is immediately available. Women are placed on a therapeutic prenatal diet with appropriate supplements. Ultrasonography is done at 16 to 20 weeks. Pregnancies complicated by risk factors or illness result in admission to a 32-bed inpatient unit with 24-hour nursing. A structured exercise program conducted by qualified staff is afforded. Social services that include information and assistance on adoption, resources and coping skills for single-parent mothers, options and skills for child care, and family planning are afforded.

FUTURE DIRECTIONS: TOWARD DECENT CARE

Santa Rita's experience shows that there is little mystery regarding the operational components required for establishing a credible, comprehensive primary care service for women. Poor correctional health care for women is not a function of staff or equipment, but rather a manifestation of pervasive and insidious attitudes, behaviors, and beliefs that influence government policy. State and local government policy makers who elect to improve the quality and availability of health care for incarcerated women in advance of a court order to do so should focus on education and training, installation of modern managed primary care models, health care finance strategies, and emphasis on diversion and aftercare.

Women offenders need to develop living skills that raise self-esteem and build confidence necessary to avoid high-risk behaviors, to negotiate the complexities of the health care system as consumers, and to adopt wellness as a primary personal value. This would seem a more worthwhile activity than, for example, insisting that women inmates learn cosmetology. Health care providers should be required to demonstrate satisfactory skills for delivery of respectful and considerate care in a sexually and culturally diverse society while in medical and postgraduate school and on a mandatory continuing medical education basis. Many medical professionals would do well to learn and adopt a less judgmental approach to their patients and trouble themselves less over whether offenders deserve their skill and effort.

Given the high proportion of mothers and nonmothers who suffer from mental and emotional disorders while incarcerated, several studies have recommended formation of self-help groups, enhancement of family-oriented group counseling, stress management training, and strategies to enhance self-esteem (Fogel and Martin, 1992).

Managed primary care for women seeks not, as the third party payors might have it, to keep the access gate to the health care system shut, but to draw all clients into promotion and maintenance of health. This requires that correctional medical departments implement aggressive protocols for identification of and intervention in medical problems, that they manage patients within diagnostic cohorts, emphasize wellness, promote continuity, and place a premium on care that is respectful and considerate. The present demand-for-service and episodic style of ambulatory care in jails and prisons treats each encounter as unprecedented, each complaint as isolated; it is the single greatest impediment to quality of care.

As the enormous growth of health care costs imperils our world economic position even as we ration health care to the poor, the United States is now compelled, however unwillingly, to adopt a universal health care access and finance system. Medicaid, the primary health finance guarantor for the poor, is summarily denied to prison and jail inmates under federal Title 42 CFR while they are incarcerated, even to those participating prior to incarceration. A great deal of preventive health care while in custody is deferred for lack of Medicaid reimbursement. There is no justifiable rationale for such an anomaly. Deferral of care benefits no one; it inflates the cost of care that inevitably must be delivered later at higher levels of acuity. Planners of universal care systems in this new century would be well advised to revisit health care financing for the incarcerated.

Incarceration as the sanction of choice for criminal behaviors is no longer socially or economically sustainable in the United States. In 1994, 1.36 million persons, about one in every 189 adults, were in jail or prison. Of these, about 83,000 were women (U.S. Department of Justice, 1995). Prison operating costs per inmate in New York have been increasing at a mean rate of 5.44 percent per year (State of New York, Office of the Comptroller, 1990). None of this appears to have any appreciable impact on crime rates. Criminal justice systems will be increasingly compelled to expand alternative and diversion programs, and the population of women offenders offers attractive opportunities in this regard. Reduction in unnecessary incarceration of women will reduce demand for scarce specialized services. For those women who must be incarcerated, planned referrals to postincarceration services with emphasis on Medicaid eligibility, family planning, drug abuse services, and coordinated health maintenance for mothers and their children should be emphasized.

The irony of Santa Rita County Jail as quite possibly the highest quality comprehensive health service provider for poor women in its community is an instructive one. The subpopulation of women offenders comes from the growing pool of poor and often victimized women in our urban centers who are quickly returned there. Their health problems and needs do not arise in prison, rather they are brought to prison with them. Informed commentators now discuss jail as the social net of last resort, providing neither punishment nor deterrence; rather respite from hopelessly untenable life situations and access to health and human service programs unavailable in their home communities (Butterfield, 1992). If this is indeed the case, then the correctional institution has, for better or worse, become integral to the community. The line between the prisoner "others" and the rest of us is no longer so clear, and the right to decent health care is no longer exclusive.

REFERENCES

Anno, J. (1991). *Prison Health Care: Guidelines for Management of an Adequate Delivery System.* Washington, DC: U.S. Department of Justice, National Institute of Corrections.

Asthma—United States, 1980–1987. (1990). *MMWR.* 39:493–497.

Bachrach, L.L. (1984). "Deinstitutionalization and Women: Assessing the Consequences of Public Policy." *American Psychologist,* 39(10): 1171–1177.

Browne, A. (1987). *When Battered Women Kill.* New York: Free Press:23.

Butterfield, F. (1992, July 19). "Are American Jails Becoming Shelters from the Storm?" *The New York Times.*

Dale, M.J. (1990). "The Female Inmate: An Introduction to Rights and Issues." *American Jails,* 4:56–58.

Dvoskin, J.A. (1990). "Jail-Based Mental Health Services." In H.J. Steadman (ed.), *Jail Diversion for the Mentally Ill: Breaking Through the Barriers.* Boulder, CO: National Institute of Corrections.

Farley, T.A., Hadler, J.L., and Gunn, R.A. (1990). "The Syphilis Epidemic in Connecticut: Relationship to Drug Use and Prostitution." *Journal of Sexually Transmitted Diseases,* 17(4):16–18.

Fogel, C.I. and Martin, S.L. (1992). "The Mental Health of Incarcerated Women." *Western Journal of Nursing Research,* 14(1):30–47.

Forney, M.A., Inciardi, J.A., and Lockwood, D. (1991). "Exchanging Sex for Crack-Cocaine: A Comparison of Women from Rural and Urban Communities." *Journal of Community Health,* 17(2):73–85.

Gibbens, T.C.N. (1975). "Female Offenders." *British Journal of Psychiatry.* Spec. 9:326–333.

Good, M.I. (1978). "Primary Affective Disorder, Aggression and Criminality: A Review and Clinical Study." *Archives of General Psychiatry,* 35(8):954–960.

Greifinger, R., M.D. (1992, December). Chief Medical Officer, NYS Department of Correctional Services. Interagency communication.

Klopf, L.C. (2000, June). Infectious Disease Control Coordinator. NYS Department of Correctional Services. Interagency communication.

Lamb, H.R. and Grant, R.W. (1983). "Mentally Ill Women in County Jail." *Archives of General Psychiatry,* 40:463–468.

Minkoff, H.L. (1987). "Care of Pregnant Women Infected with Human Immunodeficiency Virus." *JAMA,* 258:2714–2717.

Mitchell, J.L. (1988). "Women, AIDS and Public Policy." *Law and Public Policy Journal,* 3:50–51.

Mitchell, J.L., Tucker, J., Loftman, P.O., et al. (1992). "HIV and Women: Current Controversies and Clinical Relevance."*Journal of Women's Health,* 1:35-39.

Morse, D.L., Truman, D.I., Hanrahan, J.P., et al. (1990). "AIDS Behind Bars: Epidemiology of New York State Prison Cases, 1980–1988." *New York State Journal of Medicine,* 90:133–138.

Moss, S.R. (1986). "Women in Prison: A Case of Pervasive Neglect." *Women and Therapy,* 5(2–3):177–185.

New York State Commission of Correction. (1991). "In the Matter of Tammy M." (91LG026).

New York State Commission of Correction (SCOCa). (1993). *Statewide Data Compilation from Sheriff's Annual Reports: 1984–1993.* Albany, NY: Author.

New York State Commission of Correction Medical Review Board. (1991). "In the Matter of the Death of Jowana G." Albany, NY: Author.

New York State Correction Law. (1996). Section 611.

New York State Department of Correctional Services (DOCS). (1994, October). *FPMS Online Offender-Based Data Report.* Albany, NY: Author.

New York State Department of Health. (1992a, May). "HIV Seroprevalence: Semi-Annual Report." Albany, NY: Author.

New York State Department of Health. (1992b, September). "Role of Barrier Methods in HIV Prevention." Albany, NY: Author.

New York State Executive Chamber. (1994). *Women's Health. Report of the Interagency Work Group on Women's Health.* Albany, NY: Author.

Nobles, M. (1987, October 1). Testimony to the New York State Governor's Advisory Committee for Black Affairs. *Women in Crisis.* New York.

Pennsylvania Prison Society. (1983). "Women in Prison." *The Prison Journal,* 63(2).

Quinn, T.C., Glasser, D., Cannon, R.O., and Matuszak, D.L. (1988). "Human Immunodeficiency Virus Infection Among Patients Attending Clinics for Sexually Transmitted Diseases." *New England Journal of Medicine,* 318:197 –203.

Rafter, N.H. (1990). "Equal Protection Forcing Changes in Women's Prisons." *Correctional Law Reporter,* 2(4):49–52.

Resnick, J. and Shaw, N. (1980). "Prisoners of Their Sex: Health Problems of Incarcerated Women." In I. Robbins (ed.), *Prisoner's Rights Sourcebook: Theory, Litigation and Practice,* Vol. II. New York: Clark Boardman Co.

Rundle, F.L., M.D. (1988). "Report of Audit of Medical Services at the New York State Correctional Facility for Women, Bedford Hills, NY." (Unpublished manuscript.)

Ryan, T.A. and Grassano, J.B. (1992). "Taking a Progressive Approach to Pregnant Offenders." *Corrections Today,* 54(6).

Sobel, S.B. (1980). "Women in Prison: Sexism Behind Bars." *Professional Psychology,* 11:2.

State of New York, Office of the Comptroller. (1990). "Staff Study on the High Cost of Imprisonment in New York vs. Other States." Albany, NY: Author.

Sutton, G. (moderator). (1992). "Management of the Seropositive Prisoner: Medical, Ethical and Economic Perspectives. A Roundtable Discussion Among Professionals in Correctional Health Care Focusing on HIV/AIDS." *Correct Care,* 6:4. New York: World Health Communications, Inc.

Todaro v. *Ward,* 565 F.2d 48 (1977).

U.S. Department of Justice. Bureau of Justice Statistics (BJSc). (1998). *Sourcebook of Criminal Justice Statistics–1998.* Washington, DC: Author. See also: (BJSd). Women in Prison—1999.

U.S. Department of Justice. (1996, June). Bureau of Justice Statistics (BJSa). *Correctional Populations in the United States: 1994.* Washington, DC: Author.

U.S. Department of Justice. Bureau of Justice Statistics. (1998). *Prisoners in 1998.* Washington, DC: Author.

chapter 7

JAILED FATHERS
PATERNAL REACTIONS
TO SEPARATION FROM CHILDREN

JAMIE S. MARTIN
Indiana University of Pennsylvania

INTRODUCTION

For the past 20 years, the United States has waged a war against crime. The results are a decreasing crime rate and the implementation of more stringent sanctions, including the more frequent use of imprisonment. Consequently, the United States has one of the highest incarceration rates of any industrialized nation in the world (Donzinger, 1996). Current statistics indicate that approximately 1.86 million individuals are behind bars in federal and state prisons and local jails (Gilliard, 1999), with millions more cycling through our jails annually. The overwhelming majority of these inmates are men (approximately 1.7 million), and the majority of these men are fathers (Beck et al., 1993).

There is an increasing recognition of the issues surrounding incarcerated parents and their children (Dalley, 1997; Gabel and Johnston,

An earlier version of this paper presented at the annual meeting of the Academy of Criminal Justice Sciences, New Orleans, March 2000.

1995; Bloom and Stinehart, 1993; Fishman, 1990; Morris, 1965; Bakker, Morris, and Janus, 1978). However, the vast majority of studies have focused on incarcerated mothers. Unfortunately, we know relatively little about incarcerated fathers as a group. Only recently have a few researchers begun to consider the experience of being incarcerated from the perspective of fathers, providing information on their characteristics (Hairston, 1995; Carlson and Cervera, 1992; Hairston, 1989), examining their affective states (Lanier, 1993), investigating father–child interaction (Lanier, 1991), and exploring parental attitudes (Hanrahan, Martin, Springer, Cox, and Gido, 1996).

This study builds upon these earlier studies that examined incarcerated fathers. The present study represents an exploratory and descriptive effort aimed at increased understanding of an extremely understudied population—jailed fathers. That the father plays an important role in the development and prosperity of his children is becoming increasingly evident (see, for example, Lamb, 1981; Bronstein and Cowan, 1988; Marsiglio, 1995). It is also evident that a large number of children in the United States have lost their fathers to our nation's jails and prisons.

Being incarcerated is an especially stressful event. Individuals are removed from their homes and communities and remanded to an environment that strips them of their freedom and, while incarcerated, their identities as husbands, sons, brothers, and fathers. The stress of this experience is amplified when an individual enters a jail. Jails are often the "gateway into confinement" for all individuals. Whereas most prisons receive inmates who have already been detained for a period of time and have been through a classification process, jails receive individuals who, until the moment they step through the door, have been living in the relative freedom of society. Consequently, being jailed is a very chaotic, disorienting experience, and the stress is much more acute than that experienced while in prison (Gibbs, 1992).

The study reported here examines the relationships between these two experiences, (1) fatherhood and (2) the stress of being jailed. This study sought to examine the frequency and nature of contact between jailed fathers and their children and to understand whether the men's roles as fathers provided a buffer to the stress of incarceration, or conversely, whether this role exacerbated the amount of stress experienced, or both. When individuals experience stress, they often turn to family members for assistance and support. It must be recognized, however, that not all individuals were connected to their families prior to incarceration. Thus, separation from loved ones will likely result in added stress only for those individuals who had strong family relationships prior to incarceration.

The overarching questions that this study addresses are as follows:

1. What is the nature and significance of contact with family during incarceration?

2. Do the preincarceration relationships of jailed fathers impact the stress of incarceration?

METHODS AND PROCEDURES

Participant Selection Variables

For the purposes of this project, a jail inmate was deemed a "father" if he had any children. A "child" included biological, adoptive, and stepchildren, along with any child for whom the inmate was a legal guardian. If the inmate was involved in a "living together" relationship prior to incarceration, the children of an inmate's significant other were included. "Minor children" included all children under the age of 18. Fathers were identified as "parents" if they (1) resided with all of their minor children during the six months prior to incarceration or (2) had substantive (daily) contact with a minor child during the six months prior to incarceration. Men who did not reside with any of their minor children were identified as "biological fathers," and men who resided with some of their minor children but not all of their minor children were identified as "mixed parents" for this project. All variables were operationalized by securing responses to specific questions on the survey or through the interview.

Sample and Method—Phase I

The study was conducted in two phases and at two sites. The first site was a large, urban jail; the second was a small, rural jail; both jails are in the Commonwealth of Pennsylvania. The study was advertised in both sites, and the sample consisted of men who volunteered for participation. Phase I consisted of the group administration of a survey to 93 jailed fathers housed in one of two county jails. The questionnaire permitted the researcher to identify demographic information and family characteristics of the jailed fathers, collect limited information on their preincarceration parental relationships, and collect information on contact with family members during confinement.

One of the goals of this project was to determine the ways in which the preincarceration parental relationships and contact with family members during incarceration influence the stress of the jail experience. It was theorized that separation from children is a stressor for fathers who had involved relationships with their children before their incarceration. Thus, the questionnaire included a measure of negative affect, which is detailed later.

Negative Affect Measures—Emotion Index

Stress is a difficult concept to define although most people can describe a time when they have experienced it. According to Cohen, Kesslar, and Gordon (1995:3), stress can be thought of as a process in which "environmental demands tax or exceed the adaptive capacity of the organism, resulting in psychological and biological changes that may place the person at risk for disease." Using this definition, stress can be seen as a "stimulus-response" event for individuals.

The stress event has three components: (1) environmental experiences—the environmental demands, stressors, or events; (2) subjective evaluations of the stressfulness of the event—the individual appraisals or perceptions of stress; and (3) affective, behavioral, or biological responses to the stress event (Cohen et al., 1995).

It has been established previously that jail confinement is stressful (Johnson and Toch, 1988; Gibbs, 1987, 1991), and that for most individuals, separation from family is stressful. It seems reasonable that these environmental demands will result in negative affective responses for most individuals. Previous research shed some light on the kind of affective responses that might be most common among incarcerated individuals: depression, anxiety, and loneliness (Lanier, 1993; Rokach and Cripps, 1999). The negative affect measure was included in the questionnaire because "environmental demands that are appraised as stressful are generally thought to influence disease risk through negative emotional responses" (Cohen et al., 1995: 18). Gibbs and Hanrahan (1993) incorporated a measure of negative affect in their study of college students. The researchers measured depression, loneliness, anxiety, and anger. Because of the overlap between the prior prison-based research findings and the Gibbs and Hanrahan (1993) measure, the researcher utilized this negative affect measure.

The respondents were asked to report how often they experienced each emotion or feeling and then to place a slash across a 10-centimeter line to indicate the frequency of each emotion as illustrated here.

How often do you experience **loneliness?**

Never————————————————Always

The result is a score between 1–10 that reflects the relative frequency of the negative emotion. The scores for each of the four items (loneliness, anger, anxiety, and depression) were combined to form the "emotion index" (range of 0–40).

Sample and Method—Phase II

Phase II of this project consisted of face-to-face interviews with a group of 25 jailed fathers who had completed the questionnaire and indicated their interest in being interviewed. A semistructured interview protocol was used to explore the impact of incarceration on the familial relationships of the jailed fathers, including their feelings about being separated from their children, the frequency and descriptions of contact with their children, and postrelease expectations and plans.

Information from both the questionnaire and the interview was used to classify interview respondents as either "parents"—men who (1) resided with all of their minor child during the six months prior to incarceration or (2) had substantive (daily) contact with a minor child during the six months prior to incarceration, "biological fathers"—men who did not reside with any of their children, or "mixed parents"—men who resided with some of their children but not all of them. The final interview sample consisted of 6 parents, 7 mixed parents, and 12 biological fathers.

CHARACTERISTICS OF THE JAILED FATHERS

For the most part, the jailed fathers in this study were either black or white. Sixty-three percent of the respondents in this study were black ($n = 59$), and 30 percent were white ($n = 28$). Only 2.2 percent of the respondents were Latino ($n = 2$), and 2.2 percent were American Indian ($n = 2$). One respondent categorized himself as "Other," and one father did not classify himself. Because of the racial dichotomy that was present in the sample, the interviews were limited to black and white fathers.

The average age of the jailed fathers in this study is 32 years. Nearly 85 percent ($n = 79$) of the fathers had at least a high school education, and approximately 33 percent (37.6 percent, $n = 35$) reported that they had at least some postsecondary education. The postsecondary education rate in this sample is much lower than the national average of 65.6 percent (available online at http://nces.ed.gov/pubs99/condition99/Indicator-59.html).

Nearly 75 percent of the jailed fathers held jobs prior to their incarceration; 57 percent had been employed full-time, and 17.2 percent had been employed part-time. Still, the respondents had an unemployment rate that was nearly six times the national average and four to six times the local average. Approximately 23 percent of the fathers were unemployed. This is much higher than both the national unemployment average of 4.1 percent (available online at http://stats.bls.gov/ newsrels.htm) and the respective county unemployment averages, which, in October 1999 were as follows: 3.4 percent in the urban county and 5.0 percent in the rural county (available online at http://www.lmi.state.pa.us/clep/labforce.asp).

A majority of the fathers (54 percent) reported earning $15,000 or less per year prior to incarceration, with 37 percent reporting earnings of $10,000 or less per year. Approximately 21 percent earned between $15,000 and $25,000 per year. Only 20 percent of the jailed fathers earned over $25,000 per year. Thus, both the rate of employment and the earning power were quite low among respondents.

The fathers who participated in the interviews had a demographic profile quite similar to the total sample. While the subsample of interviewees appeared to be better educated than the entire sample, they had similar racial, employment, and economic characteristics.

The jailed fathers had a varied criminal history, with 74.2 percent reporting that they had been convicted of two or more offenses. The fathers' offense categories ranged from property crimes and drug offenses to interpersonal crimes.

As shown in Table 7.1, the most common offense is possession of drugs—53.8 percent of the fathers reported a conviction for this offense. Approximately 41 percent reported that they had been convicted of theft, and 35 percent had a receiving stolen property or a disorderly conduct conviction. Hence, the jailed fathers represented in this study are, for the most part, nonviolent offenders.

Parental Status of Jailed Fathers

Table 7.2 provides an overview of the parental status of the respondents. Parental status was deduced from the respondents' reports on the questionnaire regarding the number of minor children they had and the number whom they had resided with prior to incarceration. Ninety-two

TABLE 7.1 Jailed Fathers' Reported Conviction

PROPERTY OFFENSES	INTERPERSONAL OFFENSES	DRUG CRIMES	OTHER OFFENSES
Theft (40.9%)	Simple assault (31.2%)	Possession (53.8%)	Disorderly conduct (35.5%)
*RSP (35.5%)	Robbery (15.1%)	DUI (17.2%)	Failure to appear (29.0%)
Burglary (18.3%)	Aggravated assault (12.9%)		
Writing bad checks (5.4%)	Terroristic threats (9.7%)		All other offenses (21.5%)

*Receiving stolen property. Percentages do not equal 100% because of multiple convictions.

TABLE 7.2 Parental Status of Respondents

PARENTAL STATUS	NUMBER	PERCENTAGE
All children over 18	5	5.4
Child born during father's incarceration	4	4.3
"Parent" (lived with all minor children)	17	18.5
"Mixed parent" (lived with some, but not all, minor children)	20	21.8
"Biological father" (lived with no minor children)	46	50
Totals	92	100

respondents reported on their parental status. Five of the 92 respondents (5.4 percent) had adult children only, and four respondents (4.3 percent) reported that their child had been born during their incarceration. Hence, 83 respondents had minor children prior to their arrest and incarceration. Thirty-seven of the 83 respondents (44.6 percent) were residing with some or all of their minor children prior to their incarceration. The remaining 46 respondents (55.4 percent) resided with none of their minor children prior to their incarceration.

Number of Children

The fathers in the study had a total of 248 children, 115 sons and 133 daughters. Most of these ($n = 186$, 75 percent) were minor children. The fathers had 103 minor daughters, with an average age of 7.32 years, and 83 minor sons, with an average age of 8.25 years. Therefore, the jailed fathers had an average of 2.0 minor children with an average age of 7.7 years. In this respect, the respondents in the present study were strikingly similar to the 402,434 state prisoners surveyed in 1991 who had an average of 2.05 minor children (Beck et al., 1993).

As mentioned earlier, 37 of the jailed fathers who had minor children were residing with at least some of these children prior to their incarceration. The vast majority (87 percent) of these children were now residing with their mother.

ANALYSIS AND FINDINGS

This research project addresses two central questions: (1) What is the nature and significance of contact with family during incarceration and (2) Do the preincarceration relationships of jailed fathers differentially affect the stress of incarceration? The analysis begins with an exploration of the nature and extent of contact between jailed fathers and their children.

Face-to-Face Visits and Other Contact

The jailed fathers were queried about contact with their loved ones in order to explore the ways in which preincarceration relationships impact their term of incarceration. Most of the studies to date on imprisoned fathers indicate that they have little face-to-face contact with their children (Hairston, 1989; Lanier, 1991; Hairston, 1995). The reasons for the infrequent contact include distance between prison and home, traveling costs, and the preincarceration relationships that existed between the incarcerated men, their children, and the mothers of their children (Hairston, 1989; Lanier, 1991; and Hairston, 1995). More specifically, fathers who resided with their children prior to incarceration (Lanier, 1991) and married fathers were more likely to maintain regular visits with those children during imprisonment (Hairston, 1989). In the Lanier (1991) study, nearly 72 percent of residential fathers had visits from their children. It should be emphasized that all of the aforementioned studies took place in prisons.

Because jails are typically located closer to an inmate's home than are prisons, it was anticipated that jailed fathers would visit more frequently with their children than imprisoned fathers. However, this was not the case. The results of the present study suggest that the jailed fathers had less frequent contact with their children than did fathers from previous prison-based studies.

TABLE 7.3 Visits with Children by Parental Status

	LIVED WITH ALL OR SOME OF THEIR CHILDREN (N = 37)	DID NOT LIVE WITH CHILDREN PRIOR TO INCARCERATION (N = 46)	ROW TOTALS
Children have visited	56.7% (n = 21)	41.3% (n = 19)	48.2% (n = 40)
Children have not visited	43.3% (n = 16)	58.7% (n = 27)	51.8% (n = 43)

As outlined in Table 7.3, while nearly 57 percent of the respondents who resided with their minor children prior to incarceration visited with their children in jail, a full 43 percent had no visits. Similarly, only 41.3 percent of respondents who did not reside with their minor children prior to incarceration visited with their children while jailed. The fact that jail inmates are physically closer to their families appears not to increase the likelihood of visits, although the inmates' preincarceration relationships do appear to influence contact with children during incarceration.

Face-to-Face Contact: Parents and Mixed Parents

The interview data suggest various reasons for the lack of face-to-face contact between fathers and their children. Among interview respondents, 8 of the 13 men who resided with all or some of their children prior to incarceration reported that they preferred not to see their children in the jail. Several of these fathers indicated that they had never visited with their children because they believed both they and their children would have a strong emotional reaction to seeing one another through a piece of glass. As these men recounted, it would be too painful to visit with their children and too painful for their children; thus, they forgo face-to-face visits.

Other interview respondents decided to stop visits with their children after they experienced them. Generally, these fathers explained that their visits with their children were too difficult to endure. In some cases, the children were frightened of the jail environment; in other cases, they were unable to grasp why they could not have contact with their fathers. Additionally, several of the fathers indicated that the atmosphere that was present in the jail was not one they wanted their children to experience. Thus, these fathers felt it best if their children were not subjected to the emotional torment that accompanied the visits.

Five interview respondents resided with their children prior to incarceration and maintained contact through visits while they were jailed. However, none of these respondents was satisfied with the visits. In some instances, the physical design of the visiting quarters reduced the quality of the visit from the fathers' perspectives. At the large, urban jail, inmates receive visitors on the second level of the housing unit in which they reside. There are stools on both sides of a large glass window. Hence, the inmate simply moves to the second floor of the pod in which he is housed to visit with loved ones who thus remain physically outside the inmate's actual room. This does not afford much privacy for the inmate and his family.

The small, rural jail has a compact visiting area that looks like two telephone booths placed together with a common glass partition and is approximately waist high for an adult. There is a small shelf upon which a person could lean or perhaps place papers. The area below the glass partition and shelf is constructed of bricks. Inmates speak to their visitors through a telephone. When small children visit, they often have difficulty seeing the inmate and vice versa.

The important theme that emerges from discussions with fathers who resided with their children prior to their arrest and incarceration is that the jail environment is not conducive to maintaining the bonds between incarcerated fathers and their children. The "pains of imprisonment" (Sykes, 1958) for many of these men include choosing between the anguish that accompanies seeing their children through a pane of glass and the anguish of not seeing them at all.

Face-to-Face Contact: Biological Fathers

While the parents and mixed parents expressed reluctance to visit with their children or displeasure with the visits, very few of the biological fathers expressed the same concerns. Of the 12 biological fathers interviewed, 8 had not visited with their children, but only 2 fathers expressed concern that visits would be too painful for themselves or their children.

The other biological fathers who had no face-to-face visits cited other reasons for the absence of contact. In some cases, family members refused to bring their children to the jail. In other instances, the men had no contact with their children prior to their incarceration and thus no contact during incarceration. Interestingly, the four biological fathers who had face-to-face visits with their children had few complaints about the visits and suggested that their children were happy with them as well.

For the most part, the biological fathers did not report the same level of anguish with regard to visiting their loved ones as did the men who resided with their children prior to incarceration. This is not surprising, given the limited or nonexistent contact and weak emotional connection these men had with their children prior to their arrest. Consequently, when they received visits from their children, the visits caused little pain for these fathers, and they likely would not recognize that entering a jail for a visit has the potential to cause distress for their children.

Telephone and Other Contact

Many of the respondents reported maintaining contact with their children via telephone or by writing letters. Previous studies have suggested that a large majority of inmate fathers maintain regular telephone contact with their families (Lanier, 1991; Carlson and Cervera, 1992; Hanrahan et al., 1996). In the present study, telephone contact was more common than face-to-face visits for all respondents (see Table 7.4).

TABLE 7.4 Telephone Contact with Children by Parental Status

	LIVED WITH SOME OR ALL OF THEIR CHILDREN (*N* = 36)	DID NOT LIVE WITH CHILDREN PRIOR TO INCARCERATION (*N* = 46)	ROW TOTALS
Have spoken to children by telephone	75% (*n* = 27)[a]	63% (*n* = 29)	68.3% (*n* = 56)
Have not spoken to children by telephone	25% (*n* = 9)[a]	37% (*n* = 17)	31.7% (*n* = 26)

[a]One respondent failed to answer this question; thus *N* = 36.

Sixty-eight percent of respondents who had minor children prior to their incarceration maintained telephone contact with them while jailed. A common complaint of nearly all of the interviewees concerned the cost associated with making telephone calls. Most institutions do not permit incoming telephone calls. Inmates must place the calls to their families reversing the charges, which can be expensive.

Once again, the fathers who had limited or no contact with their children prior to their arrest were less likely to use the telephone to maintain contact. However, for the fathers who were attempting to maintain contact, the costs associated with making telephone calls could be prohibitive.

Impact of Separation on Children

A man's incarceration has a significant and most often negative impact on his family members (Bakker et al., 1978; Fritsch and Burkhead, 1981; Carlson and Cervera, 1992; Hanrahan et al., 1996), including his children (Johnston, 1995; Fritsch and Burkhead, 1981).

Fritsch and Burkhead (1981) suggest that children who were aware of their parent's incarceration often exhibited behavioral problems. Interestingly, the type of behavioral problems reported seemed to be related to the gender of the incarcerated parent. If a child's mother were incarcerated, the child displayed "acting-in" behaviors (withdrawal, daydreaming, increased crying, etc.); if a child's father were incarcerated, the child exhibited "acting-out" behaviors (hostility and aggressiveness, defiance, school truancy, etc.). The parents reported "problems with their children in precisely those areas where they would traditionally accept major responsibility for the rearing of children if living at home" (Fritsch and

TABLE **7.5** Awareness of Behavioral Changes by Parental Status

	PARENT AND MIXED PARENTS $N = 36^a$	BIOLOGICAL PARENTS $N = 46$	ROW TOTALS
Did not notice behavioral changes	16 (21.1%)	32 (26.9%)	48 (58.5%)
Noticed behavioral changes	20 (14.9%)	14 (19.1%)	34 (41.5%)
Column total	36^a (43.9%)	46 (56.1%)	82 (100%)

[a]One respondent failed to answer this question; thus $N = 36$. Numbers in parentheses are expected values. $X^2 = 5.25073$, DF = 1, $p = 0.0219$

Burkhead, 1981: 86). Furthermore, inmates who had contact with their children both prior to and during incarceration were more likely to report the occurrence of behavioral problems among their children (Fritsch and Burkhead, 1981).

The questionnaire data were examined to assess the jailed fathers' reports of the impact of their incarceration on their children. The respondents were asked, "Have you noticed any behavioral problems in your children?" Not surprisingly, the fathers who resided with their children prior to incarceration reported greater awareness of behavioral problems in their children, as shown in Table 7.5.

The fathers were also asked about the effect that their incarceration had had on their children's emotional and financial well-being. The reports

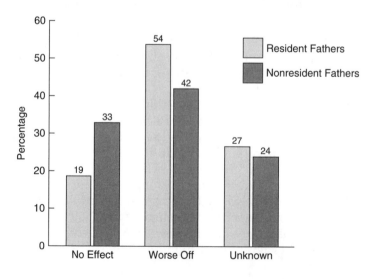

FIGURE **7.1**
Financial effect of father's incarceration on minor children ($N = 83$)

of the fathers who resided with children were compared to the reports of the fathers who resided apart from their children prior to incarceration.

As shown in Figure 7.1, the fathers who resided with their children prior to their incarceration were more likely to report financial effects than were the fathers who resided apart from their children (54 percent to 42 percent). Additionally, 33 percent of the nonresident fathers reported that their children's financial situation did not change as a result of their incarceration.

These reports could reflect the nonresident fathers' lack of financial participation in the lives of their children prior to their incarceration. It is important to note that not a single respondent reported that his children's financial situation had improved.

The respondents' reports regarding the emotional impact of their incarceration on their children were surprising. A large percentage of both resident and nonresident fathers (50 percent and 68 percent, respectively) reported that they did not know whether their children were affected emotionally by their incarceration (see Figure 7.2). Approximately 38 percent of the resident fathers reported that their children were worse off emotionally as a result of their incarceration. None of the resident fathers believed that his children were better off emotionally.

It seems possible that the questionnaire respondents were more willing to acknowledge the financial burden that their incarceration created and preferred not to acknowledge the possibility that their actions caused emotional suffering among their children. An alternative explanation is that the fathers were less aware of any effect. The interview data suggest the former may be true.

The interview data provide a different view of the perceived impact of a father's incarceration on his children. The majority (9 of 13, 69.2 percent)

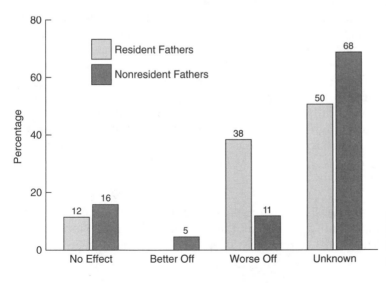

FIGURE 7.2
Emotional effect of father's incarceration on minor children (*N* = 83)

of the parents and mixed parents reported that their children had been affected emotionally by their incarceration. The emotional impact ranged from children not being able to interact with their father, feeling shame or embarrassment about their father's incarceration, to believing their father did not love them anymore and did want to live at home. The specific emotional impact often depended on the age of the children. Other effects reported by the parents and mixed parents included behavioral changes, such as their children not listening to adults or having problems in school.

The following respondent described the emotional impact of his incarceration on his children, especially his sons. He is a 27-year-old father of five children. He was residing with all of his children at the time of his arrest.

IER: How has being here changed your relationship with your kids?

R05: It moves me out of the position of father. It moves me out of the position of protector. It moves me out of the position of enforcer as far as rules go. It takes a lot away from me and my children ... [son] has asked me several times, "Daddy why don't you come home? Don't you like me no more?" He's taking this personally. He thinks it's his fault. We all know it's not that. But he's too young to realize it. And I think, I think it's going to affect him, I really do. The kid is going to think that he's unwanted. The kid is going to feel that, you know, if my daddy don't want me, who will? And you can tell the child, you can tell him over and over again, "No [son], this isn't your fault." But it doesn't matter, it doesn't matter. They think that I want to be here, that I want to be away. And that's not good for them. I don't want my kids upset at me because of this. And even if I do go home, even if I . . . even if you were God and you could snap your fingers right now and I could go home, my kids are still going to have these thoughts in the back of their head. You know, where was he? You know, to them I've been away a year. They don't know no better. Daddy's been away a long, long time. And it's going to be with them, it's going to stick with them. Why didn't daddy want to be here? You know. And now I'm stuck having to go home and sort all this out. It's pretty hard to explain to a three-year-old and a five-year-old what was going on. They don't want to hear it. So, you just do your best, you know.

In sum, the parents and mixed parents identified emotional and behavioral effects as being prevalent among their children. None of the fathers who resided with minor children prior to their incarceration reported positive effects resulting from their incarceration. Erosion of the father–child relationship concerned these fathers, and they were cognizant that their incarceration was a source of emotional strain for their children.

Interview data from the biological fathers reveal reports of a different nature. First, two of the fathers had no contact with their children prior to incarceration and no contact during their incarceration. Consequently, these respondents were not aware of any effects of their incarceration on their children.

Only two "biological" fathers reported that their incarceration had a negative impact on their relationship with their children because it served to further erode an already fragile relationship. Still, they were not able to identify the specific ways in which their incarceration affected their children's emotional state.

Two other biological fathers were not sure of the impact that their incarceration had on their children. These fathers were seeing their children infrequently (weekly or less) prior to their incarceration. Perhaps because of the infrequent contact, they were not certain of the impact, if any, of their incarceration on their children.

The remaining six biological fathers (50 percent) stated that their incarceration had a positive impact on their children. Three of these respondents reported that their incarceration had resulted in increased contact and communication with their children and in an opportunity for rebuilding their relationships. Three other biological fathers believed that their bad decisions and subsequent incarceration would serve as examples for their children and would prevent them from making the same mistakes.

In summary, the interview data suggest that the men who resided with their children prior to their incarceration were much more cognizant of and concerned about the impact of their incarceration on their children. Nearly 70 percent of the parents and mixed parents reported that their children had suffered emotionally because of their incarceration, and 50 percent reported changes in their children's behavior at home and/or at school.

Conversely, the respondents who resided apart from their children at arrest did not report negative emotional or behavioral problems among their children. Understandably, some of these respondents had no contact either prior to or during their incarceration, so it would be unlikely that their incarceration would influence their children. However, the respondents who did have contact with their children prior to incarceration were no more likely to report emotional or behavioral changes in their children. It seems plausible that these respondents chose to not see the negative impact of their incarceration on their children or to put a positive spin on the situation, such as the respondents who believed they could serve as a bad example. An alternative explanation is that these respondents are not attuned to their children and thus do not note their children's suffering.

Impact of Separation on Fathers

The next step in the analysis was to examine whether the stress of incarceration is different for fathers who resided with children prior to their arrest than for fathers who did not reside with children prior to arrest.

Data gathered from the questionnaire and interview indicate that parents and mixed parents spent more time interacting with their children and had stronger relationships with their children prior to incarceration than did the biological fathers. Because of this, it was anticipated that the parents and mixed parents would have higher levels of stress than the biological fathers because of the abrupt severance of the father–child relationship that occurs with incarceration.

For the statistical analysis, the parent and mixed parent categories were collapsed for the following reasons. First, the interview data revealed no significant differences between these two groups. Although the mixed group did not live with all of their minor children, they lived with some of their minor children prior to incarceration. The impact of the separation was no less traumatic for these fathers because they lived with only some of their children and not others. It made sense conceptually to combine these two categories. The Other category was dropped from the analysis because this group consisted of respondents who had either (1) all adult children ($n = 5$) or (2) children who were born during the respondent's jail sentence ($n = 4$). Thus, these individuals were not residing with any of their children prior to their incarceration for reasons outside of their control.

Regression analysis was completed using the emotion index and the parental status variables. As discussed earlier, the emotion index consists of four items that question how frequently respondents experience (1) anxiety, (2) depression, (3) loneliness, and (4) anger. Each item was measured using a 10-centimeter line response format. The regression analysis of the emotion index on the parental status was nonsignificant. It is the researcher's belief that because these four emotions are so different, the index should be "unbundled." Thus, each of the four negative affect items just listed was regressed on the parental status variable. The results for three of the regression analyses (anger, anxiety, and depression) were nonsignificant. The results of the regression analysis of loneliness on parental status are presented in Table 7.6.

According to Table 7.6, a statistically significant difference exists in the frequency of loneliness reported by the fathers. In this sample, the men who resided with some or all of their minor children prior to incarceration reported higher frequencies of loneliness than did men who resided apart from their children prior to incarceration.

The interview data of the respondents who resided with children prior to incarceration provide further evidence of the negative emotions experienced

TABLE 7.6 Regression of Loneliness on Parental Status

Variable	Unstandardized Regression Coefficient (b)	95% Confidence Interval		Beta
Parental status	−1.46	−2.69	−.250	−0.26

$R^2 = .0664$ $F = 5.77$ (significant at a .018 level)

by the jailed parents. This was an area in which the interviewer often had to prod the respondents because they seemed reluctant to report on their own feelings regarding separation from their children. The interviewer was interested in both (1) how the respondents felt about being separated from their children—their emotions and (2) how the respondents coped with being separated from their children—their actions.

The emotional reactions of these respondents varied. Three respondents reported feeling angry at themselves, or anger toward the criminal justice system. Three respondents reported that they "felt like crap" because of the anguish they have caused their children. Six respondents reported feeling "very hurt" or "torn apart" and powerless to change their situation. One respondent was unable to articulate his feelings regarding separation from his children.

The following respondent is a 24-year-old father who resided with his girlfriend, their three children, and her child from a previous relationship. He had previously described the jail experience as feeling like a "dream."

> IER: How have you dealt with being apart from your kids? I guess first let me ask, how does it make you feel?
>
> U28: Like crap. I think about them all day, every day. I try to go in my room and read my Bible or read a book to stop thinking about it. Or write them a letter. It doesn't help, though. It drives me crazy not to be with my kids. When they are waking up in the morning, usually I'm giving them breakfast and then I'm going to work. When I wake up here, I'm in that cell and it's wild, it's crazy.
>
> IER: Still feels like a dream.
>
> U28: Yeah. Definitely. Worse than a dream. It's like a nightmare. A bad, bad, bad, like a Freddie Krueger nightmare.

The coping strategies of these respondents ($n = 13$) can be broken down into three categories. The first strategy was "keeping busy." Six of the respondents spoke of reading, writing, identifying goals, participating in programs, and so on as a means to avoid focusing on being apart from their children. The second coping strategy identified by respondents was "turning to God." Four of the respondents reported that they had drawn strength from their religious beliefs to deal with the separation from their children. The third and final coping strategy for dealing with sepa- ration from children identified by respondents was "avoidance" or "acceptance." These respondents ($n = 3$) tried not think about being away from their children or to accept the situation because they could not change it.

This study did not examine the extent to which loneliness and the other emotions experienced by jailed fathers are related to problems within the jail. However, one of the respondents (R03) identified this link between separation from children and behavioral and emotional distur- bances in the jail. The respondent was talking about society having greater awareness and recognition of the difficulties faced by incarcerated moth- ers than it does of incarcerated fathers:

> People understand what it does to kids and mothers and stuff outside. Nobody understands what it does to [fathers] in here. Fathers ... it kills all of us. They don't see it from our perspective. They see it from the [perspective of the] ladies upstairs and how hard it is to be here, away from their kids. Fathers bringing their children over and they can't touch them and stuff. It hurts us just as much. It really does. I miss my kids a lot.
>
> Other people are going to read this somewhere, okay. [Maybe] they'll understand the impact this has. Maybe they'll be able to do something about it. It's only getting worse for [the administration] too. The more fights [the inmates] are having. The more people are trying to overdose in here. More people are trying to sneak stuff in. You know, they hate each other. They can't stand the staff. It's getting real bad. Imagine what's going to be like, you know, the closer it gets to the holidays, that's when it gets real bad for these guys. That's when a lot of the aggravation happens for them. This is a box this town put up just to put away people who were bad. They didn't care what happens to them.

It is evident that the jail experience had an effect on both the respon- dents and the children who temporarily lost a father to the criminal justice system. Not surprisingly, many respondents expressed the belief that the impact of their incarceration on their paternal role would remain after their release.

SUMMARY

The data from the current study indicate that the jail experience of fathers who resided with their children prior to incarceration is different from the experience of fathers who did not reside with their children prior to their incarceration.

The fathers who resided apart from their children prior to incarceration were less likely to maintain contact with their children while jailed but were generally satisfied with the visits when they occurred. They were less likely to report that their incarceration had negatively affected their children's emotional or financial well-being. Remarkably, one-half of the interviewees who resided apart from their children believed that their incarceration had a positive impact on their children.

In contrast, the fathers who resided with their children prior to their incarceration experienced anguish as a result of their separation from their children. These fathers either refused to permit their children to visit at the jail and/or had negative experiences when their children did visit. This group of fathers was also more likely to report that their children were worse off emotionally and financially as a result of their incarceration. The lack of contact with their children resulted in greater frequencies of loneliness for the men who previously resided with their children. These parents expressed concern of the lasting effects of their incarceration on their relationships with their children. The "pains of imprisonment" (Sykes, 1958) promise to reach beyond the walls for these fathers as they attempt to reestablish relationships with their children.

POLICY AND PROGRAMMATIC IMPLICATIONS

The present study is an exploratory and descriptive effort aimed at increasing the understanding of an extremely understudied population—jailed fathers. It is beyond the scope of this project to make broad and sweeping generalizations, but the findings make it is possible to delineate two major multifaceted policy considerations aimed at these forgotten parents. The first relates to the identification and description of jailed fathers. The second relates to maintenance of family bonds between jailed fathers and their children.

Identification and Description of Inmate Fathers

When an individual is convicted of a crime, punishment is a frequent consequence. Punishing the convicted individual, however, is a legal fiction because it is obvious that the convicted individual's loved ones are punished as well. It is certainly not debatable that our correctional policies generally overlook this reality. This observation is supported by the simple fact that there are no national statistics on the number of children affected by parental incarceration, especially with regard to incarcerated fathers. This lack of data is significant for it reflects our myopic view of male inmates, whereby we strip them of all family roles. It is much easier to incarcerate a criminal who is not viewed as a son, brother, husband, and, perhaps most specifically, father. This also reflects our arrogance and ignorance in believing that incarcerated fathers lack the capacity to be good fathers. This results in a shortsighted approach that negates our (purported) efforts to curb the cycle of crime and incarceration. Thus, it is imperative that we (1) recognize the parental status of incarcerated fathers and (2) systematically gather information on the number of men who are fathers and the number of minor children they have.

The current study presents an image of inmates that is in stark contrast to the stereotype that has become a part of our social perceptions. As would any cross-section from our society, the respondents in the current study encompassed a broad continuum of paternal behavior. The study sample included both "deadbeat" dads, who had difficulty remembering the ages of their children, and involved and loving fathers, who were the primary caregivers prior to their incarceration. Most of the prior studies have failed to recognize these differences, lumping all male respondents into one of two categories: father (has children), or not a father (has no children). This study clearly identified the differences between the fathers who were attuned to their children and those who were not; the differences were significant.

It is clear that the needs and concerns of parents differ from those of biological fathers. Hence, it is necessary to delineate the level of involvement that existed between father and child prior to incarceration. It is this author's contention that if resources do not permit large-scale programming, the men who were involved in the lives of children prior to incarceration should receive special consideration as participants.

Maintenance of Family Bonds

The respondents in the current study complained that the costs associated with telephone communication were prohibitive to maintaining contact. In addition, the unpleasant atmosphere that exists for both family members (Sturges, 1999) and for inmates during face-to-face visits made this form of family contact unappealing for many of the jailed fathers in the current study. Being forced to view loved ones through a piece of glass was more than most attuned fathers could bear. Consequently, communication and interactions between father and child are severely restricted during incarceration. Creasie Hairston (1998: 624) argues, however, that the rules pertaining to contact between inmate and family "frequently bear little relevance to correctional goals and are insensitive to the family structures and needs." The lack of, or absence of, contact during incarceration makes reunification more difficult. A separation of six months can seem an eternity to young children. The interview respondents in the current study articulated their concerns that their children would have forgotten them or would be resistant to interacting with them upon release.

The administrators of correctional facilities must accommodate many competing goals. Obviously, facility security, staff and inmate safety, and punishment are central priorities (Cripe, 1997). At first glance, these goals appear to be in direct opposition with assisting inmates to maintain contact and interaction with their children. Thus, to achieve the first set of goals, contact between inmates and their family members is highly regulated (Hairston, 1998). However, most fail to realize that programs designed to assist inmates in maintaining family relationships while incarcerated can aid administrators and staff members in achieving their primary goals of safety and security. Research has demonstrated that family maintenance programs can result in a decrease in discipline problems within the institution (Bayse, Algid, and Van Wyk, 1991), and they can improve an individual's successful release from incarceration and reintegration into his community and family (Carlson and Cervera, 1992).

Hence, a second policy implication relates to the critical need for father–child interaction during incarceration. It is imperative that jailed fathers be permitted to interact with their children in a more natural manner and that jail administrators view this as a priority. There are ways to accommodate both safety and security issues (facility, staff, and inmate) and family maintenance issues. The first step is to recognize that the father–child interaction is as critical to the effective operation of jails as these other organizational goals. This recognition would allow for the development of family-oriented policies and directives and would encourage the exploration of existing programs that permit the simultaneous accomplishment of both safety and security and family maintenance.

The following specific program recommendations are related to the policy implications just outlined. They were generated from (1) the current study and (2) a survey conducted by the Family and Corrections Network (FCN). The FCN surveyed 30 agencies that provide parenting programs in correctional facilities to identify key components of such programs (Family and Corrections Network, 1995: 6).

Evaluation and Needs Assessment of Jailed Fathers

The current study clearly identified that jailed fathers have various needs pertaining to their families. For example, many fathers desired to maintain contact with their children, but they did not want them to be exposed to the jail environment. Many fathers complained about the costs associated with telephone contact. The point that must be reemphasized is that jailed fathers, as a group, have needs that differ from other male inmates. Furthermore, fathers who lived with their children prior to incarceration have different needs than the fathers who lived apart from their children. Hence, the necessary first step of any successful family maintenance program is the assessment of needs of jailed fathers.

Programs to Meet the Needs of Jailed Fathers

The jailed fathers in the current study expressed concern about subjecting their children to the jail environment. Specifically, the environmental conditions that were most problematic were that (1) noncontact visits occurred through a piece of glass and (2) the visiting areas were either cramped or afforded no privacy. Thus, jails should provide a child-centered visiting area. This could be a relatively small space that is decorated appropriately for children and contains materials conducive to positive interactions between fathers and their children (e.g., books, board games, art supplies).

Permitting fathers contact visits is imperative. However, contact visits could be a privilege, not a right, that the jailed fathers earn by participating in parenting classes and avoiding disciplinary problems. Model programs, many of them in female correctional facilities, could be replicated in male facilities. One such program is Project IMPACT at SCI-Muncy, one of Pennsylvania's two prisons for women. This program utilizes a child-centered visiting room that resembles a day care room for visits between mothers and their children. The benefits of these types of programs affect not only jailed fathers and their children but also the correctional facilities.

Other Family Maintenance Programs

Not every incarcerated father will be able to engage in contact visits with his child(ren) while he is incarcerated. Therefore, it is critical that opportunities are afforded incarcerated fathers for maintaining contact with their loved ones in other ways. Programs are currently in place in some correctional facilities to encourage long-distance relationships. One approach permits incarcerated fathers to make either an audiotape or videotape while reading a children's book. These tapes are then sent home to their children. It seems reasonable that the reverse could happen, and children could make tapes for their fathers. Although these interactions may not be as satisfying as contact visits, they do permit communication between father and child.

Parent Education

Parenting classes can provide information to assist jailed fathers in becoming more competent parents. Numerous programs are in place in correctional facilities across the country; it is beyond the scope of this discussion to detail them. However, many of the programs contain information on child development, communication, stress management, and discipline.

A recent study (Harrison, 1997) concluded that participation of incarcerated fathers in parental training led to improved attitudes regarding child rearing. Parent education can be a way to effect positive change between parent and child both during and after incarceration. Furthermore, as we continue to expand our criminal justice policies, it seems critical that parent education programs target not only jailed fathers but also other populations (e.g., youthful offenders and probation populations).

Community-Based Support Services

Any effort to improve inmate–family relationships must recognize the critical period of reunification after release. However, most (if not all) correctional programs end when an inmate walks out the door of the jail. It seems critical that there be follow-up on parenting concerns and/or successes. It seems likely that the newly released father, in addition to readjusting to his freedom, will have to readjust to his children. Even the best-intentioned (and competent) parents can wilt when children are demanding and disruptive.

The jailed fathers in the current study expressed concern and anxiety regarding their postincarceration relationships with their children. Without a support system in place, their fears may come to fruition. Nearly 25 years ago, Jim Munro (1976) argued for an open systems view of criminal justice. This view recognizes the overlap between criminal justice and social services and acknowledges that distinct agencies (e.g., jails and social services) share common clients. Adoption of this perspective would require that jail administrators identify appropriate parenting services that exist in the community and encourage jailed fathers to hook into these community-based support services prior to their release.

CONCLUSIONS

Data from this exploratory study present an image of jailed fathers that simultaneously supports and refutes the stereotypical image of the incarcerated father. In many regards, the jail is just a microcosm of our society, with both "good" and "bad" fathers represented. The bad fathers typically resided apart from the children prior to their incarceration and interacted with them rarely. Their proclamations that fathers were important people were not matched by their behaviors in fulfilling this role. Conversely, the good fathers were involved and loving parents who spent time with their children and ached as a result of their separation.

Many of the interview respondents were reared in chaotic family situations where father absence, incarceration, and abuse were commonplace. The negative impacts of these experiences were visible in the accounts given. The children of these respondents are now experiencing similar situations, leading to a continuation of an unfortunate cycle and placing them at risk for similar outcomes. Our jail and prison populations in the year 2010 will include children who were 10-year-olds in the first year of the new millennium.

This project represents the first study known to examine jailed fathers. The findings from this exploratory study cannot be generalized to other populations, but the data suggest significant areas for additional inquiry. The data also suggest that the implementation of family maintenance programs is critical. Failure to do so will seal the fate of tomorrow's jail population, as eloquently expressed by a respondent:

> R05:   As far as I'm concerned, it's a matter of common sense. It's strictly common sense. I'm here for one reason. I'm here to be punished. My kids aren't to be punished. I'm here to be punished. So why do my children need to suffer? Is it the legal system trying to get me locked up, punish me on the left hand? On the right hand my kids are being punished. The legal system knows my kids are being punished but, hey, that's job security for them 20 years down the road. They're going to psychologically harm my children 20 years down the road and my kid's going to commit a violent act. Now they can put him in jail. Job security. Is that what it is? Or do they, is it just that they've overlooked everything? They're so ignorant to it that it doesn't matter. It's common sense. It's a matter of common sense.

REFERENCES

Bakker, L., Morris, B., and Janus, L. (1978). "Hidden Victims of Crime." *Social Work,* 23: 143–148.

Bayse, D.J., Algid, S.A., and Van Wyk, P.H. (1991, July). "Family Life Education: An Effective Tool for Prisoner Rehabilitation." *Family Relations,* 40: 254–257.

Beck, A., Gilliard, D., Greenfeld, L., Harlow, C., Hester, T., Jankowski, L., Snell, T., and Stephan, J. (1993). *Survey of State Prison Inmates, 1991* (NCJ-136949). Washington, DC: Bureau of Justice Statistics.

Bloom, B. and Stinehart, D. (1993). *Why Punish the Children: A Reappraisal of the Children of Incarcerated Mothers in America.* San Francisco, CA: National Council on Crime and Delinquency.

Bronstein, P. and Cowan, C. (eds.) (1988). *Fatherhood Today: Men's Changing Role in the Family.* New York: John Wiley.

Carlson, B. and Cervera, N. (1992). *Inmates and Their Wives: Incarceration and Family Life.* Westport, CT: Greenwood Press.

Cohen, S., Kesslar, R., and Gordon, L. (eds.) (1995). *Measuring Stress: A Guide for Health and Social Scientist.* New York: Oxford University Press.

Cripe, C. (1997). *Legal Aspects of Corrections Management.* Gaithersburg, MD: Aspen.

Dalley, L. (1997). *Montana's imprisoned mothers and their children: A case study on separation, reunification, and legal issues.* Unpublished doctoral dissertation, Indiana University of Pennsylvania.

Donzinger, S. (ed.) (1996). *The Real War on Crime: The Report of the National Criminal Justice Commission.* New York: Harper Collins.

Family and Corrections Network. (1995, June). *Parenting Programs for Prisoners.* Palmyra, VA: Author.

Fishman, L. (1990). *Women at the Wall: A Study of Prisoners' Wives Doing Time on the Outside.* Albany: State University of New York Press.

Fritsch, T. and Burkhead, J. (1981). "Behavioral Reactions of Children to Parental Absences Due to Imprisonment." *Family Relations,* 30: 83–88.

Gabel, K. and Johnston, D. (1995). "Incarcerated Parents." In K. Gabel and D. Johnston, M.D. (eds.), *Children of Incarcerated Parents.* New York: Lexington Books: 3–20.

Gibbs, J.J. (1987). "Symptoms of Psychopathology Among Jail Prisoners: The Effects of Exposure to the Jail Environment." *Criminal Justice and Behavior,* 14: 288–310.

Gibbs, J.J. (1991). Environmental Congruence and Symptoms of Psychopathology: A Further Exploration of the Effects of Exposure to the Jail Environment. *Criminal Justice and Behavior,* 18:(3) 351–374.

Gibbs, J.J. (1992). *Jailing and Stress.* In *Mosaic of Despair: Human Breakdowns in Prison,* Rev.Ed. Washington, DC: American Psychological Association.

Gibbs, J.J., and Hanrahan, K. (1993). "Safety Demand and Supply: An Alternative to Fear of Crime." *Justice Quarterly,* 10: 369–394.

Gilliard, D. (1999). *Prison and Jail Inmates at Midyear 1998* (NCJ-173414). Washington, DC: Bureau of Justice Statistics.

Hairston, C.F. (1989). "Men in Prison: Family Characteristics and Parenting Views." *Journal of Offender Counseling, Services and Rehabilitation,* 14: 23–30.

Hairston, C.F. (1995). "Fathers in Prison." In K. Gabel and D. Johnston, M.D. (eds.), *Children of Incarcerated Parents.* New York: Lexington Books: 31–40.

Hairston, C.F. (1998). "The Forgotten Parent: Understanding the Forces that Influence Incarcerated Fathers' Relationships with Their Children." *Child Welfare,* 77 (5): 617–638.

Hanrahan, K., Martin, J., Springer, G., Cox, S., and Gido, R. (1996, March). "Prisoners and Separation from Family." Paper presented at the Academy of Criminal Justice Sciences, Las Vegas.

Harrison, K. (1997). "Parental Training for Incarcerated Fathers: Effects on Attitudes, Self-Esteem, and Children's Perceptions." *The Journal of Social Psychology,* 137: 588–593.

Johnson, R. and Toch, H. (eds.) (1982). *The Pains of Imprisonment.* Prospect Heights, IL:Waveland.

Johnston, D. (1995). "Effects of Parental Incarceration." In K. Gabel and D. Johnston, M.D. (eds.), *Children of Incarcerated Parents.* New York: Lexington Books: 59–88.

Lamb, M. (ed.) (1981). *The Role of the Father in Child Development* (2d ed.). New York: John Wiley.

Lanier, C. (1991). "Dimensions of Father–Child Interaction in a New York State Prison Population." *Journal of Offender Rehabilitation,* 16: 27–42.

Lanier, C. (1993). "Affective States of Fathers in Prison." *Justice Quarterly,* 10: 49–65.

Marsiglio, W. (ed.) (1995). *Fatherhood: Contemporary Theory, Research, and Social Policy.* Thousand Oaks, CA: Sage.

Morris, P. (1965). *Prisoners and Their Families.* New York: Hart.

Munro, J. (1976). "Towards A Theory of Criminal Justice Administration: A General Systems Perspective." In J. Munro (ed.), *Classes, Conflict, and Control: Studies in Criminal Justice Management.* Cincinnati, OH: Anderson.

Rokach, A. and Cripps, J. (1999). "Incarcerated Men and the Perceived Sources of Their Loneliness." *International Journal of Offender Therapy and Comparative Criminology,* 43: 78–89.

Sturges, J. (1999). "Social Interactions Between Visitors and Correctional Officers at Two County Jails." Unpublished manuscript, Indiana University of Pennsylvania.

Sykes, G. (1958). *The Society of Captives: A Study of a Maximum Security Prison.* Princeton, NJ: Princeton University Press.

chapter 8

The Development and Diversity of Correctional Boot Camps

GAYLENE STYVE ARMSTRONG
Arizona State University West

ANGELA R. GOVER
University of South Carolina

DORIS LAYTON MACKENZIE
University of Maryland

INTRODUCTION

Correctional boot camps, also called *shock incarceration, intensive incarceration,* or *regimented discipline programs,* were first implemented as an intermediate sanction in 1983. Since then, the political appeal of boot camp programs has led to their rapid proliferation across the United States for both adult and juvenile populations. Boot camps are often perceived as an alternative sanction with "teeth," an imperative in the current political climate (MacKenzie and Parent, 1992). Currently, there are boot camp programs in state and federal prisons, local jails, and juvenile detention centers.

Boot camp programs can be difficult to identify due to vast disagreement on the definition of *boot camp*. Typically, boot camps incorporate similar basic characteristics. Boot camp prison sentences often replace an offender's traditional prison sentence. On average, offenders spend 120 days in boot camp rather than their full sentence in a traditional prison. The most distinguishing characteristic of a boot camp is the quasi-military atmosphere that resembles military basic training. This atmosphere may include military dress and titles, drill and ceremony, as well as the general organizational structure. Boot camp inmates are usually separated from the general prison population. Their entry into the boot camp program usually occurs in small groups, platoons, or squads of inmates. Boot camp inmates remain with their entry group from intake to graduation, work together as a unit, and depend heavily on their fellow "cadets" throughout their stay in the program.

This chapter begins by exploring a typical day in a boot camp. Following this background information is a section on the different perspectives and opinions about the utility and feasibility of boot camps. We then explore the diversity of boot camps. Finally, we discuss some of the varying goals of boot camps and the research examining whether the programs achieve these goals.

THE BOOT CAMP EXPERIENCE

Upon arriving at the boot camp, males are required to have their heads shaved (females may be permitted short haircuts). Inmates are informed of the strict program rules. At all times, they are required to address staff as "Sir" or "Ma'am," request permission to speak, and refer to themselves in the third person as "this inmate" or "this cadet." Punishments for minor rule violations are summary and certain, frequently involving physical exercise such as push-ups or running. Major rule violations may result in dismissal from the program.

In a typical boot camp, the 10- to 16-hour day begins with predawn reveille. Inmates dress quickly and march to an exercise area where they participate in one or two hours of physical training followed by drill and ceremony. They then march to breakfast where they are ordered to stand at parade rest while waiting in line and to exercise military movements when the line moves. Inmates are required to stand in front of the table until commanded to sit and are not permitted to converse during the 10-minute eating period. After breakfast, they march to work sites where they participate in hard physical labor that frequently involves community service, such as cleaning state parks or highways. Juveniles usually spend the first few hours after breakfast in school classrooms followed by physical labor in the afternoon. When the six- to eight-hour working day is over, inmates return to the compound where they participate in additional exercise and drill. A quick dinner is followed by evening programs that may consist of counseling, life skills training, or drug education and treatment. These rehabilitation services vary among facilities.

Boot camp inmates gradually earn more privileges and responsibilities as their performance and time in the program warrants. In some programs, a different color hat or uniform may outwardly display their new prestige. Depending upon the facility, somewhere between 8 and 50 percent of the entrants fail to complete the program. For those who successfully complete it, an elaborate graduation ceremony occurs with visitors and family invited to attend. Awards frequently are given for achievements made during the program. In addition, the inmates perform the drill and ceremony they have practiced throughout their time in the boot camp.

DEVELOPMENT OF BOOT CAMPS

Boot camps are a relatively new correctional option. The first boot camp programs were developed in Oklahoma and Georgia in 1983 (MacKenzie, 1993). These early boot camp programs emphasized the military atmosphere with drill and ceremony, physical training, and hard labor. While these components remain central to boot camps today, rehabilitative, educational, and drug treatment services now take an increasingly large share of the participants' time in the program.

Since their beginning, boot camp programs have continued to increase in size and number. By 1994, 30 states, 10 local jurisdictions, and the Federal Bureau of Prisons had boot camp programs serving adult populations (U.S. General Accounting Office, 1993). At that time, more than 8000 beds were dedicated to adult offenders. With the average offender spending 107 days in boot camp prisons, more than 27,000 offenders could complete the program in a one-year time period.

PERSPECTIVES ON BOOT CAMPS

While correctional innovations rarely attract more than minimal media attention, boot camps have received a great deal of coverage by both the local and national media. Why are boot camp programs attracting so much attention? In part, they are popular with the media because they have such a strong visual impact. Video footage and photographs of a drill sergeant yelling in the faces of boot camp participants present an evocative image for television viewers.

Another reason that boot camps have received so much attention stems from the boot camp model itself, which is in part punitive and in part rehabilitative. As such, it has wide appeal to a diverse audience. For those who are concerned that punishments should be appropriately punitive, boot camps are seen as a "get-tough" approach to crime and delinquency. For these advocates, individuals sentenced to boot camps receive their just deserts. Boots camps are among the few intermediate sanctions that are accepted as being tough on crime.

The "tough" aspects of the programs can be thought of as achieving a sentencing goal of punishment or retribution. This makes the boot camp program acceptable in lieu of a longer sentence in a traditional facility. Thus, the short, intense program is a mechanism for offenders to earn their way back to society earlier than they would have if they had been sentenced to a traditional prison. In a sense, they have paid their debt to society by being punished in a short-term but strict boot camp.

Empirical evidence supports this perception of the boot camp's punitive nature. Wood and Grasmick (1999) surveyed male and female inmates serving time for nonviolent offenses and found that they viewed boot camps as significantly more punitive than traditional imprisonment and various forms of other alternative sanctions. Thus, participants and potential participants reaffirm the belief held by the public and correctional officials that boot camps are tough and punitive.

At the other end of the punishment continuum are people who support boot camps because they believe that the educational, drug treatment, and counseling services that are part of many boot camp programs will rehabilitate offenders. By addressing the "root" causes of criminal behavior and delinquency, these therapeutic programs and services may effect positive changes in offenders. Furthermore, the potential cost savings from a reduction of time served adds to the appeal of the boot camp model for all supporters.

Support for boot camps is not universal. Their critics suggest that the confrontational nature of the program is antithetical to treatment. In fact, they argue that some aspects of the boot camps are diametrically opposed to the constructive, interpersonally supportive treatment environment necessary for positive change to occur (Andrews et al., 1990; Lipsey, 1992). Some argue that boot camps hold inconsistent philosophies and procedures (Marlowee, Marin, Schneider, Vaitkus, and Bartone, 1988), set the stage for abusive punishments (Morash and Rucker, 1990), and perpetuate a "we-versus-they" attitude, suggesting that newer inmates deserve degrading treatment (Raupp, 1978). Critics anticipate that inmates may fear staff and that the boot camps will have less individualized programming than traditional facilities. As a result, offenders will be less prepared for their return to the community.

PRISON-BASED BOOT CAMPS

The majority of prison-based boot camp programs are designed for young, male, nonviolent, first-time felony offenders who are under the jurisdiction of state departments of corrections. MacKenzie and Souryal (1994) found that, on the average, participants were 20 years old; had 11 years of education; were incarcerated for drug, burglary, or theft convictions; and were nonwhite (49 percent). However, some programs are designed specifically for drug offenders, females, or juveniles. All of these programs are generally linked to community supervision for the offenders once they are released from the boot camp program. The majority of research on boot camps is based on prison boot camp programs and will be discussed at the end of the chapter.

JAIL-BASED BOOT CAMPS

Although most of the attention has been focused on boot camps operated by state prison systems, interest in the development of boot camps for jail populations has also been growing. Jails increasingly house inmates who spend many months in confinement. Some of these offenders are state sentenced but because of the overcrowding in state prisons, they spend long periods of time in jails. In addition, significant numbers of adults violate probation or parole and must remain in jail waiting for the court's decision to revoke parole or release them. Thus, a boot camp could be used to reduce the length of stay of some of these offenders.

Austin, Jones, and Bolyard (1993) surveyed sheriffs, jail administrators, and state probation departments to add to our understanding of boot camps operated within jails. They identified 10 jurisdictions that operated boot camp prisons and 13 jurisdictions that reported that they were planning to open boot camps in the upcoming year. Of these, the earliest jail programs began in New Orleans in 1986 and in Travis County, Texas, in 1988. At the time of the survey, there were four jail boot camps in New York, four in Texas, and two in California. The size of the programs varied greatly from a low of 12 and 14 beds in Brazos County, Texas, and Nassau County, New York, respectively, to highs of 210 beds for males in New York City (with an additional 84 beds for women) and 348 beds in Harris County, Texas. However, most programs reported that they failed to operate at their designed capacity. The authors attributed this to the facts that jail inmates spend only a short term in jail, coordination among criminal justice agencies is lacking, and rigid selection procedures limited the number of eligible inmates.

Similar to prison boot camps, the daily schedule for inmates in jail boot camps involves military drill, physical training, work, and therapeutic programs such as education, vocational education, drug education, counseling, and life skills programs. After the in-jail phase of the boot camp, most programs also require participants to be supervised in the community for some period of time.

Los Angeles County's RID Program

One example of a jail-based program is the Regimented Inmate Discipline (RID) program, a unique jail-based boot camp developed by the Los Angeles County Sheriff's Department. The program was designed for defendants who were likely to receive lengthy jail sentences. RID was funded primarily by money seized from drug dealers and by the money gained from the sale of assets also seized from drug dealers. It consisted of a 90-day stay in a military-style boot camp program followed by intensive aftercare supervision in the community. RID also had a strong emphasis on programming. Inmates were required to participate in formal education, drug treatment, and counseling.

The program began in 1990 and lasted for only two years before its funding was withdrawn. With funding from the National Institute of Justice, U.S. Department of Justice, Austin, Jones, and Bolyard (1993) completed a study of the program while it was in operation. The study examined the impact of the program on recidivism rates, jail management, crowding, and cost.

Austin and colleagues found no evidence that the RID program reduced the recidivism rates of inmates who completed the program as compared to a control group. Forty-seven percent were rearrested within 12 months of release from the boot camp. There were also no differences in recidivism between those who successfully completed RID and those who were terminated prior to completing the program.

The investigators did conclude that RID improved inmate control. The participants in RID behaved very differently from the other jail inmates. RID inmates had fewer misconduct incidents, and no serious acts of violence or weapons or drug use were reported during the term of the study. However, evidence from the study suggested that the program neither reduced jail crowding nor saved money. When compared to the control group, the RID inmates spent significantly more time in jail, and the intensive programming in RID was costly. Thus, high costs combined with the program's lack of impact on recidivism led to its closing.

In conclusion, Austin, Jones, and Bolyard (1993) cautioned jurisdictions that were considering opening jail boot camps to carefully examine the goals of the program. Many jails could have problems similar to those faced by the RID program. The short length of stay and relatively rapid turnover of inmates may mean that the boot camps will increase the term of incarceration for many offenders. Prior to initiating a boot camp, jail administrators should perform a feasibility analysis to determine whether the identified goals could be achieved. This analysis should at least ensure a sufficient number of eligible offenders to approach the capacity of the planned program.

DIFFERENT MODELS

Despite shared basic characteristics across boot camps, individual facilities have unique, distinguishing features that vary (MacKenzie and Parent, 1992; MacKenzie and Piquero, 1994). Programmatic differences in boot camp programs, such as the treatment focus, selection process, and eligibility requirements, may stem from the distinct correctional goals that each program strives to achieve. These differences are not insignificant because programmatic features of a boot camp may have consequences for its ability to successfully achieve its objectives.

Drug and Alcohol Treatment

Many offenders sentenced to boot camps have drug and alcohol problems. Correctional officials and legislators are not ignorant of this fact and have included programmatic provisions in boot camp legislation that recognizes this problem. In a 1992 survey of boot camps, MacKenzie (1994) found that all camps incorporated some type of drug treatment or education into their program schedule. In addition, four states reported that their programs are specifically designed for nonviolent and drug-involved offenders. Nine states require by law that drug treatment and education be included in their boot camp's program design.

According to MacKenzie (1994), the implementation of drug and alcohol treatment and educational services in boot camps varies by program. MacKenzie found that Florida participants were required to spend 15 days in drug treatment; in comparison, New York required all boot camp participants to take part in drug treatment every day for the duration of their 180-day sentence.

Drug treatment and education also vary in the way each component is integrated into the schedule of activities of boot camp programs. For instance, New York uses a therapeutic community approach to drug treatment and education. In Illinois, counselors evaluate individual inmates' needs. Then the levels and duration of the required drug education and treatment are matched to the identified needs of each inmate. In contrast, Texas boot camp inmates receive five weeks of drug education. Additional treatment and individual counseling are provided only to offenders who volunteer.

Selection Process

One of the most important differences among boot camp programs is the selection of inmates. Generally, there are two major differences in the selection procedures. Using the first selection method, sentencing judges place offenders in the boot camp program and retain their decision-making authority over them until they exit the program. Failure to complete the program would result in resentencing of the offenders and a possible sentence of prison time.

In the second type of decision-making model, officials in the Department of Corrections decide who will enter the boot camp. Offenders are sentenced to a term in prison by the judge. The department evaluates them for eligibility and suitability. The offenders who are admitted can reduce their term in prison by successfully completing the boot camp. If they are dismissed from the boot camp, they are automatically sent to prison to complete their sentence.

Eligibility Requirements

Most boot camp programs for adult offenders restrict participation to offenders between the ages of 17 and 30 (MacKenzie and Souryal, 1994). Some programs (e.g., Louisiana) permit offenders up to the age of 40, while several other programs (e.g., Oklahoma) have no upper age limit. Participation is also frequently restricted to nonviolent, first-time felony offenders. While 10 states report that violent and nonviolent offenders are eligible for their programs, most of their participants are in fact nonviolent offenders (U.S. General Accounting Office, 1993).

Eligibility requirements can undermine the success of a boot camp program. Restrictive eligibility requirements may mean that many of the boot camp beds are unoccupied, a serious problem in this era of prison crowding. Louisiana experienced this problem when it opened its first boot camp program. Officials were forced to reduce their original strict eligibility criteria in order to identify a sufficient number of offenders to fill the available beds (MacKenzie and Souryal, 1994).

SPECIAL POPULATIONS OF OFFENDERS

The diversity of boot camps exists not only within the operation of the boot camps but also in the populations that they serve. Although initially designed for the adult male offenders, boot camps have more recently included programs for female offenders and the juvenile population.

Female Offenders

Thirteen states and the Federal Bureau of Prisons have developed boot camp programs for adult female offenders. These programs represent only 6.1 percent of the total number of incarcerated boot camp offenders. In 10 state camps, males and females are combined in one program; they live in separate quarters but are brought together for other boot camp activities. Other jurisdictions have completely separate male and female programs (MacKenzie, 1993).

In 1992, a focus group meeting composed of correctional experts, feminist scholars, and criminologists was held at the University of Maryland to discuss the special concerns regarding females in boot camps. The issues identified included equity, differential needs, detrimental influences, potential advantages for women, and alternative correctional programs.

Members of the focus group expressed concern about the impact of male correctional officers yelling at female offenders who may have been in abusive relationships prior to entering the boot camp. A confrontational environment may have a negative psychological impact on these female participants. Furthermore, questions were raised about how the programs address female-specific needs such as parenting classes and vocational training.

In response to these concerns, MacKenzie and Donaldson (1996) studied six boot camps that housed female participants. Through interviews, the researchers ascertained that women in boot camps experienced difficulties keeping up with the physical demands of the program. Furthermore, female participants reported extensive emotional stress because the majority of the boot camp staff and inmates were male. For this reason, some researchers and practitioners have argued that it is not appropriate to integrate female boot camp inmates with male inmates. MacKenzie and Donaldson concluded their study by suggesting that the boot camps they studied were designed specifically with the male offender in mind and female offenders were placed in them as an afterthought. They suggested that programs be designed for the female offender and include programming oriented toward parenting skills and responsibilities as well as education about domestic violence.

Although numerous detriments to housing female offenders in boot camps appear to exist, this option must be available. Since many of the boot camps are mechanisms for early release, women would be at a disadvantage if they did not have them as a correctional option to obtain early release. Without such an option, women would be required to spend more time away from their children. Additionally, the nontraditional demands of the program may be another advantage for women. As a result of participating in the program, women may be willing to take advantage of new opportunities such as nontraditional employment or educational programs. Certainly, more research is needed to determine the immediate and long-term impacts of the boot camp environment on female offenders' experiences.

Juveniles Offenders

The growth of boot camps for juvenile offenders was rampant during the last decade. Only one boot camp program was operating prior to 1990. By 1993, there were 19 juvenile boot camps: 6 in Florida, 4 in Texas, 2 in California, and 1 each in Alabama, Colorado, Maryland, Mississippi, Ohio, Pennsylvania, and Tennessee. Most of these programs were relatively small (30 to 175 participants) and had eligibility criteria limiting participation. In all, fewer than 300 juveniles were in the boot camps.

Since then, MacKenzie and Rosay (1996) surveyed state and local juvenile correctional administrators and found a total of 37 programs in operation as of June 1995. This rapid growth may be attributed in part to the passage of the 1994 Crime Act that permitted the Department of Justice to allocate a substantial amount of funding to juvenile boot camps. Twelve jurisdictions were awarded grants to develop new juvenile boot camp programs, and another 12 jurisdictions received funds to renovate existing correctional facilities or construct new ones. This interest in the construction and development of boot camps for juveniles has continued into the new millennium.

The typical juvenile boot camp inmate in the MacKenzie and Rosay (1996) survey was a male between the ages of 14 and 18 convicted of a non-violent offense. They found that about half of the boot camps were limited to nonviolent offenders while the other half accepted offenders convicted of violent crimes. Unlike adult boot camps, juvenile programs were not found to be limited to offenders convicted of their first serious offense and those who volunteered to participate in the program. The decision to place juveniles in boot camps varied by jurisdiction but was most frequently made by a juvenile court judge.

ISSUES IN JUVENILE BOOT CAMPS

Some additional issues in developing boot camps for juveniles are very unique to its population. Contrary to the punitive aspects of the boot camps that are often publicized by the media, the primary mission of our juvenile justice system has been treatment and rehabilitation, not retribution and punishment. To more adequately align themselves with the mission of the juvenile justice system, juvenile boot camps must be designed to address the needs of their inmates through increased treatment and programming. More recently developed models of juvenile boot camps strive to achieve this congruency. They devote a significant amount of time to academic education, rehabilitative counseling, and physical training and drill. In contrast to the amount of time adult boot camp inmates spend during the day in work activities, juvenile boot camp participants spend the majority of their day in academic classes.

Another issue that has arisen in regard to juveniles in boot camps is the definition of the type of juvenile who should be placed in the programs. The target groups for juvenile boot camps are most often nonviolent offenders with a limited criminal history. In the last 15 years, there has been a concerted effort to use incarceration less frequently for juveniles who are not a danger to themselves or others. The dilemma for the boot camps is whether to admit juveniles convicted of more serious crimes or to potentially widen the net of control to include juveniles convicted of nonviolent crimes.

GOALS OF PROGRAMS

The heterogeneity among boot camps makes broad conclusions problematic. Often program effectiveness must be examined at the state level or on a facility-by-facility basis. The determination of the "success" of a program also greatly depends on the definition of success. Toby and Pearson (1992) surveyed juvenile boot camps and found that the goals rated most important by the staff were providing safe custody for the youth in their charge, providing academic education, attempting to rehabilitate, and lowering recidivism. Punishment was relatively deemphasized—and only two states rated it as "somewhat important," while the rest did not believe that it was an important goal at all. More traditionally, program officials at boot camps have considered rehabilitation and reducing offender rates of recidivism as their top priorities of success (MacKenzie and Souryal, 1991). According to a survey of 26 boot camp programs, MacKenzie and Souryal found that the priorities next in importance were reducing prison overcrowding and providing a safe environment. This section considers the impact of boot camps on inmate attitudes, recidivism, community adjustment, prison crowding, and the prison environment.

Impact on Inmate Attitudes

Critics of the boot camp model have theorized that because of the military atmosphere, drill, and hard physical labor components of boot camp programs (i.e., the stress-producing aspects of the model), offenders would leave these programs more hostile, aggressive, and antisocial than when they entered (Morash and Rucker, 1990). In response, through a multisite study of adult boot camps, researchers examined the impact of the programs on inmate attitudes. When researchers examined the attitudes of adult offenders in eight different boot camps, they found that despite the differences between programs, boot camp participants were more positive about their experience in the program than were control groups of offenders in traditional prisons (MacKenzie and Souryal, 1994). Boot camp participants generally agreed that their experience in the program had taught them to be more self-disciplined and mature. These results were true of boot camp programs that emphasized treatment as well as those in which the military components of the boot camp model dominated. Thus, contrary to the assertions made by boot camp critics, even in boot camp programs that emphasized strict discipline, drill, and hard physical labor, participants experienced positive attitudinal change. Furthermore, when boot camp participants and the conventional prisoner groups were compared on antisocial attitudes, both groups became less antisocial while incarcerated. Researchers concluded from these findings that there was no evidence that boot camps had a negative effect on the attitudes of participating inmates.

In a national evaluation, MacKenzie, Gover, Styve and Mitchell (2000) found similar results in juvenile correctional populations. They found that boot camp juveniles became more social (less antisocial), less impulsive, and less risk taking while inmates in traditional facilities became significantly more antisocial, more impulsive, and more risk taking over time.

Impact on Recidivism

As critics predicted, offenders released from boot camps do not fare better after they return to the community. Comparisons of juvenile (Bottcher, Isorena, and Belnas, 1996; Clawson, Coolbaugh, and Zamberlan, 1998; MacKenzie, 1997) or adult boot camp inmates (MacKenzie, Brame, McDowall, and Souryal, 1995) to inmates who received a more traditional correctional option (prison, probation, training schools, detention centers) have shown no differences in recidivism rates or participation in constructive community activities such as work and school (MacKenzie and Brame, 1995). However, despite the empirical evidence, boot camps have remained a popular sentencing option for both juveniles and adults. Current recidivism data are based on programs developed from early boot camp models. As boot camps have continued to develop, so has the need for additional recidivism studies.

Impact on Community Adjustment

Offenders exit boot camps through dismissal, voluntarily dropping out (in some programs), or successful completion of the program. MacKenzie and Souryal (1994) found that some states had dismissal rates of 50 percent or more.

Offenders who successfully complete boot camp programs are placed on regular parole or intensive parole according to their assessed risk. The importance of supervision cannot be underestimated. Not surprisingly, it is very difficult for many inmates to maintain the change initiated in the boot camp once they are released back to their community. Success in many cases is linked to postrelease support. New York recognized the difficulty offenders were having returning to the community and established an innovative "after-shock" program to help them during the community supervision phase of their sentence (MacKenzie, 1993). The program incorporates work programs, employment counseling, drug treatment, and a continuation of therapeutic community meetings.

Other state correctional jurisdictions are developing additional community release innovations. For example, in Maryland, officials are developing transitional housing for boot camp graduates who do not have acceptable housing in the community. While in the program, boot camp inmates renovate the housing that will be used for the transitional housing program.

In Illinois, boot camp graduates are electronically monitored for their first three months in the community (MacKenzie, 1993). In California's boot camp program at San Quentin, participants spend 120 days in the boot camp, after which they live at a nearby naval air station for 60 days. Participants are allowed to leave the base if they have a job; unemployed participants work on the base while they look for employment. When participants do leave the base, they are intensively supervised in the community for an additional four months.

Impact on Prison Crowding

Many state correctional departments that developed boot camp prisons did so specifically to reduce prison overcrowding. By reducing the time an offender spends in prison, boot camp prisons can potentially reduce the demand for bed space and alleviate overcrowding. However, to accomplish this goal, attention must be paid to program design (MacKenzie and Piquero, 1994).

As noted earlier in the discussion on boot camp selection, decisions regarding program entry have an impact on whether boot camps can reduce crowding. Risk-averse criminal justice practitioners may potentially use alternatives to incarceration, such as boot camps, for offenders who would otherwise have been on probation or parole as opposed to incarcerated. This "net widening" makes cost savings and alleviation of overcrowding difficult to realize (Morris and Tonry, 1990).

Another factor that affects the ability of boot camp programs to reduce overcrowding is the eligibility requirement. When eligibility criteria are set too stringently, potential participants do not qualify for the programs and are sent to conventional prisons, adding to the crowding problem. Furthermore, when eligibility criteria restrict participation to offenders with a limited criminal history who have been convicted of non-serious offenses that carry short sentences, these offenders have no incentive to participate in boot camps.

Finally, graduation or completion rates must be worked into the equation in order to determine the true impact of the boot camp program on prison crowding. Programs must graduate a sufficient number of offenders to take advantage of the reduction in time served. If offenders are dismissed (i.e., fail the program) at a high rate and are then sent to conventional prisons to serve their sentences, overcrowding will not be alleviated. An interaction between failure rates and net widening is demonstrated by Parent (1994), who estimated that for boot camps with a 40 percent failure rate, the probability that the offender would have been imprisoned must be near 80 percent just to reach a "break-even" point. MacKenzie and Piquero (1994) estimate this break-even point to be 75 percent.

Impact on Prison Environment

For the past several years, quality management has played an important role in restructuring private organizations and corporations. These concepts are now also being applied to public agencies (MacKenzie, Styve, and Gover, 1998). The development of performance-based standards for corrections involved the examination of relationships between the prison environment or conditions of confinement and the desired outcomes. Quantification of environmental perceptions of prison environments has allowed researchers to compare the environment of boot camps to the environment of traditional facilities as viewed by the inmates.

Critics of boot camps assert that the camps are expected to be perceived by the juveniles as less caring, less just and have less individualized planning, fewer programs focusing on reintegration and, overall, less focus on therapeutic treatment. Furthermore, the yelling, direct commands, and summary punishments by "drill instructors" in the boot camps will result in their youth perceiving themselves to be in more danger from the staff than will the youth in the traditional facilities.

Contrary to critics, Styve, MacKenzie, Gover, and Mitchell (2000) found that inmates in a national sample of juvenile boot camps perceived the camps to have more therapeutic programming, activity, structure, control, and a more thorough preparation process for release from the facility. Boot camp inmates also perceived the facility to pose fewer dangers from other inmates and the environment and to have fewer general risks to residents. In the majority of the boot camps, inmates perceived the environments as high in the characteristics expected in a boot camp environment (i.e., structure, control, safety from other inmates), but they also viewed the environments as more therapeutic (i.e., more programming and better preparation for release).

SUMMARY

The proliferation of boot camps from their initial development almost two decades ago has led to a diversity of programs for offender populations across the country. Boot camps now exist for adults and juveniles, men and women. Boot camps have been based in jails, prisons, and juvenile detention centers. Some programs have focused on special populations such as drug offenders or nonviolent offenders while other, more modern boot camps accept a variety of offenders. Although there is some diversity among individual boot camp programs with respect to their programming, selection process, goals, and eligibility criteria, a number of basic components common to most can be used to describe a basic boot camp program.

Disagreement remains about the effectiveness, utility, and appropriateness of correctional boot camps. Researchers have found them to be perceived as significantly more punitive than traditional imprisonment and various forms of alternative sanctions. They have been shown to be effective in changing inmates' attitudes to be less antisocial than those of comparison groups. Furthermore, boot camps hold potential for reducing prison crowding if participants successfully complete the program and net widening is avoided. Although early studies on the recidivism rates of boot camps found they are no more effective than comparison facilities, recent research finds that the environment in a boot camp is perceived as more positive and therapeutic than that of comparison facilities. These perceptions suggest that updated recidivism studies on newer boot camp models are needed to completely understand their impact on offender populations.

REFERENCES

Andrews, D. A., Zinger, I., Hoge, R. D., Bonta, J., Gendreau, P., and Cullen, F.T. (1990). "Does Correctional Treatment Work? A Clinically Relevant and Psychologically Informed Meta-Analysis." *Criminology,* 28(3): 369–404.

Austin, J., Jones, M., and Bolyard, M. (1993). *Assessing the Impact of a County Operated Boot Camp.* Research in Brief. Washington, DC: National Institute of Justice, U.S. Department of Justice.

Bottcher, J., Isorena, T., and Belnas, M. (1996). *LEAD: A Boot Camp and Intensive Parole Program: An Impact Evaluation, Second Year Findings.* Ion, CA: State of California, Department of the Youth Authority, Research Division.

Clawson, H., Coolbaugh, K., and Zamberlan, C. (1998). "Further Evaluation of Cleveland's Juvenile Boot Camp: A Summary Report." Paper presented at the Annual Meeting of the American Society of Criminology in Washington, DC.

Lipsey, M. (1992). "Juvenile Delinquency Treatment: A Meta-Analytic Inquiry Into the Variability of Effects." In T. Cook et al. (eds.), *Meta-Analysis for Explanation: A Casebook.* New York: Russell Sage Foundation.

MacKenzie, D. L. (1993). "Boot Camp Prisons 1993." *National Institute of Justice Journal.*

MacKenzie, D. L. (1994). "Shock Incarceration as An Alternative for Drug Offenders." In D. L. MacKenzie and C. D. Uchida (eds.), *Drugs and Crime: Evaluating Public Policy Initiatives.* Thosand Oaks, CA: Sage.

MacKenzie, D. L. (1997). "Criminal Justice and Crime Prevention." In L. W. Sherman, D. Gottfredson, J. Eck, P. Reuter, and S. Bushway (eds.), *Preventing Crime: What Works? What Doesn't? What's Promising?* Washington, DC: National Institute of Justice.

MacKenzie, D. L., and Brame, R. (1995). "Shock Incarceration and Positive Adjustment During Community Supervision." *Journal of Quantitative Criminology,* 11: 111–142.

MacKenzie, D. L., Brame, R., McDowall, D., and Souryal, C. (1995). "Boot Camp Prisons and Recidivism in Eight States." *Criminology,* 33: 327–357.

MacKenzie, D. L. and Donaldson, H. (1996). "Boot Camp for Women Offenders." *Criminal Justice Review,* 21: 21–43.

MacKenzie, D. L., Gover, A. R., Styve, G. J., and Mitchell, O. (2000). *National Institute of Justice Research in Brief: A National Study Comparing Boot Camps with Traditional Facilities for Juvenile Offenders.* Washington, DC: U.S. Department of Justice.

MacKenzie, D. L. and Parent, D. (1992). "Boot Camp Prisons for Young Offenders." In J. Byrne, A. Lurigio, and J. Petersilia (eds.), *Smart Sentencing: The Emergence of Intermediate Sanctions.* Newbury Park, CA: Sage: 103–122.

MacKenzie, D. L. and Piquero, A. (1994). "The Impact of Shock Incarceration Programs on Prison Crowding." *Crime and Delinquency,* 40(2): 222–249.

MacKenzie, D. L. and Rosay, A. (1996). "Correctional Boot Camps for Juveniles." In *Juvenile and Adult Boot Camps.* Laurel, MD: American Correctional Association.

MaKenzie, D. L. and Souryal, C. (1991). "States Say Rehabilitation and Recidivism Reduction Outrank Punishment as Boot Camp Program Goals." *Corrections Today,* 53: 90–96.

MacKenzie, D. L. and Souryal, C., (1994). *Multi-Site Evaluation of Shock Incarceration: Executive Summary.* Report to the National Institute of Justice. Washington, DC: National Institute of Justice.

MacKenzie, D. L., Styve, G. J., and Gover, A. R. (1998). "Performance Based Standards for Juvenile Corrections." *Corrections Management Quarterly,* 2: 28–35.

Marlowee, D. H., Marin, J. A., Schneider, L. I., Vaitkus, M. A., and Bartone, P. (1988). *A Look at Army Training Centers: The Human Dimensions of Leadership and Training.* Washington, DC: Department of Military Psychiatry, Walter Reed Army Institute of Research.

Morash, M. and Rucker, L. (1990). "A Critical Look at the Ideal of Boot Camp as a Correctional Reform." *Crime and Delinquency,* 36: 204–222.

Morris, N., and Tonry, M. (1990). *Between Prison and Probation: Intermediate Punishments in a Rational Sentencing System.* New York: Oxford University Press.

Parent, D. (1994). "Boot Camps Failing to Achieve Goals." *Overcrowded Times,* 5(4): 8–11.

Raupp, E. (1978). *Toward Positive Leadership for Initial Entry Training: A Report to the Task Force on Initial Entry Training Leadership.* Fort Monroe, VA: U.S. Army Training and Doctrine Command.

Styve, G. J., MacKenzie, D. L., Gover, A. R., Mitchell, O. J. (2000). "Perceived Conditions of Confinement: A National Evaluation of Juvenile Boot Camps and Traditional Facilities." *Law and Human Behavior* 24(3): 297–308.

Toby, J., and Pearson, F. S. (1992). "Juvenile Boot Camps 1992." In *Boot Camps for Juvenile Offenders: Constructive Intervention and Early Support-Implementation Evaluation.* Final Report to the National Institute of Justice. Washington, DC: U.S. Department of Justice.

U.S. General Accounting Office. (1993). *Prison Boot Camps: Short-Term Prison Costs Reduced, But Long Term Impact Uncertain.* Washington, DC: U.S. Government Printing Office.

Wood, P. B., and Grasmick, H. G. (1999). "Toward the Development of Punishment Equivalencies: Male and Female Inmates Rate the Severity of Alternative Sanctions Compared to Prison." *Justice Quarterly,* 16(1): 19–50.

chapter *9*

DETENTION IN INS JAILS
BUREAUCRACY, BRUTALITY, AND A BOOMING BUSINESS

MICHAEL WELCH
Rutgers University

INTRODUCTION

As a result of worldwide political and economic shifts, immigration has emerged as a global phenomenon impacting most Western nations. In the United States, the issue has become increasingly politicized. Because of political forces, the Immigration and Naturalization Service (INS) has established policies that now detain more illegal aliens for longer periods of time. Greater reliance on detention, however, is controversial, particularly because it demonstrates a significant departure from earlier practices of parole. In response to the emerging trend in INS detention—which in 2000 encompassed more than 6,000 illegal aliens nationwide—critics argue that INS detention policy is ambiguous and lacks an overall rational basis. Furthermore, immigration experts conclude that for most illegal aliens, deten-tion is costly, unnecessary, and unjust; as we shall see in this chapter, INS policy continues to raise serious questions about the fairness and utility of detention (ACLU Immigrants' Rights Project, 1993;

Marks and Levy, 1994; Welch, forthcoming, 1999, 1998, 1997, 1996a, 1996b, 1993, 1991a).

For several years, immigrant advocacy groups and immigrants' rights attorneys have revealed that the conditions of confinement for illegal aliens are substandard at best and at worst violate human rights (Marks and Levy, 1994; Funk et al., 1990). Particularly distressing is the use of "Motel Kafkas" to hold travelers without visas (TWOVs) for indefinite periods of time near major airports. Inside these motels, TWOVs are detained by private security guards hired by airlines, raising sharp questions concerning government and corporate accountability. INS has expanded its detention capacity by opening large, state-of-the-art facilities in addition to using Motel Kafkas. Despite the seemingly accomodating interiors of these new facilities, the overall conditions of confinement often remain harsh. For example, at the INS detention center in Elizabeth, New Jersey—a new state-of-the-art facility—detainees were subjected to abuse by private security staff; additionally, incidents of abuse were compounded by protracted periods of confinement as well as obstructed access to legal counsel.

Characteristically, "doing time" in an INS detention center means being subjected to oppressive conditions and indefinite periods of confinement due to inefficient bureaucratic procedures. In 1995, detainees at the facility in Elizabeth rioted in reaction to the inhumane conditions and lengthy periods of detention. The disturbance at Elizabeth offers a glimpse into how even state-of-the-art facilities remain volatile institutions, especially when substandard conditions are neglected by authorities. This chapter explores several key aspects of INS policy and practice, especially as they directly and indirectly contribute to deplorable conditions and lengthy imprisonment. As INS augments its reliance on detention, it is also imperative to examine its business relations with private contractors. Amid questions over the merits of privatization, brutal business practices used to manage INS detention centers are viewed as a source of mistreatment of detainees.

DETENTION AND INS BUREAUCRACY

Efforts to warehouse large numbers of undocumented immigrants are a relatively recent development. According to the American Civil Liberties Union (ACLU) Immigrants' Rights Project (1993), the use of detention by the INS increased significantly during the 1980s. "In 1981, the average stay in an INS detention facility was less than four days. By 1990, it had grown to 23 days, with many individuals detained for more than a year" (ACLU, 1993: 1; see U.S. General Accounting Office, 1992). The General Accounting Office (U.S. GAO, 1992) reports that during the 1980s, the INS's detention budget grew from $15.7 million to more than $149 million, thereby expanding the detention capacity to hold more than 6,000 persons. In terms of expenses, the estimated daily cost to taxpayers is approximately $50 per detainee. Since the 1980s, more than 26 INS detention centers have been constructed to house more than 6,000 detainees, most of whom are people of color. Critics argue that whites seeking asylum in the United States are met with much less resistance and generally are not detained for indefinite periods of time. Seemingly, detainees from Cuba, Haiti, and Central America who seek asylum in the United States because they fear persecution in their homelands face the most difficult paths toward immigration (Welch, 1997, 1994, 1991a, 1991b; also see Arp, Dantico, and Zatz, 1990; Cook, 1993).

Policy shifts during the Reagan and Bush Administrations account for the increase in the length of detention. With the arrival of the Cuban and Haitian boat people in the early 1980s, policy was reformulated to use detention as a deterrent to illegal immigration. In 1986, the Immigration Reform and Control Act (IRCA), also known as the *Simpson-Rodino law,* was passed, requiring all workers to prove their citizenship. The major consequence of these developments was the employment of repressive measures against undocumented immigrants. Before 1980, INS detention was the exception. During the 1980s, however, "INS policy changed significantly. As a result many individuals previously eligible for release are now subject to mandatory detention" (ACLU, 1993: 3). Other detainees, although not subjected to mandatory detention, are held because they cannot meet the excessively high bonds. Because of this change in immigration policy, the use of detention by the INS increased significantly during the 1980s. The average length of detention has increased from 11 days in 1986 to 26 days in 1994, "but those figures are skewed by the inclusion of thousands of Mexicans who are detained for a day or two before they are thrown back over the border" (Solomon, 1995: 261). Immigration experts estimate that hundreds have been held more than six months and dozens for years. Taxpayers spent nearly $200 million on immigrant detention in 1994 when INS held a total of 82,000 illegal aliens for varying lengths of confinement (Solomon, 1995; also see ACLU, 1993; U.S. GAO, 1992; Welch, 1999, 1997).

BUREAUCRATIC AND INSTITUTIONAL PROBLEMS IN INS JAILS

Among the major barriers to revealing institutional problems in INS detention centers is the lack of systematic inspections and routine monitoring. One of the few comprehensive investigations of an INS detention facility was organized and coordinated by Judy Rabinovitz, staff counsel with the ACLU Immigrants' Rights Project. This project engages in litigation, public education, and advocacy and professional training to protect immigrants against discrimination and exploitation and to enforce the fundamental safeguards of due process and equal protection (ACLU Immigrants' Rights Project, 1993). In its report *Justice Detained,* the ACLU Immigrants' Rights Project (1993) summarizes a two-year investigation of the INS's Varick Street detention facility in New York City (also see Sontag, 1993a, 1993b). In addition to documenting the conditions at Varick Street, the investigation exposed egregious errors by INS. For example, U.S. citizens have occasionally been mistakenly detained by INS. During the ACLU study, researchers assisted in the release of a detainee who had been held for 14 months, long beyond the statutory release period. In this case, the detainee was held despite uncontroverted evidence of U.S. citizenship. Also during the investigation, two other detainees were in the process of verifying their U.S. citizenship. The report confirms that many detainees at Varick Street are legal permanent residents with long-standing ties to this country, with family members who are U.S. citizens with bona fide legal claims to remain in this country. Moreover, the report reveals that INS detention policies and practices subject detainees to lengthy periods of confinement in a facility that was designed solely for short-term detention. At Varick Street, detention has averaged six months, sometimes extending to three years.

According to Lucas Guttentag, director of the ACLU Immigrants' Rights Project, "Immigrants awaiting administrative hearings are being detained in conditions that would be unacceptable at prisons for criminal offenders" (Sontag, 1993a: B1). In addition to the lengthy periods of confinement, the report reveals that the Varick Street facility features inhumane living conditions, including overcrowding; staffing problems; substandard sanitation leading to poor hygiene among detainees; lack of fresh air and sunlight; inadequate food, medical, and legal services; arbitrary and punitive use of segregation; and lack of grievance mechanisms. Even when detainees are ruled deportable, oftentimes they are held for several more months or years because INS fails to promptly arrange travel and execute their departures (ACLU Immigrants' Rights Project, 1993).

Complaints over conditions at INS facilities in New York are not new. During the 1980s, INS was sued twice. In fact, the facility at Varick Street was opened following one of these lawsuits, yet the problems followed. In 1986, the General Accounting Office (U.S. GAO, 1986) issued a report criticizing the Varick Street facility for, among other things, the lack of outdoor exercise facilities and the poor quality of staffing. The investigation of the conditions at the Varick Street facility also revealed an important characteristic of the detainee population: "Virtually all of the detainees we spoke with had close family members who were either U.S. citizens or legal permanent residents" (ACLU Immigrants' Rights Project, 1993: 10):

- Mr. D had lived in the United States for 27 years, 25 as a legal permanent resident. Almost all of his relatives reside in the United States.

- Mr. C had lived in the United States almost 10 years after fleeing from Bangladesh as a political refugee. His wife is a legal permanent resident of the United States and his three children are U.S. citizens.
- Ms. A had lived in the United States for 22 years, 17 as a legal permanent resident. Her two children are U.S. citizens.
- Ms. M had been a legal permanent resident for 18 years, immigrating from Haiti with her family at the age of seven. All of her immediate family members live in the U.S., including her nine-month-old U.S. citizen daughter.

In light of these cases, serious questions are raised about the usefulness and fairness of current INS detention policy. Clearly, these detainees do not meet the most basic justification for mandatory detention since they do not pose a security risk and their chances of absconding are quite low because they have family and relatives in the U.S.

It should be noted that the problems at the Varick Street facility are generally representative of several other INS detention centers. In fact, similar problems exist with INS detention facilities in nearby Queens, New York. At Kennedy Airport, INS officials must deal with TWOV; however, the detention practice features a double standard (*New York Newsday,* 1993: 3):

INS has forced airlines to act as jailers for the TWOVs, even though the agency lets most political asylum applicants enter the country without much fuss. Applicants are simply told to show up months later when their case is called. But the INS has decided any TWOV who requests asylum should get different treatment. All TWOVs must be detained by the air carrier that ferried them into the country—at the airline's expense.

The INS detention policy costs the airline industry $8 million per year, including the expense of detaining TWOVs in neighboring motels, sometimes known as Motel Kafkas. Indeed, such detention is quite Kafkaesque. For example, the airlines hire private guards as detention officers, but these officers do not answer to the government. Moreover, while being held in a motel room for months, detainees are deprived of fresh air, telephones, and, in some cases, are shackled and sexually abused. The following cases illuminate problems with current INS detention policy (*New York Newsday,* 1993: 3; see also Hartocollis, 1990):

In August [1993], three teenagers—two boys and a girl—from Sri Lanka arrived at Kennedy Airport on a Northwest Airlines flight and requested asylum. Northwest detained them for about two months, footing the motel and security guard bills until the airline persuaded the city to arrange for foster care. During those two months, the teenagers' lawyer never knew where they were being held. And the young people weren't allowed to call him. They told him that they only were fed twice a day because the guard said there wasn't enough money for three meals.

In May 1992, Delta Airlines found itself with 13 TWOV passengers from China who requested asylum. Two escaped, a pregnant woman was paroled, and Delta ended up housing, feeding and guarding the remaining 10 until August when INS arranged for them to get an asylum hearing. Delta shelled out $181,000 which included $9,800 in medical bills for a woman who broke her arm when she leapt from her hotel room in an attempt to escape.

Major problems at INS detention centers are not confined to New York. During the past several years, the Krome Detention Center in Miami has been plagued with numerous institutional problems including complaints of sexual harassment and physical abuse. Moreover, the controversy heightened in 1990 when three people working at the Krome Detention Center were dismissed: each of them was a whistleblower who had complained of the mistreatment of the detainees (mostly Haitian). INS officials concede that there are institutional problems at Krome but point to understaffing as a major source of their difficulties (LeMoyne, 1990).

At Krome, detainees "wear orange uniforms, and the guards on the grounds are armed, and the intimidating sound of gunfire can echo through the camp from a nearby target range where I.N.S. officers practice" (Rohter, 1992: E-18). Richard Smith, the immigration service regional director, has been asked why Krome looks so much like a jail. "That's because it is a jail, albeit a minimum security jail. The sign outside may say that it's a processing center, but that's just semantics" (Rohter, 1992: E-18). Although Krome was designed for short-term detention, many detainees spend more than 90 days there. Another point of controversy is the detention of minors, who by INS regulations are not to be held in the same facility with adults. According to Joan Friedland, an immigration lawyer at Krome: "The basic problem is that there are no rules . . . . Everything is discretionary" (Rohter, 1992: E-18). INS officials at Krome deny allegations of violence and human rights abuses. Constance K. Weiss, an INS administrator at Krome, argued, "Why would we want to run a place where we beat the hell out of people?" To this, refugee advocates reply in a two-part answer: "to discourage other potential refugees and because it is easy to get away with. Detained immigrants are a powerless group . . . without recourse to normal political or legal channels" (Rohter, 1992: E-18; also see DePalma, 1992).

Elsewhere, problems have surfaced at other INS detention facilities. In June 1993, a federal class action suit was filed against INS alleging substandard conditions at its detention center in Los Angeles (San Pedro,

Terminal Island). Additionally, the suit addresses problems with access to counsel, including the following: (1) the conditions for visitation for lawyers and their clients are inadequate, (2) the law library and legal materials also are inadequate, and (3) there exists the need for more interpreters. Attorneys cite other problems at the detention center in Los Angeles: (1) there have been numerous complaints about inadequate medical care, (2) several detainees have been "lost" in the system, and (3) INS officials resort to frequent transfers, which result in the "housing" of detainees on buses (Welch, 1993).

BUREAUCRATIC NEGLECT AND INSTITUTIONAL BRUTALITY

The INS detention center at Elizabeth, New Jersey—operated by the ESMOR corporation—was one of a few facilities managed by a private contractor. In less than a year of operation, allegations of abuse and poor conditions at the ESMOR detention center quickly mounted. The institution was publicly criticized by *pro bono* attorney organizations, unidentified ESMOR guards, journalists, relatives of detainees, and U.S. Representative Robert Menendez. Subsequently, INS Commissioner Dorothy Meissner ordered a program review and investigation of the ESMOR contract on May 30, 1995. The review was conducted from June 7 to 10; however, the investigation was extended as a result of a detainee disturbance (which occurred on June 18). The scope of the investigation included probable causes of the disturbance, adequacy of response by ESMOR and INS personnel, and emergency plans that were in effect at the time of the disturbance (INS, 1995). In sum, the INS Assessment Team concluded that ESMOR guards and their mid-level supervisors failed to exhibit proper control during the disturbance. Moreover, there is considerable evidence to support the allegations of abuse and harassment of detainees by ESMOR guards. Many incidents of abuse were serious. According to the Assessment Team's report, ESMOR guards were implicated in numerous acts of physical abuse and theft of detainee property. Female detainees complained that they had been issued male underwear on which large question marks had been made in the area of the crotch. Other accounts of harassment included the unjustified waking of detainees in the middle of the night under the guise of security checks (INS, 1995).

The Assessment Team's report concluded that ESMOR did not have sufficient personnel and resorted to inappropriate uses of overtime. The ESMOR staff was hamstrung by considerable turnover, as high as 60 percent. Moreover, low salaries for guards not only contributed to turnover but also exacerbated the ongoing problem of hiring poorly qualified staff, many of whom were placed on duty without the mandatory training required by INS. Among the institutional problems, the Assessment Team found that detainees were denied proper access to natural light, privacy in some toilet and shower areas, and outdoor recreation area (INS, 1995). It should be noted that immigration lawyers complained about detainees' lack of access to counsel and the courts. Attorneys also complained that some detainees were inappropriately shackled (Peet and Schwab, 1995). At the ESMOR facility, as is the case in most INS detention centers, detainees were subjected to protracted periods of detention due to lengthy processing and inefficient administrative hearing procedures. The estimated average length of detention in the ESMOR jail was 100 to 115 days. Whereas prolonged confinement is compounded by the harshness of detention, the facility's lack of efficiency also contributed to higher institutional costs (INS, 1995).

Returning to the investigation of the disturbance, the INS Assessment Team concluded that ESMOR did not properly implement its Emergency Plan. The failure to carry out an effective emergency plan was attributed to poor personnel training, especially in the area of emergency procedures. At the moment of the disturbance, 14 ESMOR staff and one INS officer were supervising 315 detainees (among them Rumanians, Cubans, Chinese, Russians, and Indian Sikhs seeking political asylum). The disturbance commenced at 1:15 A.M. (June 18) and was brought under control at 6:30 A.M. after a tactical entry by local law enforcement officers; order was restored within 15 minutes. No significant injuries were incurred during the disturbance or during the takeover (INS, 1995). The Assessment Team determined that a ploy to create a distraction to aid an escape attempt was the underlying cause for the riot. The disturbance was precipitated by an assault on an ESMOR guard carried out by five detainees in an organized manner. When a second ESMOR guard was assaulted, the duty supervisor instructed all staff to vacate the facility—contrary to the Emergency Plan. When ESMOR guards were ordered to return to the facility by the on-site INS officer, they simply refused, leaving the facility in the hands of the detainees. The only gesture to intervene was made when the control post guard called 911 (the local emergency assistance number). Damage to the facility was limited to the interior of the building and was generally nonstructural, including broken windows, monitors, televisions, office furniture, sinks, and toilets. Among the several contributing factors to the disturbance, detainees cited harassment and harsh treatment by ESMOR staff, frustration over length of detention, lack of communication about their cases, and frustration with the inefficient hearing process.

With the closing of the INS facility at Elizabeth, detainees were either transferred to other INS detention centers or placed in one of several county jails. Unfortunately, for some of these detainees, the nightmare of detention not only continued but in some instances intensified. Twenty-five detainees (none of whom participated in the riot) were sent to the Union County (New Jersey) Jail and upon their arrival, a group of guards formed a gauntlet and punched and kicked the detainees—an ordeal that lasted more than four hours: "The guards broke one detainee's collarbone, shoved other detainees' heads in toilets, used pliers to pull out one man's pubic hair and forced a line of men to kneel naked on the jail floor and chant, 'America is No. 1'" (Sullivan, 1995a: A-1). Initially, six guards were arrested and charged with the beatings of these detainees, but prosecutors contend that at least two dozen officers participated in the beatings. Attorneys for the officers insist that the allegations of the beatings were fabricated and the detainees' injuries occurred during the riot at the ESMOR facility. However, prosecutors maintained that the detainees received brief medical checks before being transferred and such injuries were not found. Prosecutors also refuted claims that the detainees conspired to fabricate the story, especially since they had difficulty communicating with each other because they speak different languages. In 1998, three jailers were convicted of assault, misconduct, and conspiracy to obstruct the investigation; two of them were sentenced to seven years in prison and a third received a five-year sentence (Misseck, 1995; *New York Times,* 1998; Peet and Schwab, 1995; Smothers, 1998; Sullivan, 1995a, 1995b; Welch, 1999, 1997).

PRIVATIZATION AND THE TRANSITION FROM WELFARE HOTELS TO INS DETENTION CENTERS

Earlier in this chapter, reference was made to Motel Kafkas where travelers without visas (TWOVs) are subjected to various forms of abuse at the hands of private security guards. At first glance, the use of motels and residential hotels for detention purposes appears peculiar—certainly, not representative of the larger correctional enterprise. But a closer examination reveals that the link between the hotel and correctional industries is fast becoming emblematic of how prisoners, residents of halfway houses and welfare hotels, and illegal aliens are warehoused. In an effort to understand the sources contributing to deplorable conditions at INS detention centers, it is important to turn attention to the private corporations that operate some of these facilities. Perhaps the most significant development in privatization is the corporate success of ESMOR which reorganized after losing its contract with INS because of the Elizabeth riot. Currently operating under the company name Correctional Services Corporation (CSC), this private contractor has emerged as a dominant vendor in the detention of illegal aliens as well as state prisoners from various jurisdictions.

The story of ESMOR/CSC illuminates the way hotel managers have effectively made the transition into correctional management and the way that move has contributed to a pattern of abuse and mismanagement. From its inception, ESMOR/CSC became one of the most lucrative private contractors to enter the correctional sweepstakes, a bidding war produced by government's willingness to abdicate its responsibility for overseeing the supervision of prisoners and detainees. Since 1989, ESMOR/CSC has secured 11 contracts in four states, managing more than 1,900 prisoners in various detention and correctional facilities. In fiscal years 1993 and 1994, ESMOR revenues increased 72 percent to $24.27 million (Sullivan and Purdy, 1995).

Interestingly, before ESMOR/CSC formed into a private correctional company, its partners—James Slattery and Morris Horn—were managers for the Sheraton Hotel in Washington, DC. Years later, as the homeless population was surging in the early 1980s, Slattery and Horn earned a profitable contract to manage one of New York City's most notorious welfare hotels, the Brooklyn Arms (a single residence occupancy [SRO] hotel), which became synonymous with crime, vermin, and horrific conditions. According to Steven Banks, a Legal Aid Society attorney who sued the city for the inhumane conditions at the welfare hotels, the "Brooklyn Arms had dark hallways, peeling paint, rodents and a shortage of beds . . . [it] was nothing but a warehouse for desperate families that allowed the ownership to reap substantial profits by providing minimal services" (Sullivan and Purdy, 1995: 28).

In 1989, New York City officials were forced to acknowledge the inhumane conditions, including 600 housing code violations, at the Brooklyn Arms and reduced its reliance on SROs. Subsequently, Slattery and Horn, each without correctional expertise, made the profitable transition to the next housing emergency: prisons, halfway houses, and INS detention centers. ESMOR was awarded a contract to operate the Brooklyn Community Corrections Center in 1989. ESMOR received a contract from the Federal Bureau of Prisons, in 1991, to open an 84-bed halfway house at the LeMarquis Hotel in Manhattan. Controversy erupted at both locations. In Brooklyn, residents initially protested the opening of the Brooklyn Community Corrections Center, but opposition was quelled after Slattery hired William Banks, the campaign manager for Edolphus Towns, a powerful Brooklyn lawmaker. Banks embraced the task of lobbying the neighborhood and its political leaders, a service that brought him a salary of $222,000 from ESMOR in 1993 and $238,000 in 1994. Incidentally, ESMOR's president and chief executive officer, James Slattery, was paid $197,633 in salary and compensation in 1993 (Sullivan and Purdy, 1995). Controversy also followed Slattery and ESMOR to the halfway house at the LeMarquis Hotel in Manhattan where the Federal Bureau of Prisons found numerous problems in the conditions including vermin, electrical code violations, and insufficient services. Salaries for staff at the halfway house were extremely low, contributing to turnover as high as 100 percent in one year; Federal inspectors found that in 1992 it had 30 percent fewer employees than required in the contract. Equally significant was the lack of adequate food. Managers conceded that there were often 30 meals available to feed 100 inmates, thereby forcing inmates to compete, sometimes fight, for food. To cut costs and enhance profits, ESMOR also relied on inexpensive laboratories to process drug tests on inmates. Lab tests were often bungled, leading to falsely indicting inmates for illicit drug use. In fact, during that period, 12 inmates were returned to federal prison when their drug test results were given incorrect positive results, according to the Federal Bureau of Prisons. Additionally, the staff at the LeMarquis were accused of taking bribes from inmates and other forms of corruption (Sullivan and Purdy, 1995).

Despite a lengthy history of institutional problems at several locations, ESMOR continued receiving government contracts while federal officials simply overlooked a well-documented pattern of mismanagement. In 1993 ESMOR earned a $54 million contract to operate the INS detention facility in Elizabeth. Competitors for the contract fiercely charged that ESMOR's bid was egregiously insufficient to operate the facility safely and adequately. ESMOR underbid its closest competitor, Wackenhut Corrections Corporation, by a whopping $20 million. Wackenhut warned INS that ESMOR would be jeopardizing the overall safety of the facility and its population by cutting its operational costs. Wackenhut's caveat proved prophetic; the ESMOR facility erupted in mayhem in June 1995. Interestingly, INS concurred with Wackenhut as the Inspection Team determined that ESMOR hired guards who did not meet the requirements of the contract or were only marginally qualified. Investigators reported that ESMOR demonstrated a continuing cycle of contract violations (INS, 1995). Carl Frick, a veteran jail warden who was the first administrator of ESMOR's detention center in Elizabeth, remarked after the riot that ESMOR's executives "don't want to run a jail. They want to run a motel as cheaply as possible. . . . Money, money, money. That's all that was important to them" (Sullivan and Purdy, 1995: 29).

After restructuring its image by changing the company's name, ESMOR, now CSC, has continued its expansion in privatized corrections, profiting from locking up federal, state, and local prisoners. CSC became a publicly traded company in 1994 (listed on the NASDQ exchange as CSCQ), and by 1999 it had significantly increased its share of the private corrections market. Despite losing its INS contract for the Elizabeth facility, CSC has surged further into privatization. Its durable financial portfolio indicates that its stock is gaining confidence among its stockholders, even attracting a higher number of new investors. Indeed, industry analysts expect continued growth for CSC, suggesting that the future of incarcerating prisoners and undocumented immigrants promises to be a prosperous one (Welch, 1999).

In terms of the business of detention and incarceration, there is considerable speculation that privatization will continue to flourish, thus fulfilling its enormous growth potential by generating significant capital and handsome dividends. The economic formula is simple. Investors in private corrections are expecting more prisoners to be incarcerated for longer periods of time; consequently, chief executive officers and other financial players anticipate profiting opulently from the prison enterprise. Over the next five years, industry analysts project the private share of the prison market to more than double (Bates, 1998). Evidence of current—and future—financial gain in private corrections is another blunt reminder of the economic forces shaping the course of detention and imprisonment. Whereas many corporations and their investors benefit financially from the privatization of corrections, there exists a downside with tragic consequences, including the detention of undocumented immigrants who in effect become raw materials for the corrections business.

CONCLUSION

The objective of this chapter was to expose problems in current INS detention practices by drawing attention to bureaucratic inefficiency, incidents of institutional brutality, and growth of the prison business. Throughout much of its history as a federal agency, INS has been overlooked, underfunded, and understaffed. Of the more than 140,000 immigration claims filed in 1993, INS processed only 30,000. The current backlog of 300,000 cases probably will never be reviewed since it takes months (some times years) to decide a case. Whereas frivolous asylum cases should be ferreted out, legitimate claims must be identified so that they can be reviewed rather than getting lost in the bureaucratic morass. In the early 1980s, the House Immigration and Refugee Subcommittee initiated the Mazzolli-Schumer-McCollum law. If that legislation is to offer meaningful reform to immigration policy, it must improve the review process, allocate adequate resources to the INS, and create humane detention conditions. At this time, the review process often fails to discover claims by legitimate refugees. Additional funding and allocation of resources also are needed. In 1992, for instance, the INS had a staff of 297 to review all 103,447 asylum cases; Switzerland, by comparison, employed a staff of 500 to process 17,960 claims (*New York Newsday*, 1993).

As emphasized throughout this chapter, INS must ensure humane detention conditions and discontinue the practice of requiring airlines to serve as jailers. Moreover, only those persons who pose a security risk or are likely to abscond should be detained. Warehousing thousands of detainees is unnecessary, costly, and unjust. "When persons like those at Varick Street are detained by the INS without legal representation, they are deprived of an opportunity to pursue their legal claims, and the conditions of their confinement are allowed to continue, invisible to the outside world" (ACLU Immigrants' Rights Project, 1993: acknowledgments). The ACLU Immigrants' Rights Project recommends a national review of immigration detention policy, an upgrading of detention operations, and the adoption of alternatives to detention (such as supervised parole) to ensure that immigrants appear at hearings. Routine inspections of all INS detention centers are desperately needed to expose inhumane and unjust institutional conditions; such monitoring would be the first step in a long process of correcting these problems.

REFERENCES

American Civil Liberties Union Immigrants' Rights Project. (1993). *Justice Detained: Conditions at the Varick Street Immigration Detention Center, A Report by the ACLU Immigrants' Rights Project.* New York: ACLU.

Arp, W., Dantico, M. K., and Zatz, M. S. (1990). "The Immigration Reform and Control Act of 1986: Differential Impacts on Women?" *Social Justice: A Journal of Crime, Conflict and World Order,* 17(2): 23–39.

Bates, E. (1998, January 5). "Private Prisons." *Nation:* 11–18.

Cook, D. (1993). "Racism, Citizenship and Exclusion." In D. Cook and B. Hudson (eds.), *Racism and Criminology.* London: Sage.

DePalma, A. (1992, September 21). "Winds Free 40 Aliens, Stirring Second Storm." *New York Times*: A–10.

Funk, B. with E. Calvin, R. Gibbs, D. Kesselbrenner, D. Smith, J. Stansell, NLG National Immigration Project, and the Seattle, Washington NLG Immigration Law Study Committee. (1990). "United States Refugee and Immigrant Detention Policies and Practices Violate International and U.S. Law." *International Review of Contemporary Law:* 104–112.

Hartocollis, A. (1990, July 25). "A Woman Without a Country." *New York Newsday:* Part II, 8–9.

Immigration and Naturalization Service. (1995). Interim Report, *Executive Summary: The Elizabeth, New Jersey Contract Detention Facility Operated by ESMOR, Inc.* Washington DC: INS.

LeMoyne, J. (1990, May 16). "Florida Center Holding Aliens Is Under Inquiry: Additional Complaints Made of Abuse." *New York Times:* A–16.

Marks, S. and Levy, J. (1994). "Detention of Refugees: Problems in Implementation of the Asylum Pre-Screening Officer Program." New York: Lawyers Committee for Human Rights.

Misseck, R. E. (1995, October 13). "Six Guards Held in Beatings." *Star Ledger:* 1, 15.

New York Newsday. (1993, October 24). "Motel Kafka": Editorial: 2–3.

New York Times. (1998, May 2). "Prison Terms for Officers in Beatings of Immigrants,": B–6.

Peet, J. and Schwab, D. (1995, October 22). "Critics Praise INS for 'Candid' Report." *Star Ledger:* 8.

Rohter, L. (1992, June 21). "'Processing' for Haitians Is Time in a Rural Prison." *New York Times:* E–18.

Smothers, R. (1998, March 7). "Three Prison Guards Guilty of Abuse of Immigrants." *New York Times:* A–1, B–4.

Solomon, A. (1995, August 8). "The Worst Prison System in America." *Village Voice:* 25–30.

Sontag, D. (1993a, August 12). "Report Cites Mistreatment of Immigrants: A.C.L.U. Says Aliens Are Detained Too Long." *New York Times:* B1, B8.

Sontag, D. (1993b, September 21). "New York City Rights Chief Investigating U.S. Immigration Centers." *New York Times:* B3.

Sullivan, J. (1995a, October 13). "Six Guards in New Jersey Charged With Beating Jailed Immigrants." *New York Times:* A–1, B–5.

Sullivan, J. (1995b, October 16). "More Illegal Immigrants Released Since Melee Shut New Jersey Jail." *New York Times:* A–1, B–4.

Sullivan, J., and Purdy, M.(1995, July 23). "In Corrections Business, Shrewdness Pays." *New York Times:* A–1, 28.

U.S. General Accounting Office. (1986). *Criminal Aliens: INS Detention and Deportation Activities in the New York Area.* Washington, DC: U.S. Government Printing Offices.

U.S. General Accounting Office. (1992). *Immigration Control: Immigration Policies Affect INS Detention Efforts.* Washington, DC: U.S. Government Printing Office.

Welch, M. (1991a). "Social Class, Special Populations and Other Unpopular Issues: Setting the Jail Research Agenda for the 1990s." In G. L. Mays (ed.), *Setting the Jail Research Agenda for the 1990s: Proceedings from a Special Meeting.* Washington, DC: U.S. Department of Justice, National Institute of Corrections.

Welch, M. (1991b). "The Expansion of Jail Capacity: Makeshift Jails and Public Policy." In J.A. Thompson and G.L. Mays (eds.), *American Jails: Public Policy Issues.* Chicago: Nelson-Hall: 148–162.

Welch, M. (1993). *A Summary Report on INS Detention Practices.* Submitted to the ACLU Immigrants' Rights Project, New York.

Welch, M. (1994). "Jail Overcrowding: Social Sanitation and the Warehousing of the Urban Underclass." In A.R. Roberts (ed.), *Critical Issues in Crime and Justice:* Thousand Oaks, CA: Sage: 251–276.

Welch, M. (1996a). *Corrections: A Critical Approach.* New York: McGraw-Hill.

Welch, M. (1996b). "The Immigration Crisis: Detention as an Emerging Mechanism of Social Control." *Social Justice: A Journal of Crime, Conflict and World Order,* 23 (3): 169–184. Reprinted in S. Jonas and S.D. Thomas (eds.), *Immigration: A Civil Rights Issue for the Americas* (1999). Wilmington, DE: Scholarly Resources: 191–206.

Welch, M. (1997). "Questioning the Utility and Fairness of INS Detention: Criticisms of Poor Institutional Conditions and Protracted Periods of Confinement for Undocumented Immigrants." *Journal of Contemporary Criminal Justice,* 13(1): 41–54.

Welch, M. (1998). "Problems Facing Immigration and Naturalization Service (INS) Detention Centers: Policies, Procedures, and Allegations of Human Rights Violations." In T. Alleman and R.L. Guido (eds.), *Turnstile Justice: The Practice of Institutional Punishment.* Upper Saddle River, NJ: Prentice Hall: 192–204.

Welch, M. (1999). *Punishment in America: Social Control and the Ironies of Imprisonment.* Thousand Oaks, CA: Sage.

Welch, M. (Forthcoming). *Detained: Immigration Laws and the Expanding INS Jail System.* Philadelphia: Temple University Press.

chapter 10

POSTSECONDARY
CORRECTIONAL EDUCATION
THE IMPRISONED UNIVERSITY

JON MARC TAYLOR
Inmate, Missouri Department of Corrections

RICHARD TEWKSBURY
University of Louisville

INTRODUCTION

Postsecondary correctional education (PSCE) is the natural extension of, and most recent addition to, the 200-year-long progression in the field of correctional education. Since the founding of the first prison college program in the 1950s, the expansion of these educational opportunities has been prodigious, reaching nearly 800 programs in 52 correctional systems by the early 1990s. However, this growth has not been without criticism from both academe and the political front; as a result, prison-based college programs are today being substantially cut back, restricted, or closed down.

This chapter reviews (1) the history of the growth of postsecondary correctional education, (2) the common criticisms raised in opposition to providing these educational programs, (3) the political debates revolving around these opportunities, (4) synoptic analysis of programmatic evaluations, (5) institutional impact, and (6) the costs, funding structures, projected return on society's investment, and recent developments in funding and program operations.

"The most hopeful trend in prison work, in America today, is the growing realization that the term in prison can be made into an educational experience" (Craig, 1983: 102). The natural progression of this educational experience extends to offering convicts the same, albeit physically restricted, opportunities to earn a college degree from fully accredited institutions of higher education. The authors believe that PSCE is a highly efficient and cost-effective means to manage, (re) habilitate, and (re) integrate offenders as productive, tax-paying, and law-abiding citizens.

IN THE BEGINNING

Since 1844, when the first secular schoolteacher was hired to work in the Eastern Penitentiary of Pennsylvania (Roberts, 1972),[1] education programs modeled after traditional structures have consistently expanded in scope and depth within the confines of the keep. For the next century, correctional education went from tutoring in the three Rs to offering accredited prison high school programs. By the 1930s, the philosophy behind correctional education had come to be best summarized in the correctional law of New York state: "The objective of prison education in its broadest sense should be the socialization of the inmate through varied impressional and expressional activities, with emphasis on inmate needs" (Englehardt, 1939: 33).

The roots of the expansive network of PSCE programs can be found in Illinois and California fewer than 50 years ago. In 1956, Southern Illinois University matriculated the nation's first inmate college class (introductory journalism) in the State Penitentiary at Menard. The next year, courses in English, government, philosophy, and speech were also offered. By 1962, a fully accredited curriculum was in place, and by 1969, a degree program similar to the basic general studies program available on the main campus was functioning at the prison (Marsh, 1973). A decade after the commencement of higher education at Menard, a baccalaureate degree program (funded by a Ford Foundation grant) was begun at San Quentin Prison in California. The University of California at Berkeley offered a fully accredited curriculum emphasizing the social sciences: psychology, sociology, criminology, English composition, algebra, and calculus (Adams, 1968).

Stuart Adams, the San Quentin–Berkeley program project director, evaluated the program and identified nine critical issues that continue to distinguish or plague most prison college programs (1968: 15). He found the following:

1. College-level programs can operate in the penal setting.
2. Programs seldom failed on their own accord.
3. Inmate-students performed academically as well as, or even better than, students in on-campus programs.
4. Programs provided a stimulus for other education programs in prisons.
5. Consistent positive attitude and behavior changes could be observed in inmate-students.
6. These programs reach only a small percentage of the inmate population.
7. Funding is the most critical problem facing postsecondary correctional education.
8. Library resources are extremely inadequate for research purposes.
9. Poor classroom conditions detract from the educational experience.

In conclusion, Adams found it more practical to offer two-year, rather than four-year, degree curriculums in the penal setting.

The Office of Economic Opportunity initiated what was to become known as Project NewGate at the Oregon State Penitentiary in 1967. By 1969, this program had expanded to five states and was a more ambitious and comprehensive approach than any other PSCE program of the time (Baker, Irwin, Haberfeld, Seashore, and Leonard, 1973). The uniqueness of Project NewGate was that it instituted a nearly total therapeutic environment by establishing self-contained scholastic programs inside the prison. This in turn operated on a milieu therapy philosophy of immersion in academic endeavors with the intellectual and psychological growth of the inmates as primary goals. This objective was in harmony with the rehabilitative zeitgeist of the era. Project NewGate programs exemplified such a philosophy. As Craig (1983: 29) comments, "The emphasis had shifted solely from the importance of keeping an offender isolated from the community to the importance of returning to society a rehabilitated man." The end goal, as Reagen and Stoughton (1976) noted, was to invoke a metamorphosis in a social liability and change him into a social asset.

The Project NewGate program offered not only postsecondary classroom instruction to male inmate-students but also academic counseling, extracurricular activities, and psychotherapy sessions. Upon release, paroled students were sent to campus halfway houses for academic as well as community transition programming. Decreasing living and tuition stipends, administrative services, and psychological counseling were provided to the students (Baker et al., 1973). By 1972, a seventh NewGate program had been established, and 31 states had begun the process of establishing such programs. In 1974, however, the NewGate Resource

Center ceased operating under the aegis of the National Council on Crime and Delinquency because of the termination of federal funding.

The comprehensive NewGate programs were not the only PSCE opportunities available. Although by 1965 only a dozen on-site PSCE programs existed (Herron, Muir, and Williams, 1984), by 1968 Humphreys's (1972) survey of 590 prisons reported that 94 institutions provided college program opportunities to inmates, with 74 (79 percent) being exclusively via correspondence and 20 (21 percent) through some form of on-site and study release programs. The growth of these educational opportunities continued even as the rehabilitative idea faded and the just deserts model gained ascendance. In 1970, 6 percent of the national prison population was enrolled in PSCE programs. By 1977, enrollment had increased to 10 percent (Bell et al., 1979). These percentages, although fluctuating over the years and the ever-expanding prison population, translated into prolific expansion for PSCE sites. At the beginning of the 1980s, there were 350 programs with more than 27,000 enrolled inmate-students (Littlefield and Wolford, 1982). By the end of the decade, Stephan (1992) noted that 772 prison college programs were operating in 1,287 correctional facilities with more than 35,000 enrolled students. These opportunities ranged from certificates to associate degrees to baccalaureate and even graduate degrees.

For nearly 40 years, PSCE continued to expand until eventually more than 90 percent of the U.S. correctional systems offered some form of PSCE opportunities (Ryan and Woodard, 1987).[2] Yet in 1994 to 1995, the Violent Crime Control Act effectively eliminated the primary funding source for PSCE students; as a result, the number of available programs, types of programs, and number of participating inmates has been significantly decreased.

CRITICISMS OF PSCE

The critics of PSCE have raised various objections to the idea of providing educational opportunities for prisoners. Some of these criticisms focus on governmental funding of prisoner education programs, the apparent ineffectiveness of higher education in reducing recidivism, and the financial costs of such efforts. These criticisms are examined in the following sections. Here we analyze the following objections: (1) correctional systems lack the public and legal mandates to offer such programs, (2) these opportunities are fundamentally inappropriate for prisoners, and (3) the only thing that PSCE programs do is produce smarter criminals who in turn prey upon the society that provided them their education.

"The correctional movement of this century," Quinney (1979: 349) comments, "has counted on the prison as a center for rehabilitating offenders as well as confining them." Over the years, the public has affirmed reha-bilitation as the major goal of the correctional systems. Harris Polls in 1968 and 1982 (cited in Cullen, Skovron, Scott, and Burton, 1990), a 1984 *Judicature* article (Gottfredson and Taylor), a Bureau of Justice Statistics survey twice in 1987, and nationwide focus groups for the Public Agenda Foundation (Doble, 1987: 12) all revealed that the public believed that "a goal of the prison system should be to rehabilitate offenders." This public desire for offender rehabilitation is found in most of the states' constitu-tions, bills of rights, and correctional laws (Rotman, 1986). The Indiana state constitution, for example, expressly specifies that "the penal code shall be founded on the principles of reformation, and not vindictive jus-tice" (*Burns Indiana Statutes Annotated, Constitution,* 1990).

Yet this public sentiment is largely lost in the rhetoric of politics. Part of the problem, however, reports Roberts (1992), is that the "myth" that the public seems to be singularly punitive in its response to crime is due mainly to the limits of most public opinion surveys, which ask questions that are too simple based on worst-case scenarios. Both Gottfredson and Taylor's (1984) and Clark's (1985) studies of policy makers' interpretations of public criminal justice opinion found that these decision makers erro-neously assumed the public to be singularly punitive in its approach to crime control. "Despite politicians' and criminologists' continual attempts over the past fifteen years to undermine its legitimacy," Cullen and others (1990: 15) report in their analysis of support for correctional treatment, "the public believes that rehabilitation should be a goal of corrections."

This is not to suggest that the public whole-heartedly support reha-bilitation. In fact, during the late 1990s, the degree of public support for rehabilitation declined (Applegate, Cullen, and Fisher, 1997). "Neverthe-less, the public continued to recognize treatment as a legitimate correc-tional objective, especially for juvenile and nonviolent offenders" (Sundt et al., 1998: 426). Accompanying the decline in support for the rehabilitative ideal, the public is showing growing levels of support for "punishment," although the rehabilitative ideal remains the most popular purpose for the American correctional system among citizens.

Others have argued that it is just inappropriate for prisoners to receive college educations. Senator Ernest Hollings (D-SC) proclaimed during the debate over Pell Grant funding eligibility for prisoners that he believed "in education in prisons, but not at the higher education level" (*The Congressional Record—Senate,* 1991). The senator did not elaborate on why he believed this, but as the former governor and senior senator of his state, he is an influential force in the determination of public policy. William Weld (R), former governor of Massachusetts, similarly objects to PSCE as a matter of principle. Despite any demonstrated rehabilitative effectiveness and cost efficiency of such programs, he commented that "it seems to me that it's a confession that we can be successfully blackmailed by people saying, "Well, we're going to commit serious crimes unless you not only feed, clothe, and house us at your expense, but give us a great education to persuade us not to return to a life of crime; I say 'NO.'" ("60 Minutes," 1991).

These two examples highlight the fact that some people object to PSCE opportunities simply because the students are prisoners. The rationality of the wide-ranging benefits accruing from prison college programming is superfluous to these critics, which leads one to wonder whether the motivating force behind this objection is a prejudice based upon the scarlet F (for felon) imposed on all inmates.

However, the argument that the provision of PSCE programs exceeds corrections' mandate for providing rehabilitative opportunities conflicts with the legal strictures and the manifested general public sentiment. Since education is the rehabilitation/treatment program most favored by the public (Cullen et al., 1990), advanced educational opportunities are clearly within the purview of correctional administration.

Perhaps the most insidious set of objections to PSCE is that when acknowledging successes in reducing recidivism, critics attribute this result to the assumption that inmate-students are now just "smarter criminals" and thus are more difficult to catch (*New Encyclopaedia Britannica*, 1983). In fact, "the conventional wisdom has been that we need to educate the criminal by helping [him or her] to learn to read, to write or acquire job skills," observes Stanton Samenow (1986: 44); however, "what we may well produce is criminals with an education of job skills," but still criminals nonetheless. What this rationalization overlooks in regard to postsecondary education, as opposed to secondary and vocational paradigms, is the cognitive dynamic at work in higher education.

Andrews, Bonta, and Hoge (1990) contend that it is crucial to have a psychological understanding of criminal conduct to implement effective correctional treatment. Canadians Ross and Fabiano (1980) conclude from their review of 40 years of empirical research that a considerable number of offenders experience delays in the development of cognitive skills that are crucial to social adaptation. These cognitive deficits manifest themselves in individuals' inabilities "to conceptualize the consequences of their behavior and [they] are unable to use means-ends reasoning to achieve their goals" (Ross, Fabiano, and Ewles, 1988: 30). Such a conclusion reflects the earlier reasoning of Kohlberg (1970) that such adaptive insufficiencies "could lead to criminal behavior."

It is in these cognitive-social deficiencies, not in general intelligence, in the ability to deal with interpersonal conflicts and to comprehend other points of view, and the adaptive prosocial manners that higher education lends itself to (re) habilitation. As early as 1955, Cressey expressed the need to focus on the attitudes, motives, and rationalizations of criminal behavior. It is in the revision of certain cognitive deficiencies that Volpe,

Waksman, and Kearney (1985) and others (Duguid, 1981; Arbuthnot, 1984) believe that higher education provides the means to correct criminal behavior. Postsecondary education accomplishes this task, as Tope and Warthan (1986: 76) explain:

A liberal education is one which offers that student an awareness of social dynamics. For those inmates who lack the basic cognitive finesse to make conscious judgements which are consensual with the morality of our society, liberal education can help him [*sic*] fill this void, particularly for those inmates who possess the equivalence to a high school education and wish to proceed to post-secondary schooling. By igniting the spark, which starts the maturation process for a criminal, education frees the inmate from the confines of irrational judgment-making and promotes the mental and emotional transformation from adolescence to that of a communally functioning adult.

Hans Toch (1987) postulates that education is a regenerative tool for "chronically maladaptive" offenders. PSCE assists in transforming the way inmate-students view the world, and as Thomas (1983) notes, can change how they act within it. Furthermore, as Scharf and Hickey (1976: 107) suggest, if an offender "leaves prison with the same social conscience with which he entered, he faces a continuing probability of remaining morally alienated from society and its institutions." It is here, with the organized exposure to and development of a more mature sense of values (Homant, 1984) that the distinction between higher education and secondary schooling and vocational training occurs. Thus, as Taylor (1994) notes, "Prison college programs do not turn out better educated criminals; rather, they assist in elevating those involved individuals' cognitive development to new levels, enlightening their world perspective, and enhancing their moral development." Those who object to PSCE because it turns out better educated criminals (who presumably can more efficiently victimize the community) do not comprehend the mediating mechanism by which higher education can provide the impetus for change in the offenders' worldview, morals, and values. It is by virtue of the cognitive change, rather than simply vocational skill training as presented in the rational choice theory of offender rehabilitation (Orsagh and Marsden, 1985)[3] that the provision of postsecondary education opportunities for prisoners eventually protects the community. This protection is a product of an altered psychological schemata to a more prosocial mode. This alteration represents what former Attorney General Ramsey Clark (1970: 220) intended when he said, "the end sought by rehabilitation is a stable individual returned to community life, capable of constructive participation and incapable of crime." As we shall see, PSCE programs provide this service.

POLITICAL CONTROVERSY

The most prolific objections to prison college programs have come from the political arena and do not necessarily concern the provision of educational opportunities themselves but the provision of public funding for financing inmates' participation in PSCE programs. Public outcries and politicians' rhetoric about the impropriety of granting taxpayers' dollars to convicted offenders for purposes of financing higher education have led to growing widespread concerns about the existence of PSCE programs as they currently exist. The issue of state funding of prisoners' college educations has not only caused political outcries but also fueled repeated debates in Congress in regard to funding for such programs.

In 1985, New Hampshire inmates, attempting to enroll in a college program to meet the court-offered sentence reduction for exceptional rehabilitative achievement, petitioned the court to order the Department of Corrections to cover whatever educational expenses were not met by other financial aid sources. The state's supreme court ruled that an incarcerated offender had no right to a free college education when equally talented law-abiding citizens had no such right either. (See *Corrections Digest,* 1986.) Two years later, the Indiana Senate approved legislation excluding incarcerated felons from applying for state-funded higher education grants, with one senator questioning: "It's hard for me to believe what I'm hearing. We're going to deny an 18 year old from a family of 12, whose father earned only $20,000 and give it to an axe murderer?" (Niederpruem, 1987). The month the Indiana bill was signed into law, a federal court ruled that excluding only incarcerated felons from a program funded by tax dollars was discriminatory and thus unconstitutional ("Judge Says Indiana," 1987).

Beginning in 1991, senators and representatives from both political parties repeatedly introduced legislation in Congress to exclude any individual who is incarcerated in any federal or state penal institution from qualifying for Pell Grant assistance. The primary argument behind this proposal was that when inmates receive Pell Grants, a substantial number of needy or otherwise deserving students would go without financial assistance and therefore be unable to complete their education. However, as we will show, this is simply not the case.

The original force behind the exclusionary legislation was Senator Jesse Helms (R-NC), who fulminated on the Senate floor that "the American taxpayers are being forced to pay taxes to provide free college tuition for prisoners at a time when so many law-abiding, tax-paying citizens are struggling to find enough money to send their children to college" (*The Congressional Record—Senate,* 1991: 11330). The senator, however, failed to mention several critical points that clarify the validity and applicability of this argument. First, Congress has never fully funded the Pell Grant program. In fact, in the early 1990s, the Pell Grant appropriation was reduced by as much as $14 million per year. This, coupled with the fact that an infinitesimal proportion of Pell Grant dollars ever went to inmates, brings this issue into focus slightly differently.

However, the "facts" that have been used over the years to push for (and eventually achieve) an exclusion of inmates from Pell Grant funding eligibility have been used loosely and inaccurately. For instance, Representative Thomas Coleman (R-MO) declared during a 1992 House of Representatives debate that 100,000 prisoners received Pell Grants during the 1991–92 academic year (*Congressional Record–House,* 1992), and in 1993 Senator Kay Bailey Hutchinson (R-TX) stated that in 1991 to 1992, inmates "received as much as $200 million in Pell funds" (*Congressional Record–Senate,* 1993: 15746). These would be rather convincing and influential statistics; however, there is no way that they could be true. For example, if Coleman is correct, one of every eight inmates in 1991 to 1992 was a college student. In 1990, only 35,000 inmates attended college courses, nowhere near 100,000 that he claimed. And if the 35,000 inmate-college students were each awarded the $1,500 average inmate-student grant, this would equate to only one-quarter of the $200 million claimed by Senator Hutchinson.[4]

Wisconsin's Republican Representative Gunderson lamented that millions of the most needy students among us are denied Pell Grants, and by eliminating prisoners' eligibility, at least some deserving students would then receive aid (*The Congressional Record–House,* 1992). This is true. If inmates do not get this money, we may presume that it will be redirected to other financially needy students. However, this argument presupposes that inmates are neither needy nor deserving students. Instead, it implies that only traditional students are deserving and that a substantial number of such students would benefit from the exclusion of inmate-students. More than 60 percent of inmates were living below, at, or near the poverty line before their incarceration, however, and more than one-half are racial minorities (Innes, 1988). Furthermore, between 60 and 80 percent of inmates had not completed their high school educations prior to incarceration (Greenfeld and Minor-Harper, 1991). This leaves little question regarding whether inmates are among the most needy of our nation's students. During the 1993–94 academic year, 4.5 million Pell Grants were awarded to 5.5 million applicants.[5] And, in 1998 (after inmates were declared ineligible), a total of approximately 3.8 million Pell Grants were awarded (averaging $1,935), totaling more than $7.3 billion (*Federal Money Retriever,* 1999).

In the early 1990s, fewer than 30,000 inmates received Pell Grants, meaning that prisoners accounted for about one-half of 1 percent (or 1 in every 200) of all grant recipients. The Pell Grant program was created in 1972 to assist the children of the poor and working class (targeting families with less than $15,000 annual income) (Hutchinson, 1993).

Considering this objective, the previously noted demographics of inmate-college students, it is clear that the Pell Grant program (when it included inmate eligibility) was achieving its mandate.

If the facts and figures do not support the program's critics, what are the motivating factors that have driven this as a political issue? Besides reasons of obstinacy and punitiveness, as shown by Governor Weld's objections to PSCE in general, two theories have been advanced: political posturing and racism. Excluding prison inmates from Pell Grant eligibility to achieve the minimal gain for traditional students can easily be classified as an example of "sixty-second management" of the nation's higher education funding dilemma (Boyte, 1991). Such a technique can be described as the political culture of the quick fix: crisis management with a short-term calculation of gain. "Whatever the problem," according to Carl Sagan and Ann Drayan (1991), "the quick fix is generally to shave a little freedom off the Bill of Rights." Political reporter William Greider (1991) calls this political strategy coming from our nation's capital "scapegoating," which he describes as looking for minority segments to blame when things go badly and decline is visible. The call to ban prisoners from Pell Grants can thus be seen as attention-getting, tough-on-crime rhetoric meant to attract votes rather than address underlying ills.

The racism theory is based on the contention that more black males are under some form of correctional supervision than are on college campuses. With this in mind, barring prisoners from Pell Grant eligibility is a clear example of racist policy making because its results disproportionately impact black students. To exclude prisoners as a category from Pell Grant funding is to economically refuse and socially deprive minority youth from one of the few venues available to earn a higher education (Sullivan, 1991). Whatever the motivating factors behind the effort to bar inmates, an analysis of the economics, demographics, and—as we shall see in the following section—the results of PSCE do not justify prisoners' exclusion from funding.

THE EFFECTS OF PSCE

In corrections over the past 25 years, as Wreford (1990: 9) observes, "the most heated debates result from disputes concerning the efficacy of intervention strategies for the incarcerated." Perhaps even more so with PSCE, the controversy of whether college programming can bring about reductions in recidivism remains central to the debate. Opponents claim either that these programs do not reduce recidivism or if they do, that they accomplish this task with "self-selected" elites of the penal population that would successfully reintegrate, whether college educated or not.[6]

The rehabilitative ideal was strongly challenged in the 1970s by liberals and conservatives alike. The liberals criticized the programs of the medical model as control mechanisms co-opted by the state and employed to abuse and manipulate offenders (Cullen and Gilbert, 1982). Conservatives claimed that "the programs are failures; there is no evidence that they rehabilitate" (Goredki, 1979: 75). The foundation for the "nothing works" doctrine was Robert Martinson's (1974) study of 231 rehabilitative programs conducted between 1945 and 1967. Martinson's widely cited conclusions indicated that very few rehabilitative efforts have had a positive influence on recidivism.[7] Five years later, after reviewing the Martinson data, the national Academy of Sciences (Sechrest, White, and Brown, 1979) concurred with his conclusions.[8]

From the beginning of the assault on the efficacy of rehabilitation, there have been rebuttals and reevaluations of the "nothing works" doctrine. Initially, Bindman (1973) and Quay (1973) commented that it was erroneous to say corrections had failed. Corrections had not yet been tried. Proponents of the rehabilitative ethic noted that the programs had been severely underfunded[9] and adequate longitudinal follow-up evaluations had not been made to determine the efficacy or lack thereof for the programs that had been conducted. Critiques critical of the negative evaluations of rehabilitative programming continued (Martinson, 1974; Palmer, 1975; Hallack and Witte, 1977; Gendreau, 1981), while more effective evaluations of on-going, better focused, and more well-designed treatment programs were reported (Gendreau and Ross, 1979, 1987; Gendreau and Andrews, 1990). After extensive analysis of the accumulated research, DiIulio (1991: 147) has concluded that "the facile notion that 'nothing works' is ready for the garbage heap of correctional history."

The role of education in predicting recidivism is fairly clear; individuals with higher levels of completed education are less likely to return to prison even if their education was obtained either prior to being incarcerated or after being released from prison (Harer, 1993). One large-scale federal study examined the relationship between educational attainment and recidivism. Beck and Shipley (1987) observed that of 11,000 young ex-offenders with "some college," the recidivism rate was 31 percent, while high school graduates and dropouts recidivated at rates of 43 and 51 percent, respectively. Two years later, Beck and Shipley (1989), after studying the return rate of 108,000 parolees, reported recidivism rates of 30 percent for those with some college, 35 percent for high school graduates, and 40 percent for dropouts.[10] The researchers concluded that "the amount of prior education the parolees had received was related to the likelihood of rearrest" (Beck and Shipley, 1987: 3).

Postsecondary correctional education studies have traditionally failed to yield a coherent body of knowledge about program effectiveness (Maltz, 1984: 30). Much of the research to date has been methodologically flawed, thereby inhibiting the ability to draw valid conclusions. Additionally, the structure and dynamics of the penal environment make it a prohibitively difficult society to research (Sechrest, White, and Brown, 1979; Taylor and Tewksbury, 1995). Critical problems associated with correctional research, especially PSCE evaluations, include small sample sizes (fewer than 100 are common), questionable methodologies (lack of randomly selected control and experimental groups), varying definitions of recidivism (revocation of parole, rearrest, reconvictions, or reincarceration), statistically insignificant findings (or no statistical tests), and exceedingly short (or an absence of) follow-up periods. Consequently, almost all college prison program recidivism studies of the 1970s and 1980s showed inadequate samples, or insufficient follow-up periods, or both (Wreford, 1990).

Over the years, numerous reports have hinted at prison college programming successes. The reports point to the controversy surrounding determination of PSCE efficacy; they provide no scientifically acceptable design to support the validity of the outcomes reported. Holden (1982) noted that after more than 200 inmates had participated in the Indiana State Reformatory—Ball State University college extension program, none of those who had earned a degree returned as an inmate to the reformatory. This was followed by a report in *Psychology Today* (1983) that noted only 15 percent of inmate-college students (averaging 15 credit hours) in the New Mexico State Prison returned to custody, as compared with 68 percent from the general prison population. Assad (1986) reported that not one graduate of the Boston University program at MCI—Norfolk had returned to prison.

The problems with these reports, as mentioned, include the lack of defined methodology (if one was used at all). No matched control groups were used; no definition of recidivism was used other than return to the specific prison,[11] and even if definitions of recidivism and adequate time spans were provided (as in the federal studies), there was no definition of the programming structure or delivery location ("some college" prior to parole leaves open the question of the amount and type of academic achievement and whether educational attainment was earned prior to initial arrest, during incarceration, or after parole and before reincarceration). Finally, no statistical evaluations were completed analyzing cause-effect relationships. The value of these reports, other than their presentation of interesting phenomena, is scientifically muted in the debate regarding PSCE's role in reducing recidivism.

In the early reviews of PSCE evaluations (Lewis, 1973; Seashore, Haberfield, Irwin, and Baker, 1976), no relationship was found between postsecondary education and recidivism. However, Linden and Perry (1982) reviewed the data from Project NewGate and found that the five separate programs achieved most of their goals but did not influence recidivism rates. Yet when analyzed individually, the Pennsylvania program, which had the most extensive postrelease transition program,[12] did have a lower recidivism rate than those at other sites. This result supports Haviland's (1982: 78–79) observation that

> Isolating the impact of postsecondary education on inmates alone without consideration of the configuration of the prison setting makes meaningful evaluation difficult. . . . College placement services, counseling, curriculum development and admission procedures must be integrated into the inmates' education experience in order for meaningful conclusions to be made.[13]

In quasi-scientific evaluations,[14] the results of the effect of PSCE ranged from no statistically discernible relationship to significantly positive relationships between higher education and reduced levels of recidivism, but all suggested that an influence did exist to some degree. Haviland (1982) evaluated 193 inmate associate degree graduates (ranging from vocational to liberal arts fields of study) from an entire midwestern correctional system's PSCE program, and after three years compared these men with others at similar risk of recidivism from the general prison population. The results revealed no substantial difference between the two groups' recidivism rates (new conviction and reincarceration after release). However, "if the study focused only on those inmates who were paroled for the first time, one would realize higher success rates than those experienced in this study."[15] Also, by analyzing specific risk categories, well over half of recidivists came from the high to very high assaultive risk categories (i.e., those most categorically likely to recidivate).

Craig (1983) also found no evidence in the recidivism relationship in a northeastern penitentiary between those who earned college credits as compared with those with only secondary educations (GEDs and high school diplomas). Yet the college students were three times as likely to have a sentence of at least 10 years, three times as likely to be incarcerated before age 18, three times as likely to have less than 8 years of formal education (because they went right into the PSCE program),[16] and twice as likely to have been unemployed at the time of their arrest. Although the two studies (Haviland, 1982; Craig, 1983) did not find a significant difference between the experimental (PSCE) and control groups,[17] the higher risk classifications of the experimental group members suggest an educationally induced mediating effect. Similar return rates for different classification groups suggest that an intervention has affected the experimental group.

A series of other PSCE evaluations noted a relationship between postsecondary education and reduced recidivism. Thompson (1976) reviewed the recidivism rates of students in one Alabama junior college's PSCE and found that college students recidivated at a rate of 16 percent compared with a national average of 70 to 75 percent. More recently, Gainous (1992) reported a recidivism rate of 5 percent for all Alabama inmates released between 1987–1991 who had completed college courses compared to a recidivism rate of 35 percent for other inmates. Blackburn's (1979) examination of the Maryland Correctional Training Center's college program compared students and other offenders, reporting a positive effect in recidivism reductions. In 1980, the Texas Department of Corrections also stated its belief that junior college enrollment results in lower recidivism rates (Gaither, 1980). In Canada, Duguid (1981) reported that inmate-students in the University of Victoria's PSCE program showed a recidivism rate of 14 percent while nonstudents had a rate of 52 percent. Perhaps most remarkably, California's college program at Folsom prison reported a recidivism rate of 0.0 percent for students earning baccalaureate degrees. This compares with what at the time was a recidivism rate of 21.9 percent within the first year and 55.0 percent in three years (Chase and Dickover, 1983).[18] Utilizing a computer model to compare actual recidivism rates of PSCE graduates in New York to projected recidivism rates based on past departmental analysis, Thorpe, MacDonald, and Bala (1984: 87) "found that a sample of offenders who earned college degrees while incarcerated had a substantially lower return rate than the projected rate based on departmental overall data."[19] A Federal Bureau of Prisons recidivism study reported an average recidivism rate of 40 percent, while those with college degrees returned at a 5 percent rate (Harer, 1993).

Most of the preceding evaluations suffer from the lack of carefully selected and matched control groups. Critics of these studies cite the "self-selection" bias that skews results. This suggests that simply enrolling in a college program distinguishes inmates as among an elite of the institutional population. This could suggest, according to Holloway and Moke (1986: 15), that "perhaps they would have succeeded on parole without college participation." In other words, based on these evaluations, we simply do not know whether the lower rates of recidivism result from education or whether these inmates would have failed to recidivate no matter the conditions.

Perhaps the most methodologically rigorous PSCE evaluations have accounted for self-selection bias in their analyses. These studies are focused on individual institutional programs and when viewed as a body, present compelling evidence regarding the positive effects that PSCE can have on recidivism. Four major evaluations have been conducted to date involving prison college programs in Pennsylvania, Ohio, New York, and Michigan.

Blumstein and Cohen (1979) compared all PSCE participants at the State Correctional Institution at Pittsburgh, Pennsylvania, with a control group of randomly selected offenders with secondary educations. They identified postsecondary education as the single statistically significant factor on recidivism out of 108 possible variables but only for those inmates at the highest risk of recidivating. In Ohio, Holloway and Moke's

(1986) evaluation of the college program at the Lebanon Correctional Institution employed a similar, although less sophisticated, methodology. These researchers worked with two groups of offenders: college students and secondary school graduates. The two groups were matched for key variables, allowing education's impact to be assessed. Holloway and Moke (1986: 16) conclude:

> The only significant difference, then, between the two groups was what they were able to do with their time in prison. Group One earning college degrees and Group Two completing high school/GED then pursuing other institutional assignments. . . . [The conclusion] supports the hypothesis that even persons who have a high likelihood of recidivating, based on their criminal backgrounds and lack of employment and educational histories, derive substantial benefit from access to college while in prison.

In New York, a follow-up study of all male offender participants (986) in the Inmate College Program during the 1986–87 academic year (and released in 1990) examined recidivism rates for inmates who earned degrees (356) or had dropped out of or had been administratively removed from the college program (630). The degree-earning students had a statistically significant lower rate of recidivism compared with others (26 percent versus 44 percent). This finding led to the following conclusion: "Earning a college degree while incarcerated is positively linked to successful postrelease adjustment as measured by return to the Department's custody" (Clark, 1991: 1).[20]

Finally, Wreford (1990) reviewed 907 graduates of the Michigan Department of Corrections–Jackson Community College program. The students were compared with the Michigan and national penal populations on 27 variables. College students were slightly older (28 versus 34) and more likely to be minorities. In terms of criminal history, current offense, and length of sentence, students were identified as "some of the most hardened criminals to be found in the United States" (Wreford, 1990: 62).[21] However, even with these characteristics, examination of recidivism rates three years after release shows a statistically significant difference between college graduates (23.8 percent) and the state's inmate population in general (30.0 percent). College graduates were statistically significantly less likely to return for a new felony, meaning that "graduates not only returned to prison significantly less often than the norm, but when they did it was generally for less egregious violations and thus, presumably, for shorter periods of incarceration" (Wreford, 1990: 109).

All told, whether PSCE opportunities actually have a cause-effect relationship in reducing recidivism still can be debated. It remains to be shown whether offenders who participate are somehow elite or special in ways that make their subsequent successful reintegration more likely than for the average inmate. Effectively determining this issue may be impossible: Selection of true control and experimental groups for a PSCE evaluation raises difficult ethical considerations.[22] Ross and McKay, the Canadian researchers who spent more than two decades studying offender rehabilitation, have concluded (1978: 290) that "nowhere else in the literature [of correctional programming] can one find such impressive results with the recidivistic adult offender." It is reasonable to suggest, as Palmer (1984: 254) comments, that "studies need not be nearly perfect in order to yield valuable results or strong clues" that prison college programs produce significantly lower rates of recidivism. This means that PSCE not only can make society safer but also—as we shall see in the following sections—is economically efficient.

INSTITUTIONAL IMPACT OF PSCE

Reducing recidivism is the *socially centered* goal of rehabilitative efforts; this, as we have seen, can be achieved through postsecondary correctional education. The *offender-centered* goal of rehabilitation is a positive attitude change and the development of healthy coping skills. These also have been shown to be achievable through the development of cognitive abilities ingrained in PSCE programming.[23] These changes in attitudes and coping skills become evident long before the time of release and thus can have direct positive impacts on institutional environments.

In general, as Luttrell (1991: 55) observes, "Educational programming has long been recognized as an important management tool" for correctional administrators. Colvin (1992) explains that an institution with a full range of programs is more likely to have stable and peaceful inmate-staff relations than an institution that warehouses inmates or operates on a paramilitary model with few programming opportunities. DiIulio (1991) notes that although not a guarantee of peace, programs increase interactions between staff and inmates. Consequently, these contacts break down barriers that may contribute to stressful (or even hostile and violent) relations. The direct impacts of PSCE, then, focus on both the achievement of individual-level goals and the structured operations of a prison. On the individual level, PSCE students have fewer misconduct incidents, improved relations with other inmates and staff, greater acceptance of responsibilities, and increased levels of self-esteem. On an institutional level, benefits are gained when the presence of a PSCE program offers an additional tool for staff recruitment and retention.

Participation in correctional programming is sometimes similar to a privilege linked to institutional behavior. Violent or chronic rule violators are often denied participation opportunities (DiIulio, 1991). Evidence suggests that those who participate in prison college programs are perceived and documented as being better behaved than the general inmate population. However, it has not been determined whether this is a cause-and-effect relationship or whether the phenomenon is actually a function of unique characteristics of those likely to seek out such opportunities.

In their evaluation of a Canadian maximum security PSCE program, Gendreau, Ross, and Izzo (1985) found no statistically significant effects on students' institutional conduct. However, although no documented impact was found, staff impressions of students known as troublemakers were noticeably improved as a result of their enrollment. A similar evaluation compared inmate-students' behavior with that of offenders participating in a conjugal visitation program. It found that conjugal visitation enhanced institutional control only when participants were not college educated (Davis, 1988). The level of an offender's education provided the best predictor of positive behavior. Taylor (1993a) surveyed inmates who retained full-time institutional employment along with full-time academic enrollment and reported that worker/students incurred only one-fourth as many conduct violations as other inmates, with the PSCE students displaying almost no violent behavior.[24]

With cognitive-moral development suggested as the mediating influence of PSCE, evidence of such psychological change can be seen in several studies of such influence on offenders. A 1982 national survey of correctional education directors noted that 88 percent believed that college programming had a positive influence on the relationship between inmates and staff; 77 percent reported an increase in acceptance of personal responsibility for actions taken; and 94 percent reported positive impacts on inmate-students' self-esteem (Peak, 1983). Additionally, 70 percent of the directors observed improved relationships among offenders. Duguid (1987: 5) reported a similar result in Canadian PSCE programs and found that "some administrators credit university students with creating a 'calmer' atmosphere in the prison and with 'defusing' potentially violent eruption."[25] Pass (1988), working in the same prison as Davis, explains the Peak and Duguid observations as being a result of higher levels of education creating less social distance between inmates and staff.[26] Numerous researchers have noted that ethnic and racial divisions are a leading cause of tension and violence in prisons (Carroll, 1974, 1982; Kruttschnitt, 1983; Kauffman, 1988; Hunt, Riegel, Morales, and Waldorf, 1993). These divisions can be bridged by higher education that may enhance social interactions and harmony rather than exasperate the consequences of overcrowding and anomic racial and ethnic interactions.

Another, perhaps complementary, explanation for reduced conflict and improved relations among PSCE students and graduates is traced to increased levels of self-esteem. Benson (1991) argues that incarceration breaks an inmate's sense of adequacy and promotes feelings of worthlessness. In turn, Roundtree, Edwards, and Dawson (1982) report that prison self-esteem increases with educational attainment. Anklesaria and Lary (1992) note significant reductions in hostility and aggression with increased offender self-esteem. With nearly universal increases in inmate-students' self-esteem (Peak, 1983) and the noted positive relationship between behavior and self-esteem, the impact of PSCE programming on correctional populations becomes an important management tool.

Inmate-college students provide positive peer role models in a setting commonly devoid of such characterizations. PSCE students have been cited as "inspirations" (Begovich, 1990) and "precedents" (Harrell, 1991) in the penal environment. This influence is gained not only through the status of their educational attainment, but also through positive involvement in the community. Duguid (1987: 14) expands on the inmate-student's role in the culture of the institution:

> The prisoner-student is expected to assume specific obligations toward his less fortunate or less able fellow prisoners. Thus this new academic elite is encouraged to attract other men to education programs, to work with men pursuing the GED certificates or reengaged in Adult Basic Education programs, and [to improve] their skills to identify and work with men with literacy problems. It is here in this realm of community involvement, more than with the success of individual university students, that the real value of the program to the prison is to be found.

While the overall impact of positive peer role models may be difficult to identify empirically, such impacts clearly are not difficult to identify subjectively.

Finally, PSCE programs not only can bring benefits to inmates and the administration of institutions but also can provide convenient educational opportunities for institutional staff. It is not uncommon for the occasional correctional officer or administrator to participate in college classrooms alongside inmate-students (Nelson, 1975; Kiser, 1987a). Another way that programs can provide direct benefits to institutional staff is to offer separate, but similar, courses on-site for staff enrollment (Yarborough, 1989). This option encourages staff education but removes the potential dilemmas involved in staff and inmates being "peers." In this way, the inmate population is being educated and staff can pursue personal and professional advancement.

The Task Force Report on Corrections for the President's Commission on Law Enforcement and Administration of Justice (1967) cited the need for recruiting and retaining qualified personnel. These tasks were directly linked with the recruitment of college-educated staff. Not long afterward (1974), the American Correctional Association encouraged institutions to work with local colleges to develop associate degree programs for their personnel. The assumption here is that a more educated staff is a better staff. Education can also prepare personnel for the psychological, social, and technological challenges presented by a job in corrections. Ross (1989) argues that corrections today combine the task of a high-tech security guard with the abilities of a social worker. As corrections continue to evolve into a complex social service bureaucracy, "advancement with an agency will depend more on one's qualifications and education and less on seniority" (Ross, 1989: 264). Therefore, by providing correctional staff opportunities to continue their educations in a convenient and low-cost fashion, PSCE programs can enhance all aspects of institutional management.

Thus, PSCE programs can provide correctional institutions and systems a valuable tool for staff recruitment, training, and retention while working to rehabilitate inmates and positively influence the institution's social environment. Furthermore, the involvement of postsecondary institutions in prisons can provide unique research opportunities in a host of fields, including (but certainly not limited to) criminal justice (Taylor, 1993a), adult education (Gubar and Hedlin, 1981), and sociology (Kandal, 1981). "This research in turn enhances the educational programs and professional well-being of both university and correctional staff" (Duguid, 1987: 12).

Postsecondary correctional education programs benefit the institutional environment by helping to resocialize offenders by modifying attitudes, improving coping skills, and enhancing self-esteem. Offenders in these programs positively influence the institutional environment by being positive role models who do not return to prison as recidivists. These programs can also offer educational opportunities to correctional personnel that would not be available without offender-centered programs. As we see in the next section, these programs can be offered in a cost-effective manner and provide significant returns on society's investment.

THE ECONOMICS OF PSCE

For fiscal year 1993–94, the United States spent nearly $22 billion on corrections (Lillis, 1993). This sum is $10 billion more than it spent only five years earlier. Morris Thigpen, commissioner of corrections in Alabama, has warned that "we're on a train that needs to be turned around. It doesn't make sense to pump millions into corrections and have no effect on the crime rate" (Ticer, 1989: 80). With governments' demands exceeding their fiscal capabilities, "smart programs" that invest now to reduce greater demands later and even strengthen the economic base of the nation are more necessary than ever before. PSCE is a program opportunity that achieves these goals.

To begin with, much of the financing of PSCE programs originates in correctional department budgets. From a correctional administrator's viewpoint, this can be a highly advantageous position. Prison industries and maintenance work engage, at best, only one-half of the penal population.

When this is contrasted with the fact that 10 percent to 15 percent of inmates enroll in college classes (when they are available), PSCE is seen as a major programming option.

Littlefield and Wolford (1982) reported that in the early 1980s, the most common funding sources for such programs were as follows (in descending order of investment):

1. Pell Grants.
2. State-funded student aid grants.
3. Veterans benefits.[27]
4. Individual student payments.
5. Correctional departments' education budgets.
6. Scholarships from the sponsoring college or university.

However, this order differs today. According to directors of correctional education programs in state correction systems, in the 1997–98 academic year, the most commonly cited available sources of funds for inmates' post-secondary education were private foundation grants and general state funds (Tewksbury, Erickson, and Taylor, 2000). However, the majority of correctional education directors, when asked what funding opportunities are available for postsecondary education, report that none are available in their states. Therefore, three years following the elimination of Pell Grant eligibility for inmates, most states do not have funds or programs. Among the remaining states, the most common funding sources for post-secondary educational programs are as follows (in descending order of availability; note the indication of ties):

1. Privation foundation grants
1. General state funds
3. Students' own money
3. State educational grants
5. Perkins Grants (federal funds)

At an average annual cost of $25,000 to incarcerate an individual (Zedlewski, 1987) with a substantial number of those incarcerated being recidivists (Greenfeld, 1985; Beck and Shiplet, 1987), the possible savings from reducing the numbers of recidivists are great. Even with the average expense of $2,500 per year in tuition, texts, and fee costs (Taylor, 1989), the return on the investment can be substantial. For 1 percent ($250) of the cost of one year of incarceration ($25,000), one year of PSCE programming can be funded. If such programming is continued over two to four years, the demonstrated recidivism rate for participants can be drastically reduced. Even figuring the provision of baccalaureate-level education, the cost is only 40 percent of one year of incarceration. And, as we have seen, this will most likely result in single- (rather than high double-) digit return rates for graduates.

The possible cost savings that PSCE programs can provide through reduced recidivism have been well documented (Greenwood and Turner, 1985; Wreford, 1990; Chancellor, 1992; Elliott, 1994). Haber (1983) argued that if the Lorton, District of Columbia, Prison college program did indeed achieve a near-zero recidivism rate for its participants (approximately 10 percent of the institutional population), approximately 10 percent of the District of Columbia's prison budget would be saved: "This amount of money is no doubt between several thousand and million dollars" (Haber, 1983: 54). Or, as Elliott (1994) showed, a recidivism rate of less than 5 percent over the course of five years for Illinois inmates who attended college classes while incarcerated has substantial economic savings. Additionally, when considering cost savings in terms not only of reducing criminal justice expenses but also of adding to public funds through earned wages, income taxes, consumer spending, and sales taxes, the economic benefits of PSCE programming are great.

On a national scale, Taylor (1992b) developed a model for analyzing the potential cost savings of PSCE programming. This argument holds that if PSCE programming were expanded so that 15 percent of the offenders released annually had earned at least an associate's degree,[28] with an annual recidivism rate of 15 percent compared with the standard return rate of 50 percent, this would result in a savings of $120 million annually in incarceration costs. Taking this model a step further, the savings this outcome would produce in crimes not committed would range from $2 to $20 billion in nonincurred victimizations. Taylor (1992b: 137) concludes by observing:

> By either measure presented, and these are only the crudest of projections, the return on investment that postsecondary education provides the nation is substantial, thus lending credibility to the notion that the most cost-effective way to control crime is through prevention rather than through retaliation.

In general, the financial benefit society realizes for its investment in public and private higher education exceeds a 12 percent rate of return (Bernstein and Magnusson, 1993), and the total return from its investment in PSCE is far greater. From a social investment viewpoint, the observation by Chase and Dickover (1983: 94) of the Folsom Prison college program speaks for the PSCE opportunity as a whole: "It seems evident that the public, whose tax dollars on both the state and federal level support these programs[s], have realized a high return on their investment." However, as we will see in the next section, tax dollars are no longer invested in PSCE, leading some to question whether there is any hope for a payoff.

The Current State of PSCE

As Kiser (1987b: 102) has observed, "One of the most dramatic twentieth century developments in American penitentiaries has been the widespread introduction of college programs for inmates." However, as has been noted throughout this chapter, this "dramatic development" has not been without criticism or without reduction. The criticisms have been serious and successful in curtailing the availability of PSCE programs. Ryan and Woodard (1987) noted that 92 percent of the states reported some form of PSCE programming. By 1992 Sarri (1993: 2) noted that this had dropped to 84 percent of states reporting "some type of postsecondary educational programming." Since that time, Congress has successfully eliminated inmates from the pool of eligible applicants for Pell Grants, and the resulting loss of funds has seriously reduced the number of programs and participating inmates.

The most recent research (Tewksbury and Taylor, 1996; Tewksbury, Erickson, and Taylor, 2000) shows that following the elimination of inmates' eligibility for Pell Grants, the number of correctional systems and the number and proportion of inmates enrolled in PSCE have continued to decline. Passage of the 1994–95 Violent Crime Control Act marked the elimination of all state and federal inmates' eligibility for educational assistance through the Pell Grant Program. During the following academic year (1995–96), enrollment in PSCE programs decreased 44 percent to just over 21,000 inmate-students. In part this drop in enrollment can be attributed to the fact that the proportion of correctional systems offering PSCE programs dropped from 82.6 percent to 63.0 percent (Tewksbury and Taylor, 1996).

In the next two years, however, an even more dramatic drop in program availability and student enrollment occurred. By the 1997–98 academic year, only 54.9 percent of reporting correctional systems reported any form of PSCE programming offered. Furthermore, the range of programming and degree options had been significantly curtailed. Between 1994–95 (prior to the elimination of Pell Grant eligibility) and 1997 to 1998, the proportion of correctional systems offering associate degrees decreased from 71.0 percent to 37.3 percent. The availability of bachelor's degree programs dropped from 48.0 percent of all systems to 19.6 percent, and graduate degrees (in any discipline) dropped from 13.0 percent to only 6.0 percent. The one form of education that has not suffered significantly has been in the area of certificate programs; in 1994 to 1995, 52 percent of all correctional systems offered at least one such program, but this dropped only 3 percent to 49 percent of all correctional systems in 1997–98 (Tewksbury, Erickson, and Taylor, 2000).

The proportion of correctional systems offering postsecondary educational opportunities not only has dramatically decreased, but we have also seen a substantial decrease in the proportion of prison inmates enrolled in postsecondary education programs. In 1994 to 1995, 1.0 of every 13.7 adult prison inmates was enrolled in some form of higher education program. By 1997–98 this dropped to 1.0 in every 26.3 adult inmates (Tewksbury and Taylor, 1996). The primary reason for this decrease is the lack of funds to pay for inmates' education. Although correctional officials report that 41 percent of all adult inmates meet institutional requirements to permit their enrollment, only 10 percent of these students do enroll, principally because of an inability to pay tuition and other costs (Tewksbury and Taylor, 1996).

In short, the current state of postsecondary correctional education is rather bleak. Programs are being eliminated or are shrinking significantly. Funding sources are being eliminated, and a once popular and promising means of rehabilitation and behavioral administration is disappearing from our correctional system.

CONCLUSION

Postsecondary correctional education involves a program structure that "promotes civility, develops cognition and encourages confidence. These three Cs should guide the thinking of our approach to criminal rehabilitation" (Pendleton, 1988: 83). Without an effective rehabilitation strategy, our current correctional policies will eventually deplete society's resources, thereby draining the funds allocated for education, health care, and investments for the future. PSCE is an effective and cost-efficient means by which to offer offenders opportunities to break the costly cycle of crime perpetuation, victimization, and reincarceration. We believe that by implementing short-term, cost-saving strategies to reduce or eliminate educational opportunities, crime will be perpetuated in the long term. This, in turn, will produce even higher levels of victimization, pain, and expense to us all.

In one of the original evaluations of a prison college program, Lockard (1974: 22) poignantly suggested a policy prescription that carries as much, if not more, wisdom today than it did then: "Simply, and aside from humanitarian concerns—it is cheaper in the not-so-long run to pay (adequately) for effective anti-recidivism measures, than to finance law enforcement, justice administration, and penal services and apparatus." It is clear, however, that this is not the path our policymakers have chosen.

ENDNOTES

1. Correctional education had its foundation in the late 1700s when the Quakers employed religious teachings at the Walnut Street Jail. In 1825, Louis Dwight, who believed that criminality was spawned in the lack of familiarization with the scriptures, sponsored the Sabbath Prison schools, which utilized chaplains, theology students, and volunteers to teach literacy through Bible readings (McKelvey, 1936).

2. However, this growth has not been continuous or smooth. For example, Wolford and Little-field (1985) report that 58 prison college programs were discontinued between 1976 and 1982.

3. Andrews, Bonta, and Hoge (1990) point out that effective correctional treatment depends on the type of programming provided to which type of offenders in which type of setting. Orsagh and Marsden (1985) suggest that by employing the rational-choice theory of crime causation, treatment programs aimed at "economically motivated offenders" who place a high value on income and work should prove effective when they enhance work and income-generating skills. Ross, Fabiano, and Ewles (1988: 30) focus more on the irrational behaviors of offenders caused or at least influenced by cognitive deficits and note that white collar criminals (economically motivated offenders) "are less likely to have such cognitive deficits." Thus, even though PSCE obviously can impart strong employment and income-generating skills, the "treatment" aspect lies in the cognitive development area of the programming. As such, neither theory conflicts with the other; rather, they serve to complement one another.

4. No one knows how many inmates receive Pell Grants each year. The application form has no specific designation that would declare that an individual is incarcerated, and the lack of income, although suggestive of incarceration, by no means ensures such a situation. In 1982, the Department of Education reported that 37 percent of inmate-students relied on Pell Grants for their primary source of funding a college education (O'Hayre and Coffey, (1982). In 1994, Senator Pell's staff calculated that only 27,771 inmates received grants during the 1993–94 academic year.

5. In 1992, the Higher Education Reauthorization Act was signed into law. It increased the program's appropriation, raising the family income ceiling to $42,000 (90 percent coming from below $39,000), and increased the number of grant recipients by nearly 1 million. Iron-ically, Senator Helms, who initiated the movement against inmates' Pell Grants because of a stated concern about traditional students not receiving aid, cast the only dissenting vote against the Reauthorization Act (Krauss, 1992).

6. Ross and McKay (1978) call this the YAVIS syndrome accusation. He defines this as the charge that only young, attractive, verbal, intelligent, and successful candidates are selected for treatment programming.

7. The issue that rehabilitative programming was not achieving reductions in recidivism had been known more than 15 years preceding the publication of Martinson's findings (Wootan, 1959; Bailey, 1966; Robison and Smith 1971). The reason Martinson's article had such a profound impact was not necessarily its intellectual argument, but following the turmoil of the 1960s, it was published in the midst of a conservative campaign to provide "objective data" to advance a particular vision of criminal justice (Cullen and Gendreau, 1989).

8. The same year the National Academy of Sciences issued its affirmation of Martinson's 1974 findings. Martinson (1979: 243), upon continuing evaluations of correctional treatment, stated that "on the basis of the evidence in our current study I withdraw this conclusion" that nothing works. Additionally, the conclusions of both Martinson and the Academy of Sci-ences studies were misinterpreted by those seeking to discredit the rehabilitative ethic. What was reported was that based on the available data, the relationship between treat-ment and rehabilitation efficacy measured by recidivism rates was ambiguous.

9. Chaneles (1976) reported that, on average, less than $100 per year was spent per inmate for social services and extended rehabilitation programming. Furthermore, this was for only 5 percent of the penal population. A decade later, Ryan and Woodard (1987) noted that, on average, the amount devoted to education in correctional budgets barely exceeded 3 percent.

10. *Recidivism* was defined in three ways: rearrest, reconviction, and reincarceration for a new offense. Primarily, however, recidivism in this study refers to rearrest.

11. This means a parolee on a technical violation could return to another prison in the state or a reconvicted offender could be sent to another prison system entirely, and both situations could be counted as program successes.

12. A 1972 study identified 11 needs of ex-offenders (e.g., financial help, counseling, living arrangements, medical care, substance abuse treatment) that if unmet tend to correlate with higher levels of recidivism. The U.S. Department of Labor (1977) and Mallar and Thornton (1979) each reported that providing temporary financial assistance was quite suc-cessful in reducing recidivism rates of parolees.

13. Complicating the evaluations of PSCE effectiveness, Peak (1983) observed that many consider recidivism an unreliable "method of assessing correctional effectiveness .... The common opinion is that there are simply too many other variables impacting on recidivism that should be taken into account." Others (Martinson, 1974) have identified recidivism as the quantifiable measure of the efficacy of treatment programs, and (Taylor, 1992) notes that virtually all PSCE evaluations have employed recidivism barometers as their measure of efficacy. If return rates (treatment failures) are utilized, then what standards are to be employed to evaluate program effectiveness?

14. Quasi-scientific studies are defined by the following methodology: (1) defined experimental and control groups, (2) evaluation periods of at least one year, with most analyzing at least three years of postrelease behavior, and (3) a percentage comparison between groups, with most but not all determining statistical significance.

15. Several researchers (Wallerstedt, 1984; Greenfield, 1985; Beck and Shipley, 1987) have noted that a relationship generally exists between the number of incarcerations and the propensity to recidivate.

16. The control group had a "significantly higher percent of inmates with a high school diploma than the college (experimental) group" (Craig, 1983: 76). This is noteworthy for the ongoing debate over the actual educational value between a high school diploma and general equivalency degree (GED).

17. The Haviland (1982) study revealed a lower recidivism rate for the experimental group as compared with the control group, while Craig's (1983) study revealed a higher recidivism rate for the experimental group. However, both results failed to achieve statistical significance.

18. The evaluation period for the college graduates was for only six months after release, which tends to dilute the results. This is especially true in light of Glaser's (1964) and Gottfredson and Ballard's (1965) observation that at least 75 percent of recidivism occurs within three years after release. Consequently, it is suggested that three years should serve as the minimum period of study in determining programming effectiveness.

19. None of these studies determined the statistical significance of a relationship between postsecondary education and reductions in recidivism. However, the substantial differences in return rates are suggestive of a possible true relationship.

20. This result coincides with Glaser's (1964) findings 25 years earlier that prison education was related to lower recidivism rates only when the education was extensive and occurred over prolonged periods of confinement.

21. All of these factors are commonly associated with a high likelihood of recidivism (Kirchener, Schmidt, and Glaser, 1977; Harer, 1993).

22. The central ethical question in a truly scientific design is how to select control and experimental groups, which must come from a common pool-desiring enrollment (to eliminate the self-selection bias). The question that blocks such assignment is who has the authority to grant and deny access to those who desire a college education? Even if such a study were set up, legal challenges could well be raised, with a strong possibility of such an experimental design being voided by the courts.

23. The terms *socially centered* and *offender-centered* were originally proposed by Palmer (1983).

24. These results mirror Petersilia and Honig's (1980) observation that offenders involved in treatment programs and work assignments experienced significantly lower infraction rates. The significance of this finding is that Gottfredson and Adams (1982) found that institutional behavior is correlated to postrelease success, a fact validated by Harer (1993).

25. Similarly, Taylor witnessed such an influence in 1991 at a midwestern maximum security prison when the inmates protested institutional conditions. The initial form of that protest was to be a violent eruption; however, many college students (who were respected among the population) suggested a tactic based on Gandhi and King (whom the inmate-students had studied in the prison's PSCE program) that entailed peaceful demonstrations over four days during recreation periods. This tactic did not violate institutional rules and allowed the entire population an opportunity to participate. This strategy was successfully implemented, avoiding what could have been a violent altercation (Taylor, 1992).

26. *Social distance* is defined as "the degree of closeness or remoteness one desires in interaction with members of a particular group" (Parrillo, 1985: 491).

27. McCollum (1994) explains that prison college funding received an unexpected boost in the 1960s and 1970s when an increased number of those incarcerated were also military veterans who utilized their G.I. Bill educational benefits to enroll in prison college programs.

28. Taylor based the choice of 15 percent of the released population achieving PSCE graduation on a theorized 60 percent parity of the 25 percent of the adult U.S. population with postsecondary educations. This parity is chosen because of the associated educational learning disabilities and pathologies concentrated in penal populations, leaving Taylor to believe true parity to be unrealistic.

REFERENCES

Adams, S. (1968). *The San Quentin Prison College Project.* Berkeley, CA: University of California Press.

Andrews, D., Bonta, J., and Hoge, R. (1990). "Classification for Effective Rehabilitation: Rediscovering Psychology." *Criminal Justice and Behavior,* 17: 19–52.

Anklesaria, F., and Lary, S. (1992). "A New Approach to Offender Rehabilitation: Maharishi's Integrated System of Rehabilitation." *Journal of Correctional Education,* 43 (1): 6–13.

Applegate, B. K., Cullen, F.T., and Fisher, B.S. (1997). "Public Support for Correctional Treatment: The Continuing Appeal of the Rehabilitative Ideal." *Prison Journal,* 77 (3): 237–258.

Arbuthnot, J. (1984). "Moral Reasoning Development Programs in Prisons: Cognitive Development and Critical Reasoning Approaches." *Journal of Moral Education,* 34(2): 112–123.

Assad, G. (1986, August). "A Beacon of Light: Exemplary Education at MCI—Norfolk." *Corrections Today:* 150–154.

Bailey, W. (1966). "Correctional Outcome: An Evaluation of 100 Reports." *Journal of Criminal Law, Criminology and Police Science,* 57: 153–160.

Baker, K., Irwin, J., Haberfed, S., Seashore, M., and Leonard, D. (1973). *Summary Report: Project NewGate and Other Prison College Education Programs.* Washington, DC: Office of Economic Opportunity.

Beck, A. and Shipley, B. (1987). *Recidivism of Young Parolees.* Washington, DC: Bureau of Justice Statistics.

Beck, A. and Shipley, B. (1989). *Recidivism of Prisoners Released in 1983.* Washington, DC: Bureau of Justice Statistics.

Begovich, R. (1990, May 31). "Pendleton Inmates Earn Degrees." *Muncie Evening Press.*

Bell, R., Conrad, E., Laffey, T., Lutz, J., Miller, P., Simon, C., Stakelon, A., and Wilson, N. (1979) *Correctional Education Programs for Inmates.* Washington, DC: U.S. Department of Justice.

Benson, I. (1991). "Prison Education, and Prison Education in the UK." *Yearbook of Correctional Education.* Burnaby, BC: Institute for the Humanities, Simon Fraser University: 3–10.

Bernstein, A. and Magnusson, P. (1993, February 22). "How Much Good Will Training Do? *BW:* 76–77.

Bindman, A. (1973). "Why Does Rehabilitation Fail?" *International Journal of Offender Therapy and Comparative Criminology,* 17(3): 309–324.

Blackburn, F. (1979). "The Relationship Between Recidivism and Participation in Community College Associate of Arts Degree Program for Incarcerated Offenders." Unpublished doctoral dissertation, Virginia Polytechnic Institute and State University.

Blumstein, A. and Cohen, J. (1979). "Control of Selection Effects in the Evaluation of Social Problems." *Evaluation Quarterly,* 3(4): 583–608.

Boyte, H. (1991, Summer). "Democratic Engagement: Bringing Populism and Liberalism Together." *American Prospect:* 55–63.

Burns Indiana Statutes Annotated, Constitution. (1990). "Article 1, Section 18." Charlottesville, VA: Michie Company.

Carroll, L. (1974). *Hacks, Blacks and Cons: Race Relations in a Maximum Security Prison.* (Reissued 1998). Prospect Heights, IL: Waveland Press.

Carroll, L. (1982). "Race, Ethnicity, and the Social Order of the Prison." In R. Johnson and H. Toch (eds.), *The Pain of Imprisonment,* Beverly Hills, CA: Sage.

Chancellor, F. (1992). *A Study of Alabama Prison Recidivism Rates of Those Inmates Having Completed Vocational and Academic Programs While Incarcerated Between the Years of 1987 thru 1991.* A Special Report by the Department of Post-Secondary Education. Montgomery, Alabama, Department of Corrections.

Chaneles, S. (1976). "Prisoners Can Be Rehabilitated Now." *Psychology Today,* 10(5): 129–133.

Chase, L. and Dickover, R. (1983). "University Education at Folsom Prison: An Evaluation." *Journal of Correctional Education,* 34(3): 92–95.

Clark, P. (1985). *Perceptions of Criminal Justice Surveys, Executive Summary.* Michigan Prison and Jail Overcrowding Project.

Clark, P. (1991). *Analysis of Return Rates of the Inmate College Program Participants.* Albany: New York Department of Correctional Services.

Clark, R. (1970). *Crime in America.* New York: Simon and Schuster.

Colvin, M. (1992). *The Penitentiary in Crisis: From Accomodation to Riot in New Mexico.* Albany: State University of New York Press.

Congressional Record—House. (1992, March 26) "Amendment Offered by Mr. Coleman of Missouri": 1892–1898.

Congressional Record—Senate. (1991, July 30). "Amendment No. 938": 11329–11334.

Congressional Record—Senate. (1993, November 16). "Crime Bill": 15746.

Corrections Digest. (1986, January 29). "Ruling on Free College Educations for Inmates": 6.

Craig, J. (1983). "A Study of Inmate Participation in College-Level Academic Programs and Recidivism." Unpublished doctoral dissertation. Teachers College, Columbia University.

Cressey, D. (1955). "Changing Criminals: The Application of the Theory of Differential Association." *American Journal of Sociology,* 61(5): 116–120.

Cullen, F. and Gendreau, P. (1989). "The Effectiveness of Correctional Rehabilitation: Reconsidering the 'Nothing Works' Debate." In L. Goodstein and D.L. MacKenzie (eds.), *The American Prison: Issues in Research Policy.* New York: Plenum.

Cullen, F. and Gilbert, K. (1982). *Reaffirming Rehabilitation.* Cincinnati: Anderson.

Cullen, F., Skovron, S., Scott, J., and Burton, Y. (1990). "Public Support for Correctional Treatment: The Tenacity of Rehabilitative Ideology. *Criminal Justice and Behavior,* 17(1): 6–18.

Davis, R. (1988). "Education and the Impact of the Family Reunion Program in a Maximum Security Prison." *Journal of Offender Counseling, Services, and Rehabilitation*, 12(2): 153–159.

Dilulio, J. (1991). *No Escape: The Failure of American Corrections.* New York: Basic Books.

Doble, J. (1987). *Crime and Punishment: The Public's View.* New York: Public Agenda Foundation.

Duguid, S. (1981). "Rehabilitation Through Education: A Canadian Model." In L. Morian (ed.), *On Prison Education.* Ottawa: Canadian Publishing Centre.

Duguid, S. (1987). *University Education in British Columbia.* Burnaby, BC: Prison Education Program, Simon Fraser University.

Elliott, M. J. (1994). *Department of Corrections Program Performance Indicates October, 1988 to September, 1994: Alternative Solutions to Metropolitan Chicago's Problems of Crime, Employment, Welfare & Education.* Chicago: Roosevelt University.

Englehardt, N. (1939). "Fundamental Factors Governing Success of a Correctional Education Program." *Correctional Education Today.* American Prison Association.

Federal Money Retriever. (1999). "Student Financial Aid." Available at http:www.fedmoney.com.

Gainous, F. J. (1992). *Alabama: Correctional Education Research.* Montgomery: Department of Postsecondary Education.

Gaither, C. (1980). "An Evaluation of the Texas Department of Corrections' Junior College Program." Huntsville, TX: Department of Correction Treatment Directorate, Research and Development Division.

Gendreau, P. (1981). "Treatment in Corrections: Martinson Was Wrong." *Canadian Psychology,* 22(4): 332–338.

Gendreau, P. and Andrews, D. (1990, January). "Tertiary Prevention: What the Meta-Analyses of Offender Treatment Literature Tells Us About 'What Works.' " *Canadian Journal of Criminology:* 173–184.

Gendreau, P. and Ross, R. (1979). "Effective Correctional Treatment: Bibliotherapy for Cynics." *Crime and Delinquency,* 25: 463–489.

Gendreau, P. and Ross, R. (1987). "Revivification of Rehabilitation: Evidence from the 1980s. *Justice Quarterly,* 4(3): 349–407.

Gendreau, P., Ross, R., and Izzo, R. (1985). "Institutional Misconduct: The Effects of the UVIC Program at Matsqui Penitentiary." *Canadian Journal of Criminology,* 27(2): 209–217.

Glaser, D. (1964). *The Effectiveness of a Prison and Parole System.* Indianapolis: Bobbs-Merrill.

Goredki, J. (1979) *A Theory of Criminal Justice.* New York: Columbia University Press.

Gottfredson, D. and Ballard, K. (1965). *The Validity of Two Parole Prediction Scales: An Eight Year Follow-up Study.* Vacaville, CA: Institute for the Study of Crime and Delinquency.

Gottfredson, M. and Adams, K. (1982). "Prison Behavior and Release Performance." *Law and Policy Quarterly,* 4 (3): 373–391.

Gottfredson, S., and Taylor, R. (1984). "Public Policy and Prison Populations: Measuring Opinions and Reforms." *Judicature,* 68 (4–5): 190–201.

Greenfeld, L. (1985). "Examining Recidivism." NCJ-96501. Washington, DC: Bureau of Justice Statistics, U.S. Department of Justice.

Greenfeld, L. and Minor-Harper, S. (1991). *Women in Prison.* Washington, DC: U.S. Department of Justice.

Greenwood, D. and Turner, S. (1985). *The Vision Quest Program: An Evaluation.* Santa Monica, CA: Rand Corporation.

Greider, W. (1991, September 5). "The Politics of Diversion: Blame It on the Blacks." *Rolling Stone:* 32,33,96.

Gubar, S. and Hedlin, A. (1981). "A Jury of Our Peers: Teaching and Learning in the Indiana Women's Prison." *College English:* 779–789.

Haber, G. (1983). "The Realization of Potential by Lorton, D.C. Inmates with UDC Education Compared to Those without UDC Education." *Journal of Offender Services, Counseling and Rehabilitation,* 7: 37–55.

Hallack, S., and Witte, A. (1977). "Is Rehabilitation Dead?" Crime and Delinquency, 23: 372–382.

Harer, M. (1993). *Recidivism Among Federal Prison Releases in 1987: A Preliminary Report.* Washington, DC: Federal Bureau of Prisons, Office of Research and Evaluation.

Harrell, G. (1991, January). "Bar Exam: Prisoners Finding Rehabilitation from Ball State's School of Hard Knocks." *The Indianapolis New Times:* 8–9.

Haviland, J. (1982). "A Study of the Differences Between Prison College Graduates and the Total Released Inmate Population on Recidivism by Risk Category." Unpublished doctoral dissertation, Western Michigan University.

Herron, R., Muir, J. and Williams, D. (1984). *National Survey of Post-Secondary Education Programs for Incarcerated Offenders.* Hackensack, NJ: National Council on Crime and Delinquency.

Holden, A. (1982, July 9). "MEMO: Indiana State Reformatory—RE: Ball State University Program." Indianapolis: Indiana Department of Correction.

Holloway, J. and Moke, P. (1986). *Post-Secondary Correctional Education: An Evaluation of Parole Performance.* Wilmington, OH: Wilmington College.

Homant, R. (1984). "On the Role of Values in Correctional Education." *Journal of Correctional Education.* 35(1): 8–12.

Humphreys, T. (1972, April 24). "Inside Prison and on Study Release Plans, More Convicts Are Given College Training." *The Chronicle of Higher Education:* 3.

Hunt, G., Riegel, S., Morales, T., and Waldorf, D. (1993). "Changes in Prison Culture: Prison Gangs and the Case of the 'Pepsi Generation.'" *Social Problems,* 40(3): 398–409.

Hutchinson, D. (1993, November 15). "Dear Colleagues: (CORRESPONDENCE)." Washington, DC: U.S. Senate.

Innes, C. (1988). "Profile of Inmates, 1986, Special Report." NCJ-109926. Washington, DC: Bureau of Justice Statistics, U.S. Department of Justice.

"Judge Says Indiana Can't Deny College Aid Inmate Students." (1987, April 18). *Indianapolis Star.*

Kandal, T. (1981). "Behind Closed Doors: Teaching Sociology in Prison." *Social Policy,* 11: 53.

Kauffman, Kelsey. (1988). *Prison Officers and Their World.* Cambridge, MA: Harvard University Press.

Kiser, G. (1987a). "Disciplinary Problems Among Inmate College Students." *Federal Probation,* 51(2): 42–48.

Kiser, G. (1987b). "Teaching College Courses to Inmates." *Journal of Correctional Education,* 38(3): 102–107.

Kitchener, H., Schmidt, A., and Glaser, D. (1977). "How Persistent Is Post-Prison Success?" *Federal Probation,* 41(1): 9–15.

Kohlberg, L. (1970). "The Just Community Approach to Corrections: A Theory." *Journal of Moral Education,* 4(3).

Krauss, C. (1992, February 21). "Senate Votes to Expand Aid to College Students." *New York Times:* 6.

Kruttschnitt, C. (1983). "Race Relations and the Female Inmate." *Crime and Delinquency,* 29: 578–592.

Lewis, M. (1973). "Prison Education and Rehabilitation: Illusion or Reality?" College Station, PA: Institute for Research on Human Resources, Pennsylvania State University.

Lillis, J. (1993). "DOC Budget Nearly $22 Billion." *Corrections Compendium,* 18(9): 7, 10.

Linden, R. and Perry, L. (1982). "The Effectiveness of Prison Education Programs." *Journal of Offender Counseling, Services and Rehabilitation,* 7: 43–57.

Littlefield, J. and Wolford, B. (1982). "A Survey of Higher Education in U.S. Correctional Institutions." *Journal of Correctional Education,* 33(1): 14–18.

Lockard, R. (1974). "Outside Evaluation of the Educational Media Technology Technician Program." Burlington County College: Pemberton, NJ. 1–21.

Luttrell, M. (1991). "The Impact of Sentencing Reform on Prison Management." *Federal Probation,* 55(4): 54–57.

Mallar, C. and Thornton, C. (1979). "Transitional Aid for Released Prisoners: Evidence from the Life Experiment." *The Journal of Human Resources,* 13(2): 208–236.

Maltz, M. (1984). *Recidivism.* Orlando, FL: Academic Press.

Marsh, J. (1973, March). "Higher Education in American Prisons." *Crime and Delinquency Literature:* 139–144.

Martinson, R. (1974). "New Findings, New Views: A Note of Caution Regarding Sentencing Reform." *Hofstra Law Review,* 7: 243–258.

McCollum, S. (1994). "Prison College Programs." *The Prison Journal,* 73(1): 51–61.

McKelvey, B. (1936). *American Prison.* Chicago: University of Chicago Press.

Nelson, T. (1975). "Prisons and Colleges." *Adult Leadership,* 23(12): 373, 383.

New Encyclopaedia Britannica. (1983). Vol. 5. Chicago: Helen Hemingway Benton: 268.

Niederpruem, K. (1987, January 31). "Senate Passes Bill Denying Jailed Felons State Education Funds." *Indianapolis Star.*

O'Hayre, B. and Coffey, C. (1982). *The Current Utilization of Pell Grants by Men and Women Incarcerated in State Correctional Facilities.* Washington, DC: U.S. Department of Education.

Orsagh, T. and Marsden, M. (1985). "What Works When: Rational-Choice Theory and Offender Rehabilitation." *Journal of Criminal Justice,* 13: 269–277.

Palmer, T. (1975). "Martinson Revisited." *Journal of Research in Crime and Delinquency,* 12: 180–191.

Palmer, T. (1983). "The Effectiveness Issue Today: An Overview." *Federal Probation,* 47: 3–10.

Palmer, T. (1984). "Treatment and the Role of Classification: A Review of Basics." *Crime and Delinquency,* 30: 245–267.

Parrillo, U. (1985). *Strangers to These Shores.* New York: John Wiley.

Pass, M. (1988). "Race Relations and the Implications of Education Within Prison." *Journal of Offender Counseling, Services and Rehabilitation,* 13: 145–151.

Peak, K. (1983). "Directors of Correctional Education Programs: A Demographic and Attitudinal Profile." *Journal of Correctional Education,* 34: 79–83.

Pendleton, E. (1988). "Student Centered Instruction: A Prison Model for Building Self-Esteem. *Journal of Correctional Education,* 39(3): 82–84.

Petersilia, J. and Honig, P. (1980). The Prison Experience of Career Criminals. Santa Monica, CA: Rand Corporation.

President's Commission on Law Enforcement and Administration of Justice. (1967). *Task Force Report: Corrections.* Washington, DC: Author.

Psychology Today. (1983, April). "Learning Maketh the Honest Man": 77.

Quay, H. (1973, May 24). "What Corrections Can Correct and How." *Federal Tribune-Star.*

Quinney, D. (1979). *Criminology* (2d ed.). Boston: Little, Brown.

Reagen, M. and Stoughton, D. (1976). *School Behind Bars: A Descriptive Overview of Correctional Education in the American Prison System.* Metuchen, NJ: Scarecrow Press.

Roberts, A. (1972). *Sourcebook on Prison Education.* Springfield, IL: Charles C. Thomas.

Robinson, T., and Smith, G. (1971). "The Effectiveness of Correctional Programs." *Crime and Delinquency,* 17(1): 67–80.

Ross, D. (1989). "Educational Requirements for Correctional Officers: Standards for Entry Level and Promotion." *Yearbook of Correctional Education.* Burnaby, BC: Institute for the Humanities, Simon Fraser University: 263–277.

Ross, R. and Fabiano, E. (1980). *Time to Think: Cognition and Crime Link and Remediation.* Ottawa: Ministry of the Solicitor General.

Ross, R., Fabiano, E., and Ewles, C. (1988). "Reasoning and Rehabilitation." *International Journal of Offender Therapy and Comparative Criminology,* 32: 29–35.

Ross, R., and McKay, H. (1978). "Behavioral Approaches to Treatment in Corrections: Requiem for a Panacea." *Canadian Journal of Criminology,* 20 (2): 279–295.

Rotman, E. (1986). "Do Criminal Offenders Have a Constitutional Right to Rehabilitation? *International Journal of Offender Therapy and Comparative Criminology,* 32: 29–35.

Roundtree, G., Edwards, D., and Dawson, S. (1982). "The Effects of Education on Self-Esteem of Male Prison Inmates." *Journal of Correctional Education,* 332(4): 12–17.

Ryan, T. and Woodard, J. (1987). *Correctional Education: A State of the Art Analysis.* Washington, DC: National Institute of Corrections.

Sagan, C. and Drayan, A. (1991, September 8). "Real Patriots Question." *Parade Magazine.*

Samenow, S. (1986). "Making Moral Education in Prison Living Reality." *Journal of Correctional Education,* 37(1): 44–46.

Sarri, R. (1993). "Educational Programs in State Departments of Corrections: A Survey of the States." Paper presented at the annual meetings of the American Society of Criminology, Phoenix, AZ.

Scharf, P. and Hickey, J. (1976). "The Prison and Inmates Conception of Legal Justice: An Experiment in Democratic Education." *Criminal Justice and Behavior,* 3(2): 107–122.

Seashore, M., Haberfield, S., Irwin, J., and Baker, K. (1976). *Prison Education Project NewGate and Other College Programs.* New York: Praeger.

Sechrest, L., White, S., and Brown, E. (1979). "Report on the Panel." *In the Rehabilitation of Criminal Offenders: Problems and Prospects.* Washington, DC: Academy of Sciences.

"60 Minutes" (1991, May 5). "Prison U."

Stephan, J. (1992). *Census of State and Federal Correctional Facilities, 1990.* Washington, DC: Bureau of Justice Statistics.

Sullivan, C. (1991). "Dear Board Members (CORRESPONDENCE)." Washington, DC: Citizens United for the Rehabilitation of Errants.

Taylor, J. (1989). "The Economics of Educational Rehabilitation." *Journal of Prisoners on Prison,* (Fall): 57–63.

Taylor, J. (1992a, June). "Where's a Reporter When You Need One?" *Indiana Defender:* 16.

Taylor, J. (1992b). "Post-Secondary Correctional Education: An Evaluation of Effectiveness and Efficiency." *Journal of Correctional Education,* 43(3): 132–141.

Taylor, J.M. (1993a). "Quierer Es Poder: A Call for Criminal Justice Educators to Teach in the Penal Setting." *The Criminalist,* 18(4): 1, 6–8.

Taylor, J.M. (1993b). "College Student/Worker Survey: Indiana State Reformatory." (Unpublished manuscript).

Taylor, J.M. (1994). "Should Prisoners Have Access to Collegiate Educations: Questions and Answers." *Educational Policy.*

Taylor, J. and Tewksbury, R. (1995). "From the Inside Out and Outside In: Team Research in the Correctional Setting." *Journal of Contemporary Criminal Justice,* 11(2): 119–136.

Tewksbury, R., Erickson, J.D., and Taylor, J. (2000). "Opportunities Lost: The Consequences of Eliminating Pell Grant Eligibility from Correctional Education Students." *Journal of Offender Rehabilitation.*

Tewksbury, R., and Taylor, J., (1996). "The Consequences of Eliminating Pell Grant Eligibility for Students in Post-Secondary Education Programs." *Federal Probation,* 60(3): 60–63.

Thomas, J. (1983). "Teaching Sociology in Unconventional Settings: The Irony of Maximum Security Prisons." *Teaching Sociology,* 10: 231–250.

Thompson, J. (1976). "Report on Follow-up Evaluation Survey of Former Inmate Students of Alexander City State Junior College." Alexander City, AL: Alexander City State Junior College.

Thorpe, T., MacDonald, D., and Bala, G. (1984). "Follow-Up Study of Offenders Who Earn College Degrees While Incarcerated in New York State." *Journal of Correctional Education,* 35(2): 86–88.

Ticer, S. (1989, May). "The Search for Ways to Break Out of the Prison Crisis." *Business Week:* 80–81.

Toch, H. (1987). "Regenerating Prisoners Through Education." *Federal Probation,* 51(3): 61–66.

U.S. Department of Labor. (1977). *Unlocking the Second Gate: The Role of Financial Assistance in Reducing Recidivism among Ex-Prisoners.* Washington, DC: Employment and Training Administration.

Volpe, R., Waksman, M., and Kearney, C. (1985). "Cognitive Education in Four Canadian Prisons." *Journal of Correctional Education,* 36(2): 66–74.

Wallerstedt, J. (1984). *Returning to Prison.* Washington DC: Bureau of Justice Statistics.

Wolford, B. and Littlefield, J. (1985). "Correctional Post-Secondary Education: The Expanding Role of Community College." *Community / Junior College Quarterly,* 9: 257–272.

Wootan, B. (1959). *Social Science and Social Pathology.* London: George Allen & Unwin.

Wreford, P. (1990). "Community College Prison Program Graduation and Recidivism." Unpublished Doctoral Dissertation, University of Michigan.

Yarborough, T. (1989). "An Analysis of Why Inmates Drop Out of Higher Education Programs." *Journal of Correctional Education,* 40: 130–135.

Zedlewski, E. (1987). *Making Confinement Decisions.* Washington, DC: U.S. Department of Education.

chapter 11

COMMUNITY PERCEPTIONS ABOUT PRISON CONSTRUCTION
A CASE STUDY

RANDY MARTIN
Indiana University of Pennsylvania

DAVID CHAMPION
University of Pittsburgh

TODD GIBNEY
Indiana University of Pennsylvania

INTRODUCTION

From the mid-1970s through the 1980s and into the 1990s, there were new record highs for numbers of prisoners (Carlson, 1992; Shichor, 1992). The Bureau of Justice Statistics (BJS) reports that, since 1985, the average annual increase in the prison population has been more than 7 percent. At the beginning of 1999, 1,302,019 persons were confined in state and federal prisons, making the rate of imprisonment 4.6 per 1,000 (BJS, 1999).

This steady and dramatic increase in incarceration rates has created a correctional crisis. One strategy for addressing this crisis has been (and likely will remain) prison construction (Krause, 1992). Since the 1970s, the

United States has experienced unprecedented increases, not just in the number of individuals who are incarcerated but also in the number of new prisons being built (Grieco, 1978; Carlson, 1992; Abrams et al., 1992). The most recent data from BJS indicate a 41 percent increase in prison bed space between 1990 and 1995 when 213 prisons were constructed and more than 280,000 beds were added (BJS, 1997). Despite this unprecedented level of construction, at the beginning of 1999, state prisons were operating at between 13 and 22 percent over capacity, and the federal system was at 27 percent above capacity (BJS, 1999). If this trend continues, the need for more prison space will not soon change.

To build new prisons, departments of correction (DOCs) must find appropriate locations. Siting is one of the major problems and largest obstacles relating to prison construction (Shichor, 1992; Abrams et al., 1992). Given rates of prison construction over the past 15 years, issues relating to siting have become increasingly important. However, despite the importance of the issues and the heated public debate surrounding the process, little solid empirical evidence is available concerning the impact of prison construction on host communities. Only a limited number of studies have been conducted, and the focus of these assessments has tended to be on more objective economic indicators with minimal attention having been paid to community attitudes and perceptions. In their comprehensive review of the literature on the effects of prisons on communities, McShane and her colleagues (1992: 105) conclude that "most information is unsupported by good research design." They also conclude that in many studies, the "results are misleading and the limitations of the data are improperly explained" (p. 106).

The study reported in this chapter was conducted in collaboration with the Pennsylvania Department of Correction (PDOC). It is one component of a larger project designed to assess, over time, the impact of the construction of a state correctional institution on the immediate surrounding communities and the entire county. This study, the Community Attitude Survey (CAS), is a pre- and postassessment of the attitudes and perceptions of community and county residents about the impact that the new prison will have on their lives. The results reported here represent the first phase, the preassessment, of the CAS.

LITERATURE REVIEW

Prisons as LULUs

The literature on prison siting overlaps with that on the (locally unwanted land use) LULU and (not in my back yard) NIMBY models for conceptualizing the views and reactions of affected communities. LULUs are regionally needed facilities, such as power plants, toxic dumps, halfway houses, homeless shelters, and prisons that are unwanted locally because of their feared impact on the community (Krause, 1992). NIMBY refers to the reactions of people faced with the siting of such facilities. In other words, the need for the facility may be recognized, but the attitude is "build it somewhere else." The theme in this literature is that "conflict over facility siting has become increasingly common across facility types and neighborhoods throughout the United States" (Takahashi and Gaber, 1998: 184). While these conclusions refer to a wide range of facilities, they have also been attributed more specifically to prisons. Citing a specialist from the National Institute of Corrections, Silas (1984) indicates community resistance in 80 percent of prison siting cases.

Communities' concerns over siting such facilities range from having their image tarnished, to safety fears, and to worry over declining property values among others. In one of the most comprehensive studies to date, the Daniel Yankelovich Group (DYG) conducted a national survey of resident attitudes toward 18 facility types classified as LULUs (cited in Takahashi and Gaber, 1998). Four separate levels of acceptance were identified in the data. The level representing the highest rejection rating included landfills, prisons, and factories. It was found that facility types that were perceived to have the greatest potential for environmental impact were viewed more negatively than most human service facilities. Because prisons are human service facilities, these findings may seem a bit inconsistent. However, in a 1995 Gallup Poll, 22 percent of Americans viewed crime and drugs as the most important problems facing our nation. Hence, human service facilities that cater to and house populations dealing with substance abuse, HIV disease, and other associated serious problems often are perceived to constitute detrimental environmental impact similar to facilities such as toxic dumps (Takahashi and Gaber, 1998).

Dear (1992) indicates that public attitudes toward those who are different tend to be hierarchically organized (i.e., some folks who are different are good neighbors and some are not). Citing the DYG study, Dear identifies good neighbors as those with physical disabilities and problems most common to all of us (e.g., old age, terminal illness). Neighbors who were identified in the middle range were individuals with mental disabilities. Those rated as the worst neighbors were people with social diseases, such as criminals, alcoholics and drug addicts.

Given the complexity of the issues and the varying interests involved, it is difficult to predict how communities will react to the proposed openings of LULUs (Dear, 1992). Depending on the configuration of factors, a range of reactions is possible, but when the facility is a prison, the general view has been that the community will respond negatively and with fear (Grieco, 1978). Because of the negative perceptions about prisons and those whom they house and the anticipated resistance to having one as a neighbor, prison siting has often operated from "social scripts calling for win-lose antagonism and incivility in the community interactional field" (Krause, 1992: 35). The developer knows that the task is to site an unwanted facility, and the locals come to be seen as "obstacles to be surmounted," rather than as partners in the siting process (Krause, 1992: 35).

Rodgers and Haimes (1987) point out that prison siting decisions tend to become embroiled in local politics, engendering strong reactions of an often diverse nature. Some leaders and members of the community see the introduction of a prison as a needed economic boost, but for others, it generates a host of fears and concerns. While proponents present arguments based on predicted economic gains, opponents often express concerns about personal and family safety (Carlson, 1988).

Attitude/Perception Assessment. Community attitudes and reactions are major factors in prison siting (Shichor, 1992; Abrams et al., 1992). Rodgers and Haimes (1987: 30) conclude that "existing research indicates that these subjective 'fears' and attitudes are more powerful than objective measures of prison impact in explaining community resistance to potential siting." In spite of this avowed importance, there exist very few good, systematically collected data concerning the impact that the construction of a correctional facility has on the attitudes and perceptions of community members. From the research (and common sense), it can be assumed that there is a fairly broad range of possible cognitive and emotional reactions and that these reactions are influenced by a variety of factors (e.g., distance from the facility, property ownership). It is also reasonable to assume that individual and community perceptions change over time. However, research to date has come up short in identifying and assessing the relevant attitudinal and perceptual variables, especially in terms of changes over time.

Studies have more likely looked post hoc at objective indicators, such as property values, median incomes, crime rates, and the addition of new industry, to assess the impact of the introduction of a prison into a community. Of those few studies that have attempted to investigate more personal, subjective variables, none has utilized a pre-post design to assess change/impact. Rather, the studies have employed only postdesigns, relying on retrospective reports to estimate attitude change. These studies also have generally suffered from small and ill-defined samples (McShane et al., 1992).

Understanding how more personal subjective factors evolve over time is important for host communities and for departments of correction. Such knowledge will allow both parties, in this often reluctant partnership, to better maximize the positive aspects, minimize the negative, and create a smoother process for all involved.

Perception Studies: Selected Review. In the limited research that has been done, a variety of social/personal indicators have been used to assess the influence of prisons on the host communities. Abrams et al. (1985) conducted telephone interviews with a total of 399 residents of Dade County Florida. Respondents were asked to assess the quality of their neighborhood before and after the introduction of the prison. Generally, individuals thought their neighborhood had either stayed the same or improved (53 percent and 25 percent, respectively).

Extending the earlier work, Abrams and colleagues (1992) conducted a series of studies using seven prison sites in four states. A variety of economic and other objective indicators was examined, but of interest here is the assessment of public perceptions. Respondents near four facilities were asked about the safety of their neighborhoods and about the general quality of life. The majority of respondents (50–75 percent) saw no impact from the prison, and 78–99 percent believed that the quality of life had not declined. There are, however, several factors that make this study different from the one discussed in this chapter. The prisons about which perceptions were solicited had been in operation from 6 to 10 years and were located in populous counties. Also, sample sizes were moderate (ranging from 334–419) and were from a rather narrow geographic area; "the target area was defined by a circle, several miles in diameter, drawn using the facility as its center" (Abrams et al., 1992: 3).

Maxim and Plecas (1983) also conducted a study focusing on resident concerns. Two hundred and thirty-eight people participated in face-to-face interviews about their concerns relating to having a prison in their neighborhood. Factor analysis of the responses revealed four types of concerns (rooted in social interactional contexts): family safety, general quality of life, the value of the neighborhood, and neighborhood instability. Four hypotheses corresponding to the different concerns and their related factors were derived (see Maxim and Plecas, 1983, for more detail). Mixed support was found for the hypotheses.

Carlson (1988) adopted a slightly different approach, asking residents in the host community (six months after the prison had opened) to indicate which of 15 effects (8 positive, 7 negative) they expected as a result of having the prison in the community. Not surprising, the researcher found that persons who were opposed to the prison's construction were significantly more likely to expect negative effects. Carlson also assessed beliefs held by the respondents and found significant concerns about demands placed on local law enforcement, increased crime rates and drug use, and a negative community image. (It is not clear from the report to what extent these expressed concerns might translate into more personal variables such as fear for personal and family safety.) Carlson (1988) received completed surveys from 47 percent of the households in the community ($n = 170$), which would be considered a good response rate. However, it does beg the question as to whether those with more concerns and negative expectations were more likely to respond.

In summary, the post hoc assessments of perceived impact indicate that the individuals sampled generally do not hold strongly negative views. The existing data do suggest that persons who initially oppose prison construction in their community tend to become more neutral or supportive once they are informed about the economic benefits (Carlson, 1988). Clear conclusions about attitude change cannot be derived, however, because the data are virtually all retrospective. Only one study that included perceptual data collected using a pre-post design was found (see Krause, 1992). Also, the general view expressed in the literature that prison siting has met with strong community opposition is not actually supported with systematic data.

METHODS AND PROCEDURES

Methodology

Arguments for prison siting have most often been framed in economic terms. Opposition, on the other hand, takes more varied forms, many of which relate to the perceptions and attitudes of the members of the affected community. Consequently, DOCs must not only attend to the technical concerns involved in the siting process but also should be attentive to social considerations. Community attitudes and reactions are major factors in facility siting (Shichor, 1992). Abrams (1988) suggests that the impact of facilities should be assessed in two ways: (1) evaluation of objective factors (e.g., economic indicators, crime rate) and (2) assessment of subjective factors (e.g., attitudes, opinions, and perceptions). Obviously, there can be debate over what exactly to measure in addressing these two areas, but there are also issues that relate to when such factors are assessed.

McShane et al. (1992) identify three phases of impact: (1) during site selection, (2) during construction, and (3) during opening and operation. One of the main criticisms of research that has been done on prison siting is that measurement of impact has been almost exclusively ex post facto, which results in an inability to draw solid conclusions about time order. In other words, studies generally lack good baseline measures of key concepts (McShane et al., 1992). This issue has less salience for objective measures because archival data that can provide baselines for comparisons usually exist.

The study reported here may be seen as falling somewhere between phases 1 and 2 identified by McShane et al. (1992). Data were collected after the site had been selected but during the very early stages of construction.

The present study utilized a community attitude survey (CAS) (see Appendix A), focusing on four types of data: personal/demographic variables, awareness and knowledge about the institution, concerns about safety, and perceptions about economic impact and the quality of life. The survey was mailed (with one follow-up) to specific adults and/or addresses throughout Indiana County, Pennsylvania. The sampling design, the survey instrument, and study procedures are described in the following sections.

About the Prison

At this point, before proceeding to more detailed discussions of the methods and results, it seems that it would be useful to describe the facility that is the focus of this study. In 1996, the State of Pennsylvania enacted legislation (Act 33) that created a category of violent youthful offender whose status before the law is that of adult. These individuals are young adult offenders (YAOs) who have committed one or more of eight specified violent offenses with a deadly weapon. A projection study at the time the legislation was being enacted estimated that Act 33 would produce an additional 500 prisoners for the Pennsylvania Department of Corrections to house. Subsequently, $52 million was allocated to construct a separate facility for these YAOs (Pennsylvania Juvenile Court Judges Commission, 1996). As a result, a maximum security prison, the State Correctional Facility at Pine Grove (SCI Pine Grove), was constructed to incarcerate juveniles who have been remanded, as adults, to the DOC. The mission of SCI Pine Grove is to provide a secure, safe, and humane facility for YAOs, ranging in age from 15 to 18 (SCI Pine Grove Project Office at Indiana University of Pennsylvania, 2000).

Sampling

In their review of prison siting research, McShane et al. (1992) identify the use of small, nonrandom samples as major limitations of many studies that have been conducted. The study reported here employed what can best be described as a stratified, disproportionate sample ($n = 3,795$) of the entire county. Three separate location samples were constructed using different sampling strategies. Two samples were developed for communities immediately surrounding the site. In the first, all identifiable residences within a two-mile radius of the prison site were surveyed ($n = 596$). For the second, a random sample of individuals from the local borough and the immediately surrounding township (excluding any overlap with sample number 1) was drawn from sewage records ($n = 999$). To obtain a sample for the remainder of the county ($n = 2,200$), a technique from archeology, systematic transect sampling, was employed (Redman, 1974). All residences within one-half mile on either side of three transects were surveyed. One transect, a state route (roughly) divides the county from east to west, and another route divides it from north to south. The third transect (route) was included to ensure that a small town and some other locales in closer proximity to the prison were included. This mutlimethodological sampling design was utilized in an attempt to enhance reprentativeness and to address key variables such as distance from the site.

Survey Instrument

Prison siting research has been generally criticized for exhibiting a lack of care in the conceptualization of relevant variables. The underrepresentation of key concepts creates construct validity problems, because the resulting variables represent only portions of the relevant concepts. Additionally, the variables that have been used have often been inadequately operationalized (McShane et al., 1992).

In an attempt to avoid the pitfalls described, the CAS (see Appendix A) not only was based on variables culled from the literature but also drew on information provided by the DOC and the community. From these various perspectives, several sets of salient variables were developed. The first set consists of demographic/control variables. The second set assesses awareness of and knowledge about the prison. The third set relates to safety concerns. The final set focuses on perceived economic impact and other quality of life aspects.

Support for the inclusion of these diverse types of variables can be found in the work of Guest and Lee (1983), who describe two types of feelings towards one's community, evaluative and sentimental. The evaluative aspect deals with satisfaction relating to "residential environment" type variables. These evaluations tend to be based more in logical and rational assessment of physical things, such as economic conditions. The sentimental aspect derives from deep-seated emotional elements, relating to more subjective, quality of life issues. McShane et al. (1992) also generally site lack of adequate control variables as a major limiting factor in prison siting research relating to the inclusion of a broad range of demographic items.

Before proceeding with further discussion of specific variables, we should reiterate that all perception studies done to date have assessed perceptions/attitudes after the fact. The current study assessed community perceptions very early in the prison construction process and therefore asked respondents to indicate their perceptions based on the anticipated impact of the prison.

Several variables relevant to community fears can be identified in the literature. Some of these variables have been assessed in perception studies, and others have been assessed using more "objective" data. Concerns/fears for general safety over prisoners' families visiting and/or moving into the community, rising crime rates, escapes, and prisoners staying in the area upon release have been addressed (see, for example, Shichor,

1992; Carlson, 1991, 1992; Grieco, 1978). Variables relating to perceived fear are assessed on the CAS with items 17– 20.

The area that has received the most empirical attention in prison siting impact studies has been economics. A variety of indicators has been used to measure economic impact, ranging from changes in property values, to tax revenues, to growth of new business, to employment rates (e.g., Smykla et al., 1984; Grieco, 1978; Carlson, 1991; Abrams and Lyons, 1987). These economic variables have most often been operationalized through existing community statistics or sometimes through anecdotal evidence. There is a dearth of systematically gathered data relating to perceptions about economic impact, and the data that do exist have been gathered after the fact, not prior to the opening of the prison in a community. The expected economic impacts of the prison on the surrounding communities were assessed with items 21, 22, 23, and 25 on the CAS.

There are two additional perceptual items on the CAS. One (item 24) is an evaluative quality of life measure, asking about the perceived impact on public services. The second (item 26) is a sentimental type item, asking whether the respondent's intention is to remain where he or she is or to relocate because of the introduction of the prison.

A range of factors affects community and individual reactions to the siting of a prison. Under differing conditions, prisons may produce negative, neutral, or positive perceptions (McShane et al., 1992). Because of this varied potential for reaction and impact, it is essential that salient control (independent) variables be measured. Several such variables have been identified in the literature.

One powerful control variable when measuring individual and neighborhood perceptions is distance from the facility. Proximity to the site is often cited as one of the most salient factors affecting individuals' reactions to the construction of facilities such as prisons (e.g., Maxim and Plecas, 1983; Dear, 1992, Shichor, 1992). Given the importance attributed to distance/proximity as a variable influencing perceptions about facilities such as prisons, two strategies for operationalizing it were employed. It was assessed by the location sample (i.e., in the aggregate, site is the closest, borough/township is next, and the county sample is the most removed). A more precise measure is provided by item 15, which provides an estimate of how far the respondent lives from the site. To assist in obtaining good data for this item, a county map was provided, with the prison site and key landmarks identified. The distances in miles from the site to known locales were also provided.

In his review of the NIMBY literature, Dear (1992) identifies several other key control variables. Those relating to the respondent are home ownership, household size, income level, education level, occupation, and marital status. Facility characteristics, such as size and type, have also been found to influence reactions. These factors are addressed with the CAS, along with other control variables (e.g., age, gender).

Procedures

Each person/address in the three location samples was mailed a packet containing a cover letter, the CAS, the map, a postage-paid return envelope, and a self-addressed, postage-paid postcard. The procedures described to the prospective respondent were that he or she should return the survey in the postage-paid envelope and mail the postcard separately. Three address labels were printed for each individual/address in the sample. One label was used to send the initial mailing, the second was affixed to the postcard, and the third was for the follow-up mailing (if needed). This technique has been demonstrated to be an effective way to allow for the identification of those who have and have not responded for the follow-up while maintaining the anonymity of survey responses (Babbie, 1989). Upon receipt of the postcard, the third address label was destroyed. After approximately four weeks, those address labels that remained were used to identify the individuals/addresses for the follow-up mailing. The follow-up packet contained a new (different) cover letter, another copy of the CAS and the map, and a postage-paid return envelope.

ANALYSIS AND RESULTS

The total number of residences surveyed was 3,795; 1,659 responses were received (a 44 percent response rate). The response breakdown by location sample is reported later. The results presented relate only to the aggregate sample. Analyses comparing the different location samples were conducted, but discussion of these results is beyond the scope of this work.

Comparison of Sample Demographics

Before discussing the survey data, it is important to briefly examine the concordance between the sample and the county population. It is difficult to construct a direct comparison because the sample for the CAS was not drawn from the general population of the county. Instead, adult property owners were targeted because it is this group whose views are identified as being most relevant and most potentially oppositional. The comparisons presented in Table 11.1 are based on the most congruous county statistics that were available. Table 11.1 breaks the county population and CAS sample into two subgroups, the Indiana Borough and White Township (combined) and the remainder of the county. The latter group refers to statistics representative of the county, other than Indiana Borough and White Township. These generally correspond to two of the three location samples from the study. The third location sample, the site, cannot be specifically

TABLE **11.1** Comparison of County Demographics with CAS Sample Demographics

SAMPLE	OVERALL COUNTY DEMOGRAPHICS		CAS SAMPLE DEMOGRAPHICS[a]	
Location	County (remainder)	Borough (plus township)	County (sample)	Borough (plus township)
Variable	Valid % (Total)	Valid % (Total)	Valid % (Total)	Valid % (Total)
Gender[b]				
Male	47.0 (11,997)	44.1 (5217)	48.4 (465)	60.3 (234)
Female	53.0 (13,516)	55.9 (6607)	51.6 (496)	39.7 (154)
Marital status[c]				
Single, never married	23.1 (10,061)	45.6 (13,299)	10.0 (96)	10.1 (39)
Married	62.5 (27,175)	42.5 (12,398)	65.9 (633)	69.2 (267)
Separated/Divorced	6.1 (2635)	5.7 (1662)	9.5 (91)	11.4 (44)
Widowed	8.3 (3588)	6.2 (1779)	14.7 (141)	9.3 (36)
Household income				
Less than $30,000	77.5 (31,642)	75.3 (17,186)	48.4 (418)	32.3 (116)
$30,000 and higher	22.5 (9200)	24.5 (5650)	51.6 (445)	67.7 (243)
Occupation type				
Professional	11.2 (3215)	24.2 (4507)	19.8 (166)	35.3 (122)
Skilled	30.7 (8836)	33.2 (6183)	12.8 (107)	8.4 (29)
Unskilled	27.0 (7750)	20.0 (3731)	34.9 (293)	19.4 (67)
Retired[d]	31.1 (8940)	22.6 (4225)	24.1 (202)	29.8 (103)
Other[e]	N/A	N/A	8.5 (71)	7.2 (25)
Education level[f]				
Less than h.s. diploma	29.9 (10,731)	18.0 (3150)	7.6 (72)	2.3 (9)
High school/equivalent	49.2 (17,663)	35.0 (6137)	40.7 (387)	21.1 (82)
Some college	12.6 (4512)	20.0 (3479)	26.3 (250)	23.2 (90)
Bachelor's degree	5.3 (1905)	14.5 (2556)	15.5 (147)	21.9 (85)
Graduate/Professional	3.0 (1055)	12.5 (2196)	9.9 (94)	31.4 (122)

[a]CAS sample demographics site sample could not be distinguished as county or borough and has been excluded.
[b]Overall county demographics variable Gender is limited to residents age 40 and older.
[c]Overall county demographics variable Marital Status refers to residents age 15 and older.
[d]Overall county demographics Occupation Type category Retired is composed of residents age 65 and older.
[e]Overall county demographics variable Occupation Type category Other is not applicable due to the lack of available data.
[f]Overall county demographics variable Education Level refers to residents age 25 and older.

addressed because there is no way to unbundle those residences from the other two subgroups.

The county population and the CAS demographics have some key differences. The gender breakdown for the county location sample is very similar, but women are substantially underrepresented in the borough sample. This difference is most likely attributable to the use of sewage records as the sampling frame because the vast majority of the names listed on these records are male. The other two location samples did not use names but identified only residences. It is likely that this bias had an impact on the findings. Women were found to be generally more concerned about the potential impact of the prison, and if they are underrepresented, so too will be the level of concern indicated. This impact would apply specifically to the borough location sample findings and, to a lesser extent, to the aggregate samples.

The categories relating to marital status also have some large differences. Given that property owners were the focus, the CAS sample is generally older (and probably more well established). The county marital status statistics are based on individuals 15 and older, whereas the mean age for the CAS sample is 54. The differences that are exhibited would likely be reduced if county population data that reflected the same age group as the CAS data were available.

Of greater concern are the divergences in income and education levels. Both groups of CAS respondents are significantly higher on these variables than the levels reflected in the county population statistics. This may be partly related to the age and property ownership status of the CAS sample, but it also may reflect a response bias. It is possible that income and education level influence a person's willingness to respond to such a survey. It should be noted, however, that the literature generally indicates that opposition and negative reactions to LULUs are positively associated with both income and education; those with more education and those in higher income brackets are more likely to oppose such facilities.

There are also some differences in types of occupations. Both CAS groups seem to underrepresent those in professional and skilled positions. The CAS county sample overrepresents unskilled workers, and the borough is virtually identical to the county population in this category. Given these differences, it is difficult to ascertain what, if any, impact there might be. The literature generally indicates that those who depend less on a facility for employment are more likely to see it negatively. If it can be assumed that professional and skilled workers have broader employment opportunities and would therefore depend less on such a facility, they could be expected to be more negative in their perceptions. If this were the case, the likely impact of the differences in occupation between the CAS sample and the county population would create a bias in the direction of less opposition. It is also possible that differences in coding schemes may account for some of the areas of divergence.

Given the differences in the comparison groups, the discrepancies between the county population statistics and the CAS sample statistics are difficult to interpret. However, the differences identified across the variables seem to vary in their potential impacts, which would lead to the conclusion that it is not likely that a consistent and systematic bias is operating. Nonetheless, anytime that there are discrepancies between the population and a sample, some caution is required in interpreting the results.

The CAS Data

All variables except location were operationalized by having individuals respond to the survey items. The operational definitions should be clear from a review of the survey (see Appendix A). Location was operationalized by precoding the response envelopes by sample location (site, borough/township, county).

Simple descriptive statistics were computed for all items on the CAS. Measures of central tendency and dispersion were computed where appropriate. For all other variables, frequency distributions were constructed. The demographic data are presented in Table 11.2, and the responses to the perceptual questions are presented in Table 11.3.

Demographic Profile

The average respondent is approximately 54.0 years of age, with a mode of 45.0 and a standard deviation of 16.33. These results are what would be expected given that the survey targeted adult property owners. Of the respondents, 52 percent are male and 47 percent female (1 percent gave no response to this item). Consistent with the age statistics, 68 percent of the sample is married and has an average of less than one child (0.78) living at home. The vast majority of the sample (approximately 86 percent) report income of $30,000 or above, and more than 30 percent are in the $45,000 and above ranges. Approximately 60 percent of the respondents are employed (94 percent in full-time positions), and of those who are not, 57 percent (368/645) are retired. Ninety-four percent have, at a minimum, a high school diploma or equivalent. Fifty-nine percent have had at least some college-level education, with almost 35 percent having earned a bachelor's or graduate degree. Consistent with those targeted for the sample, the vast majority of the respondents are permanent residents of the county. The mean length of time at the current address is more than 20.0 years (247.48 months), with a standard deviation of 196.53 months (see Table 11.2).

TABLE 11.2 Demographic Variables: CAS Sample

VARIABLE	FREQUENCY/RESPONSES	PERCENT (VALID)
Location—Site		
Location—Borough	389/1659	23.4
Location—County	974/1659	58.7
Age (mean, in years)	53.47 mean/1634 responses	N/A
Gender—Male	859/1641	52.3
Gender—Female	782/1641	47.7
Marital status—Single, never married	155/1641	9.4
Marital status—Married	1129/1641	68.8
Marital status—Separated	19/1641	1.2
Marital status—Divorced	136/1641	8.3
Marital status—Widowed	202/1641	12.3
Mean number of children	0.78/1615 responses	N/A
Income—$15000	225/1482	15.2
Income—$15000–$29999	392/1482	26.5
Income—$30000–$44000	325/1482	21.9
Income—$45000–$59999	213/1482	14.4
Income—$60000<	327/1482	22.1
Employed—Yes	990/1635	60.6
Employed—No	645/1635	39.4
Permanently employed	900/954	94.3
Temporarily employed	54/954	5.7
Part-time employed	148/929	15.9
Full-time employed	781/929	84.1
Occupation—Professional	349/1442	24.2
Occpation—Skilled	167/1442	11.6
Occupation—Unskilled	444/1442	30.8
Occupation—Retired/Disabled	369/1442	25.6
Occupation—Other	113/1442	7.8
Education<High school diploma	97/1630	6.0
Education—Diploma/Equiv.	569/1630	34.9
Education—Some college	396/1630	24.3
Education—Bachelor's degree	292/1630	17.9
Education—Grad/Prof. degree	276/1630	16.9
Length of residence (mean, in months)	461.52 mean, in months/1638 responses	N/A
Permanent resident—Yes	1618/1645	98.4
Permanent resident—No	27/1645	1.6
Length of time at address (mean, in months)	247.48 mean, in months/1642 responses	N/A
Own	1488/1629	91.3
Rent	141/1629	8.7

TABLE 11.3 Perceptual Variables: CAS Sample

VARIABLE	FREQUENCY/RESPONSES	PERCENT (VALID)
Aware of prison—Yes	1555/1635	94.5
Aware of prison—No	90/1635	5.5
Familiar with location of prison—Yes	1552/1635	93.6
Familiar with location of prison—No	83/1635	5.1
Mean miles from prison	7.479 miles/1612	N/A
Security—Minimum	111/1610	6.9
Security—Medium	253/1610	15.7
Security—Maximum	641/1610	39.8
Security—Did not know	605/1610	37.6
Escape—Not very worried	911/1637	55.7
Escape—Somewhat worried	564/1637	34.5
Escape—Very worried	162/1637	9.9
Likely visitor problems—Not very	989/1632	60.6
Likely visitor problems—Somewhat	474/1632	29.0
Likely visitor problems—Very	169/1632	10.4
Personal safety—Not at all worried	918/1644	55.8
Personal safety—Somewhat worried	550/1644	33.5
Personal safety—Very worried	176/1644	10.7
Family safety—Not at all worried	775/1567	49.5
Family safety—Somewhat worried	579/1567	36.9
Family safety—Very much worried	213/1567	13.6
Crime—Decrease	96/1621	5.9
Crime—Remain same	1284/1621	79.2
Crime—Increase	241/1621	14.9
Property values—Fall	399/1607	24.8
Property values—Remain same	1060/1607	66.0
Property values—Rise	148/1607	9.2
Resident employment—Not very likely	311/1633	19.0
Resident employment—Somewhat likely	860/1633	52.7
Resident employment—Very likely	462/1633	28.3
Economy—Bad for economy	101/1602	6.3
Economy—No effect on economy	512/1602	32.0
Economy—Good for economy	989/1602	61.7

TABLE 11.3 Perceptual Variables: CAS Sample (continued)

Public services—Go down	116/1616	7.2
Public services—Remain same	1272/1616	78.7
Public services—Improve	228/1616	14.1
Cost of living—Go down	30/1623	1.8
Cost of living—Same	1328/1623	81.8
Cost of living—Rise	265/1623	16.3
Move—Farther from prison	55/1621	3.4
Move—Out of county	70/1621	4.3
Move—Stay	1496/1621	92.3
Comments—Yes	170/1659	10.2
Comments—No	1489/1659	89.8

Knowledge/Awareness of the Prison

In terms of their knowledge and awareness of the prison, 95 percent of those responding report having been aware of the prison before receiving the survey, and 95 percent are familiar with its location. There is, however, a fair amount of uncertainty about the security level, with 23 percent either misidentifying it as minimum or medium and 37 percent indicating that they do not know (see Table 11.3).

Perceptual Profile

Safety Concerns. Respondents were asked how worried they are about the possibility of a prisoner escaping. Of the 1637 individuals who responded to this item, 56 percent are "not very" worried, 34 percent are "somewhat" worried, and only 10 percent (162) are "very" worried. In response to a question about how likely it is that visitors to the facility will cause problems in the area, 61 percent of the respondents believe it to be "not very" likely, 29 percent see it as "somewhat" likely, and only 10 percent (169) answered "very" likely.

Respondents were also asked how much the introduction of the prison makes them worry about their personal safety and the safety of their family. In regard to personal safety, of the 1,644 who responded, 918 (56 percent) are "not at all" worried, 550 (33 percent) are "somewhat" worried, and only 176 (11 percent) are "very much" worried. The responses were similar for concern for family safety, with a slightly higher percentage (approximately 14 percent) indicating that they are "very much" worried and 37 percent report being "somewhat" worried. When asked about the potential impact on the crime rate, most (1,284, or 79 percent) believe that it will remain the same. Ninety-six (6 percent) responded that the rate will decrease, and 241 (14 percent) report that it will increase (see Table 11.3).

Economic Impact and Quality of Life. Using several different indicators, respondents were asked to assess the potential economic impact of the prison on the county. A substantial majority (1,060, or 66 percent) believe that property values will remain the same. Three hundred and ninety-nine (25 percent) think that they will fall, and 148 (9 percent) believe that they will rise. In assessing the employment potential of the new prison, 19 percent report it to be "not very" likely that county residents will gain employment there, 52 percent consider it to be "somewhat likely," and 28 percent think it "very likely" that the prison will employ local residents. Most respondents are hopeful about the overall economic impact for the county. Sixty-two percent believe that the prison "will be good for the economy," 31 percent responded that there will be no effect, and only 6 percent think that the prison "will be bad" for the local economy. A final economic question relates to the cost of living. More than 80 pcent of the respondents think that there will be no effect, and 16 percent expect it to rise.

The survey also asked how the quality of public services would be affected by the presence of the prison. Most (79%) responded that public services would remain the same. Fourteen percent believe that they will improve, and 7 percent think that the quality will go down. The final question asked whether individuals plan to relocate as a result of the prison's being built. The response choices were to remain in the county but move farther from the prison, to move out of the county altogether, or to stay where they are. Of those who responded to this item (1621), 92 percent plan to stay where they are, and only 4 percent (70) indicate a desire to move out of the county altogether (see Table 11.3).

Summary

From these data, it is clear that, for the sample as a whole, the level of concern over the potential negative impact of SCI Pine Grove on the Indiana County community is quite low. The majority of the residents surveyed are generally neutral in their responses to all 11 of the perceived impact items (see Appendix A, items 17–26). On only two items did the number of respondents perceiving negative impact exceed 15 percent. When asked about the cost of living (item 25), 16 percent believe that it will go up as a result of the prison, and 25 percent believe that property values "will fall" (item 21).

The Weighted CAS: Describing the County

To accommodate key variables, such as distance from the site, a disproportionate sampling strategy was used. Given this disproportionality, to construct a representative view of the county's overall perceptions, it is necessary that the three different location samples be appropriately weighted. To the extent the sample in this study is representative, the weighted aggregate sample indicates what would be expected if all residents of the county had been surveyed. The location samples were weighted by dividing the total number of households in the location by the number of households from that location sample that responded to the survey. This procedure adjusts for both the disproportionality in the original sampling process as well as the differential response rate that was obtained for the three location samples. The total number of households in the site location is 628, and the number of households that responded to the survey is 296. Therefore, the weight is 628/296, or 2.12. There are 9,800 households in Indiana Borough/White Township, and 389 people responded, making the weight 9800/389, or 25.19. The (remainder) of the county contains 21,175 households. Dividing this number by 974 respondents indicates that the county location sample weight is 21.74.

Based on the numbers and rates of responses obtained from the three location samples, if the survey had been mailed to all households in the county (i.e., weighted sample), the expected number of responses would be 13,831 (site = 312; Indiana Borough/White Township = 3,816; county = 9,703). As with the original sample, simple descriptive statistics were computed for all items on the CAS. Weighted measures of central tendency and dispersion were computed where appropriate.

For the purposes of this chapter, it is not necessary or fruitful to describe the results of the weighted sample analysis in detail. Generally, the weighted data indicate that, if all households in the county were to be surveyed, the low levels of concern and negative expectations about the impact of SCI Pine Grove identified through the original sample would likely be even lower and less negative.

Cross-Tabular Analyses: Gender, Income, Education Level, Occupation

To gain some insight into the possible influence of some of the control factors on the perceptions of county residents, cross-tabular analyses were conducted using gender, income, education level, and occupation as independent variables. These variables have been linked to a wide range of beliefs and attitudes in the literature. It is beyond the scope of this chapter to report the results of these analyses in detail, but a general summary of the findings should be instructive.

While cross-tabular analysis does not allow for interpretation of complex interactions or multiple influences at once, the results of the analyses suggest several things. First, it is clear that the perceptions of the respondents are influenced, in relatively complex ways, by a variety of factors, and the saliency of factors may vary depending on the specific type of perception. Second, the variation in patterns of associations and responses would seem to indicate that the respondents generally exhibit high levels of discriminativeness in their perceptions. Third, it seems that gender may be a significant variable in determining perceptions related to safety concerns. (The roles of education and income levels are less clear.) Finally, the diversity of findings from these analyses indicates the utility of further analysis. The results from some specific cross-tabular analyses are discussed in the "Discussion and Conclusion" section.

Comments

Respondents were invited to include written comments as part of the survey. Of the 1,659 total respondents, 170 (10 percent) included comments of some type. While the overall number of respondents offering comments is small, making comments is significantly associated with location. Respondents from the site sample were the most likely to provide comments (17 percent, 50/296), those from the county were next (9 percent, 88/974), and the borough respondents were third (8 percent, 32/389).

The comments ranged from one- or two-word opinions referring to a particular item to detailed editorials. Some were focused specifically on issues pertaining to the prison and some addressed other less related or unrelated issues. Content analysis identified three major themes: (1) hope for jobs for local residents and a positive impact on the economy, (2) fear/concern for neighborhood, family, and personal safety, and (3) anger (or expressed sense of betrayal) at local political leaders for not having been included in the decision-making process. Given the small number of respondents making comments, more detailed analyses were not possible.

Summary of Results

In reviewing the results from the survey, three general findings stand out. First, the level of concern and negative perceptions expressed is rather low overall and does not reach the levels that might be expected from the literature on prison and other LULU siting. As described earlier, the modal response on all 11 perceived impact items is either the most positive or, at the worst, the neutral response category. On only two items does the percentage of respondents indicating the most negative response exceed 15 percent. There are several possible explanations for these outcomes, which are discussed in the following section.

By weighting the location samples, it was possible to estimate the results of a survey that would be sent to every household in the county. From this analysis, it can be concluded that the CAS sample results provide what would be considered a slightly conservative estimate of county concern and negativity. In other words, it is likely that the sample data generally overestimate levels of concern and negative perceptions relative to the entire county.

DISCUSSION AND CONCLUSIONS

Abrams (1988) suggests that the impact of prisons on communities can be assessed in two ways: by examining subjective factors (i.e., attitudes, beliefs, opinions, and perceptions) and/or through the evaluation of objective indicators (e.g., property values, crime rates, employment). Abrams observes that objective factors are mainly used in the promotion of siting a facility, and those offered most in opposition are subjective. Abrams also indicates that subjective considerations, rather than objective information, influence many issues relating to the siting of prisons. Consequently, there is clearly a need to assess community perceptions, a need that has not been adequately addressed in the siting research. The main goal of the CAS was to gauge community opposition and/or support across the entire county by assessing residents' perceptions about the potential impact of SCI Pine Grove.

According to Takahashi and Gaber (1998), facility types with increased potential for environmental impact are viewed more negatively than most human service facilities. Prisons, however, are rated among the most undesirable facility types, along with landfills and factories. What differentiates prisons from other types of human service facilities and creates such strong opposition is the fact that they house members of populations (e.g., drug abusers, people with HIV/AIDS, criminals) who are associated with serious problems. Given concerns about crime and drugs, it is generally believed that negative sentiments about prison siting run strong.

Despite the apparent clarity in the literature on the issue of community reactions to prison siting, closer scrutiny raises questions about the actual level of negative reaction and resistance; none of the sources consulted offers a clear empirical assessment of the extent of the resistance. The uncertainty over levels of negativity and resistance is greatly attributable to the fact that all of the studies identified have been post hoc assessments of community perceptions. No systematically gathered data that represent community perceptions prior to a prison coming on-line were found . This issue is important in interpreting the results of the CAS because there exists no empirically derived benchmark against which to judge the (a)typicality of the level of concern and negative perceptions identified in the Indiana County community.

To the extent that the image of serious and high levels of opposition and concern portrayed in the literature is accurate, the levels encountered in Indiana County are lower than would be expected. In the context of what the DOC might generally anticipate in the siting process, it seems safe to conclude that the concern and negative perceptions exhibited would not exceed expectations. The extent to which they might fall below that expected is not discernible from the information available to the researchers.

Several possible scenarios relating to the findings should be considered:

1. The levels of opposition and negativity portrayed in the literature provide an inaccurate image, and the levels obtained with the CAS are consistent with the actual norm.

2. The levels obtained with the CAS are below the norm. If this is the case, there are three possible explanations: (a) The DOC and community leaders did a good job of working with the community and proactively addressed concerns and allayed fears, (b) the residents of Indiana County were able to make more accurate assessments of the potential impact than have been residents in other communities, and (c) the residents of Indiana County possess unique characteristics that can account for their deviation from the norm.

3. The sample was biased and generated a systematic underestimation of negative perceptions and concerns. Two factors could have created such a sample: A biased procedure could have been used to develop the sample, or a response bias occurred. The response bias would have to take the form of a disproportionate number of residents who are opposed to the prison and see its impact as being mainly negative not responding.

4. Negative reactions were attenuated by the fact that the facility is to house "juveniles." It is possible that a public perception developed that SCI Pine Grove is not the same as another prison because the offenders are "just kids."

Normal Levels of Opposition

There is no way to adequately assess the standard levels of opposition and negative perceptions that community residents express prior to the opening of a prison because no studies that included premeasures of such variables were found. Some studies have found negative attitudes about prisons in surrounding communities (e.g., Carlson, 1992; Abrams et al., 1992; Krause, 1992; Grieco, 1978), but there is no way to know the nature of the preopening attitudes. If the levels of concern and negative perceptions found in this study are actually the norm, it would seem that considerably more has been made out of such issues in the literature than is warranted.

Below Normal Levels of Opposition

Assuming that the results of the CAS indicate lower than normal levels of community concern and opposition, three possible explanations need to be explored.

Because no profiles of the typical prison-siting community or community resident exist, it is not possible to do normative comparisons to assess the congruence of Indiana County and its residents with the norms. It seems likely that aspects of the entire county and the more immediate surrounding communities are both similar and dissimilar to other communities in which prisons have been sited. Like many other prison sites, Indiana County is rural and, as a whole, is economically depressed. Less typically, the more immediate communities contain a substantial percentage of residents with higher than average levels of education and income and greater occupational stability.

These and other characteristics relevant to the CAS sample have been identified as important predictors of reaction to prison siting. Age and education have been found to be important factors in attitudes about prisons and other LULUs (Shichor, 1992; Hamilton, 1985), with objections often coming from those who are younger and more educated than the general population (Hamilton, 1985). It has been concluded that such individuals are better able to ascertain risk and negative impact and are better able to secure livelihoods not connected to the facility (Hamilton, 1985). The age ranges for the three location samples were rather broad, but the mean ages were all in the mid-50s, which, according to Hamilton, would be consistent with lower levels of objections. The education data, however, are not consistent with Hamilton's observations. In the CAS sample, education was found to be inversely and strongly associated with safety concerns and variably associated with perceptions about economic impact.

Dear (1992: 293) identifies income as the "single best predictor," with the most affluent being the least welcoming of a LULU facility. Again, the results from the CAS do not fit this pattern. Income was positively related to several of the economic impact and quality of life variables (i.e., the higher income, the more positive the perceived impact), and variably associated with safety concern variables, with higher income being a bit more associated with greater concern.

Another factor that has been linked to rejection of LULUs is property ownership (Takahashi and Gaber, 1998). The CAS targeted property owners for this reason. Because of this, the percentage of respondents who are not property owners is too small (about 9 percent) to support specific analysis. However, the data are suggestive. The county location sample contains 83 percent of all nonproperty owners who responded, and this location sample is consistently more concerned and negative than is the borough sample, which has the lowest percentage of nonproperty owners.

Shichor (1992) observes that prisons are often sited in low prestige areas. If one looks at the overall economic state of Indiana County, the siting of the prison may appear to be consistent with this observation. However, the proximity of the prison to the county seat and to the largest university in the state system of higher education does raise some interesting questions about the issue of community "prestige."

The last issue relates to the influence of proximity on resident perceptions. Considerable attention has been paid to the importance of this variable in the literature, prompting Dear (1992: 29) to caution that the rule of "closer proximity, more resistance" should never be underestimated. However, considerable fuzziness exists in the literature, with no clear operational definitions or parameters for proximity being provided. Dear (1992) does indicate that the closer residents are to the site, the more likely they are to oppose the facility, and goes on to say that "opposition runs high among those on the same block...two to six blocks away...interest or awareness declines to the point of indifference" (p. 29). Perceptions of proximity are somewhat relative to the nature of the area under study. Certainly, a simple linear model of the impact of proximity is not applicable to the CAS data, but neither is Dear's observation.

In summary, it is not possible to clearly assess the extent to which the residents of Indiana County are different from or similar to residents in other communities where prisons have been sited. The deviations from the findings reported in the literature do raise some questions about the similarity, but other than these discrepancies, there is no compelling reason to assume significant overall differences. In fact, a more tenable conclusion is that the literature on resident perceptions to prison siting is incomplete and that extrapolating too liberally from the literature on other LULUs may not be appropriate. It is also feasible that the way in which the DOC and community leaders handled the siting had some positive impact on resident perceptions.

If the following are true, there may well have been something about the siting process that (positively) impacted the perceptions: (1) the county residents are not somehow unique, (2) their perceived levels of concern and opposition are below the norm and, (3) their perceptions about the potential impact of the prison are relatively consistent with what has been found to actually happen in communities with prisons (see the following discussion). The influence attributable to the types of information that were presented, the timetables for providing information, and other processual variables cannot be estimated from the CAS data. No assessment of the siting process and strategies was carried out to support such analysis.

Sample and Response Bias

The issues relating to sample bias have been discussed elsewhere, but several observations are in order here. Despite the difficulties in comparing the CAS sample with overall county demographics, there do not appear to be differences between the sample and (corresponding components of) the general county population that would systematically bias all of the results. The three differences that appear to hold the greatest potential for biasing the results are the underrepresentation of women in the borough location sample and the overall overrepresentation of individuals in the higher income and education levels. The underrepresentation of women would generally serve to underestimate the levels of concern, especially in the borough sample, whereas the overrepresentations of income and education would likely have the opposite effect. The exact impacts of these biases cannot be measured, nor can the extent to which they might counteract each other be determined.

There is no way to know, without collecting additional data, whether any response bias exists and, if it does, the nature of its impact. There are, however, several issues that relate to this possibility. First, the response rate for the CAS is quite good by most standards. This does not ensure against a bias, but it does make one less likely. Second, conventional wisdom is that, in cases such as this, the most likely bias would be to get a disproportionate number of unhappy residents responding. So, if a response bias does exist, it seems more likely that it would serve to overestimate the level of concern.

Youthful Offenders

As indicated earlier, it is possible that community perceptions were affected by the knowledge that SCI Pine Grove was to house young offenders. The age range of the offenders to be housed at SCI Pine Grove was well publicized. However, on the CAS, no attempt was made to assess this knowledge as a variable, so it is not possible to draw any clear conclusions about the extent of the impact it may have had on community perceptions.

A question was asked about the security level of the facility. The modal response (by a slight margin) was the correct one, with 39.8 percent (641/1610) of the respondents indicating "maximum security." However, a combined 22.6 percent incorrectly identified the facility as either "minimum" or "medium," and 37.6 percent did not know. It is possible that had more residents been aware of the security level, the responses would have reflected a more negative tone overall. It is also possible that knowledge of the offender age range led some people to underestimate the level of security. It is a limitation of this study that this issue cannot be more fully explored from the data.

Specific Findings

Another issue warranting discussion is the fit between the specific results on the perceptual items and the findings on the real impact of prisons on their surrounding communities.

Economic Impact and Quality of Life. The data on economic impact are very consistent across the different studies. In a study comparing prison and no-prison counties, Smykla et al. (1984: 522), found that the counties with prisons exhibited increased levels of "economic and social prosperity" in the form of higher property values, increased retail sales, new businesses, and higher quality of social services. They also cite three earlier studies that reported no adverse impacts on local economies. The perceptions relating to potential economic impact that were reported on the CAS are generally consistent with these findings. Using the results from the weighted sample, 63.0 percent of the respondents would expect that the prison would be good for the local economy and only 5.5 percent would see it as being bad. Similarly, 82 percent expect that there would be no effect on the cost of living, and only 16 percent see the potential for an increase. As for the likelihood that county residents will be employed at the prison, the results indicate a bit more pessimism, with only 30 percent of the respondents falling into the Very Likely category. The expectations about the impact on the quality of public services are consistent with those about economic impact. More than 93 percent of the respondents would be expected to fall into the Stay the Same (79.7 percent) or Improve (13.6 percent) categories. Although these results may underestimate the potential positive impact, they reflect more neutral or optimistic outlooks than negative expectations and pessimism.

One other economic issue and the one that, according to the literature, is typically of greatest concern is the impact on property values (Shichor, 1992; Abrams and Lyons, 1987; Stanley, 1978). In this respect, the residents of Indiana County appear to be no exception. This variable yielded the highest rate of negative responses of all of the perceptual variables. In the weighted sample, almost 23 percent of the respondents would be expected to indicate that property values will fall as a result of the prison, and only 9 percent would anticipate a rise. The data presented in the literature on property values generally focus on objective indicators, not on community perceptions. From these data, it does appear that the perceptions of the county residents are overly pessimistic because it has been generally found that property values do not decline; in fact, they often increase (Shichor, 1992; Abrams and Lyons, 1987; Abrams and Martin, 1987; Smykla et al., 1984). Also Abrams and Lyons (1987) point out that, in cases where property values have fallen, the decline could be linked to strong public opposition to the prison siting. If this is a main factor, it would be expected that declines in property values in this case are unlikely.

One other finding from the literature relating to economic impact is pertinent to this discussion. It has been found that local individuals or groups who are less likely to gain financially from the introduction of a prison (e.g., retirees, those employed in occupations that are not likely to depend on the prison for livelihood) are more likely to object (Shichor, 1992). Cross-tabular analysis yielded significant relationships between Occupation and three variables relating to economic impact (Cost of Living, Impact on the Economy, and Likelihood of Residents Being Employed). These findings do not appear to be totally consistent with the literature. The retirees, who made up approximately 25 percent of the respondents, were not the most negative in their perceptions. Those in the Unskilled occupation category consistently indicated the most negative perceptions concerning potential economic impact, and respondents in the Professional and Skilled occupation categories were the most positive. It should be noted that respondents in the Unskilled occupation category were significantly less likely to be employed than were those in the Professional and Skilled categories (74 percent, 98 percent, and 93 percent, respectively), which seems to be even more confusing.

Safety Concerns. As discussed earlier, common objections to prison siting relate to fears about increasing levels of crime, escapes, and problems being created by the families of the prisoners as they visit or relocate into the area. It has also been found that such fears tend to be higher in small communities with low crime rates (Silas, 1984).

Looking at the weighted sample data, it can be seen that the vast majority of respondents would perceive very little impact at all on the crime rate because only 13 percent believe that it will increase. Concern over escapes is equally low, with an expected 8 percent expressing the highest level of concern and 58 percent being "not very worried at all." The expected findings for concerns over personal safety are virtually identical, with 9 percent being "very much" concerned and 58 percent being "not at all" worried. The percentages for concern over family safety are slightly higher (which is not surprising): 12 percent would be worried "very much" and 52 percent "not at all." Again, no perceptual data are available against which to compare these findings, but the image that is portrayed in the literature seems to indicate that substantially higher levels of fear than these should exist.

As for the indicators of real impact, escapes are generally a very rare occurrence, especially from maximum security facilities. Studies on local crime rates have generally shown that communities with prisons have no higher crime rates than do comparable communities without prisons (Smykla et al., 1984; Abrams and Martin, 1987), and Hawes (1985) found lower crime rates in prison communities. Shichor (1992) reports the studies of Millay (1989), Lidman et al. (1988), Farrington and Parcells (1989), and Caillier and Versteeg (1988). In an assessment of crime rates in a community before and after prison construction, Millay found no significant change. There have, however, been some conflicting findings. In two studies conducted in Washington state, Lidman et al. and Farrington and Parcells found higher crime rates in prison communities. A similar finding is also reported by Caillier and Versteeg in a study of Salem, Oregon. Caillier and Versteeg attribute their findings to release and after-care policies that made it likely that nonresident prisoners would remain in the area to access services.

As for the concern over prisoners' families causing problems in the community, again the vast majority of county residents would be expected to express low levels of concern (9 percent in the Very Likely category). This low level of concern is consistent with the data, which generally identify very little community impact that is attributable to prisoner families (Shichor, 1992).

Conclusions

If it can be assumed that the CAS sample is not significantly biased, it can be concluded that county residents currently hold perceptions about the possible impact of SCI Pine Grove that are generally consistent with objective indicators of real impact reported in the literature. It also appears, although empirically based comparisons are not possible, that the residents of the county may be less negative in their perceptions than might be expected. Carlson (1992) concludes that the most significant factors affecting adverse prison–community relations are the siting process and public relations. If Carlson is correct, it would seem that, as discussed, the low levels of concern and accurate perceptions about prison impact might well be attributable, at least in part, to the way the siting process was conducted.

IMPLICATIONS AND RECOMMENDATIONS

Prisons are not generally listed among additions to a community that bring with them high prestige. They are sited by extralocal entities and, for a variety of reasons, are often unwanted, at least by some segments of the community. Because of these factors, the siting process can (and often does) take on an air of incivility and antagonism (Krause, 1992).

Three general siting strategies have been identified in the literature: early predesignation of land use; closed siting, which includes legal overrides and similar strategies; and open discussion (Sechrest, 1992; Abrams,

1988). Given the extremely limited application of predesignation, the third approach is generally considered to be the most efficacious (Abrams, 1988; Shichor, 1992). Its successful negotiation, however, requires that three sets of issues be addressed: public confidence (i.e., trust), public risk, and power sharing (Abrams, 1988). Shichor (1992) observes that most people are aware of the stigma attached to having a prison in their community, and this awareness can result in feelings of powerlessness and/or a lack of community efficacy. In cases in which a prison is being introduced into a community, there is a general underlying concern over the level of community disruption. This concern is not just about changes occurring but is more focused on the direction of change (Krause, 1992).

As indicated previously, no data that directly address the siting strategies employed were gathered. However, the general results of the CAS do offer some insights about their possible effectiveness. It would seem that the general process for siting SCI Pine Grove would be considered as open discussion. Although there are most certainly some community residents who believe that they were not given any, or at least adequate, input, the process would qualify as having been an open one. It would seem that the DOC and community leadership have done at least a respectable job in addressing the three open discussion issues identified by Abrams (1988). The lack of strong negative perceptions and the overall low levels of concerns would seem to imply a reasonable level of trust in the process and indicate low perceived risk. This interpretation is further supported by the (guarded) optimism about the potential economic impact and the accurate assessment of likely changes in public risk. The issue of power sharing was not assessed with the CAS, but because the affected communities do not express strong negative perceptions, it might be concluded that there is not a pervasive feeling of having been excluded from the process or of having been victimized in some way. It must be kept in mind, however, that these are extrapolations. It is possible that residents may have responded quite differently to direct questions about power sharing. In fact, although not numerous, some responses did include (at times in rather strong language) comments about not being included in the decision-making process. It is also possible that some level of resignation may have already set in because by the time the CAS was administered, the prison was a "done deal."

One recommendation that can be derived from the preceding discussion is that, in the future, efforts should be made to directly assess and systematically monitor aspects of siting processes. Such data would prove useful in identifying those aspects of the siting process that are more and less effective in addressing public concerns and fears. This information could assist in fine-tuning the siting strategies for future facilities and could thereby help to create more cooperative relationships with host communities in both the short and long terms.

REFERENCES

Abrams, K.S. (1988). "Prisons as LULUs: A Sequel, Part 2." *Environmental and Urban Issues,* 15: 24–27.

Abrams, K.S. and Lyons, W. (1987). "Impact of Correctional Facilities on Land Values and Public Safety." North Miami, FL: FAU-FIV Joint Center for Environmental and Urban Problems.

Abrams, K.S. and Martin, A. T. (1987). "Prisons as LULUs: A Sequel." *Florida Environmental and Urban Issues,* 14: 18–21.

Abrams, K.S. et al. (1985). "The Socioeconomic Impacts of State Prison Siting on the Local Community." Joint Center for Environmental and Urban Problems, Florida International University.

Abrams, K.S. et al. (1992). "Issues in Siting Correctional Facilities" (An Informational Brief). Available at www.nicic.org/pubs/1992/010591.pdf.

Babbie, E. (1989). *The Practice of Social Research* (5th ed.). Belmont, CA: Wadsworth.

Bureau of Justice Statistics. (1997). *Census of State and Federal Correctional Facilities, 1995.* Washington, DC: U.S. Government Printing Office.

Bureau of Justice Statistics. (1999). "Corrections Statistics." Available at http://www.ojp.uddoj.gov/bjs/correct.htm.

Carlson, K. A. (1988). "Understanding Community Opposition to Prison More Citing: More Than Fear and Finances." *Corrections Today,* 50: 84–90.

Carlson, K. A. (1991). "What Happens and What Counts: Resident Assessments of Prison Impacts on Their Communities." *Humboldt Journal of Social Relations,* 17(1,2): 211–237.

Carlson, K. A. (1992). "Doing Good and Looking Bad: A Case Study of Prison/Community Relations." *Crime & Delinquency,* 38(1): 56–69.

Dear, M. (1992). "Understanding and Overcoming the NIMBY Syndrome." *Journal of the American Planning Association,* 58(3): 288–300.

Grieco, A. L. (1978). "New Prisons: Characteristics and Community Reaction." *Quarterly Journal of Corrections,* 2: 55–60.

Guest, A.M. and Lee, B.A. (1983). "Sentiment and Evaluation as Ecological Variables." *Sociological Perspectives,* 26: 159–184.

Hamilton, L. C. (1985). "Concern About Toxic Wastes: The Demographic Predictors." *Sociological Perspectives,* 28: 463–486.

Hawes, J. A. (1985). *Cities with Prisons: Do They Have Higher or Lower Crime Rates?* Sacramento, CA: Senate Office of Research.

Krause, J.D. (1992). "The Effects of Prison Siting Practices on Community Status Arrangements: A Framework Applied to the Siting of California State Prisons." *Crime & Delinquency,* 38(1): 27–55.

Maxim, P. and Plecas, D. (1983). "Prisons and Their Perceived Impact on the Local Community: A Case Study." *Social Indicators Research,* 13: 39–58.

McShane, M.D., Williams, F.P. III, and Wagoner, C.P. (1992). "Prison Impact Studies: Some Comments on Methodological Rigor." *Crime & Delinquency,* 38(1): 105–120.

Pennsylvania Juvenile Court Judges Commission. (1996). The Juvenile Act. 42 PA C.S. Sec. 6301. et. seq. Harrisburg, PA: Pennsylvania Juvenile Court Judges Commission.

Redman, C. L. (1974). *Archeological Sampling Strategies.* (An Addison-Wesley Module in Anthropology No. 55). New York: Addison-Wesley.

Rogers, G. O.and Haimes, M. (1987). "Local Impact of a Low-Security Federal Correctional Institution." *Federal Probation,* 51(3): 28–34.

Sechrest, D. K. (1992). "Locating Prisons: Open Versus Closed Approaches to Siting." *Crime & Delinquency,* 38(1): 88–104.

Shichor, D. (1992). "Myths and Realities in Prison Siting." *Crime & Delinquency,* 38(1): 70–87.

Silas, F.A. (1984). "Not in My Neighborhood." *American Bar Association Journal,* 70(27): 27–29.

Smykla, J. O., Cheng, D. C., Ferguson, C. E., Trent, C., French, B., and Waters, A. (1984). "Effects of a Prison Facility on the Regional Economy." *Journal of Criminal Justice,* 12: 521–539.

Stanley, C.E. (1978). *The Impact of Prison Proximity on Property Values in Green Bay and Waupun, Wisconsin.* Milwaukee, WI: Wisconsin Division of Corrections and Bureau of Facilities Management.

Takahashi, L. M. and Gaber, S. L. (1998). "Controversial Facility Siting in the Urban Environment: Resident and Planner Perceptions in the United States." *Environment and Behavior,* 30(2): 184–215.

This project was supported by funding from and in cooperation with the Pennsylvania Department of Corrections and Secretary Martin Horne. The authors would also like to acknowledge the support of Dana Henry and the Indiana County Chamber of Commerce and to thank Dr. Chris Zimmerman, Dawna Komorosky, and Kraig Kiehl of the Pine Grove Project Office at Indiana University of Pennsylvania for their assistance.

APPENDIX A

Pine Grove Prison Community Survey

Please answer the questions below by either writing your response on the line or by checking the appropriate box.

1) **What is your age in years?**_____

2) **Gender**
   ( ) Male   ( ) Female

3) **Please indicate your marital status**
   ( ) Single, never married
   ( ) Married
   ( ) Separated
   ( ) Divorced
   ( ) Widowed

4) **How many children currently live with you?** _____

5) **Please estimate your annual household income for 1997.**
   ( ) less than $10,000
   ( ) $10,000–$24,999
   ( ) $25,000–$50,000
   ( ) over $50,000

6) **Are you employed?**
   ( ) Yes   ( ) No
   If yes:
     a) Is your job
       ( ) Permanent   ( ) Temporary
     b) Do you work
       ( ) Part time   ( ) Full time

7) **What is your occupation?**
   _____

8) **Which category best describes the highest level of education that you have completed?**
   ( ) Less than high school diploma
   ( ) High school diploma or equivalent
   ( ) Some college
   ( ) Bachelor's degree
   ( ) Graduate degree

9) **How long have you lived in Indiana County?**
   Years _____   Months _____

10) **Are you a permanent resident of Indiana County?**
    ( ) Yes   ( ) No

11) **How long have you lived at this address?**
    Years _____   Months _____

12) **Do you own or rent the property at this address?**
    ( ) Own   ( ) Rent

13) **Before you received this survey, were you aware that the PA Department of Corrections had selected Indiana County as the location for a new prison?**
    ( ) Yes   ( ) No

Please use the enclosed map to answer questions 14 and 15.

14) **Are you familiar with where the prison will be located?**
    ( ) Yes   ( ) No

15) **As accurately as you can, estimate in miles how far you live from the location of the new prison**

_____ miles

( ) Cannot estimate, do not know where it is at all.

Please answer questions 16 through 26 on the back of the survey.

16) **What level of security best describes the new prison?**

( ) Minimum security
( ) Medium security
( ) Maximum security
( ) Don't know

17) **How worried are you about an inmate escaping from the prison?**

( ) Not worried at all
( ) Somewhat worried
( ) Very worried

18) **How likely is it that persons coming to Indiana County to visit inmates will cause problems in the local community?**

( ) Not very likely
( ) Somewhat likely
( ) Very likely

19) **Does the new prison being built in the county make you worry about**

a) **your personal safety**
( ) Not at all
( ) Somewhat
( ) Very much

b) **the safety of your family**
( ) Not at all
( ) Somewhat
( ) Very much

20) **What effect will the prison have on crime in Indiana County?**

( ) Crime will decrease
( ) Crime will stay about the same
( ) Crime will increase

21) **How will the prison affect property values in the Indiana County area?**

( ) Property values will fall
( ) Property values will stay about the same
( ) Property values will rise
( ) Unable to decide

22) **How likely is it that current residents of Indiana County will be employed at the prison?**

( ) Not likely
( ) Somewhat likely
( ) Very likely

23) **Overall, how do you think the prison will affect the economy of Indiana County?**

( ) It will be bad for the economy
( ) It will have no impact on the economy
( ) It will be good for the economy

24) **How do you think the prison will affect the quality of public services in the County?**

( ) The quality will go down
( ) The quality will stay about the same
( ) The quality will improve

25) **How do you think the prison will affect the cost of living in Indiana County?**

( ) The cost of living will go down
( ) The cost of living will stay about the same
( ) The cost of living will rise

26) **As a result of the prison locating in Indiana County, which of the following do you think that you are more likely to do?**

( ) Remain in the county, but move farther from the prison
( ) Move out of the county
( ) Stay where you are

Thank you for your participation. Feel free to offer any comments you might have on a separate sheet of paper.

chapter 12

Building Local Networks
A Guide for Jail Administrator Leadership

DAVE KALINICH
BRUCE BIKLE
Grand Valley State University

Introduction

Jails are complex systems. Jails confine both pretrial and sentenced offenders (Carlson and Garret, 1999). The population is typically made up of the economic underclass, many of whom have health and substance abuse problems that must be addressed by the jail staff (Irwin, 1985). Over the years, the number of inmates with mental health problems has increased, making control of inmates more difficult (Jerrell and Komisaruk, 1991). The majority of "fresh arrests" brought into the jail manifest recent use of drugs or alcohol, making the potential for suicide among jail inmates high. Detention of individuals is usually short, especially for pretrial inmates, creating, on a regular basis, a new group of inmates with a new set of problems for staff to address (Kerle, 1999).

    Jail personnel are faced with controlling a number of tasks. First and foremost are controlling cell blocks and providing a safe environment. Extra attention and effort must be expended to control mentally ill and

Shortly after lights out one night, 20 inmates, carrying their bedrolls, quietly exited their jail through a door into a darkened alley. It was not an escape. Two deputies accompanied them as they quietly moved down the alley and across the street to the old police lockup that had been closed by the city. The 20 inmates were lodged there until the morning inmate count had been taken in the jail. By "sneaking" 20 inmates into the condemned lockup from the jail, the court-mandated population cap had been met for yet another day (Kalinich and Klofas, 1988). This incident took place more than two decades ago, but it is a good description of the creative skills that jail administrators often applied in managing the internal environment of the jail system when they were bettered by external forces beyond their control. It also summarizes the lack of leadership skills that many administrators have exhibited in dealing with forces and constituents in the system's external environment. Moreover, this tale exhibits the paradox that jail administrators face as they are held accountable for the conditions of their jails but lack any formal authority or influence with agencies and individuals that affect jail conditions and resources.

potentially suicidal inmates. In addition, inmates must be fed, clothed, taken to and from the local courts, and provided with visitation privileges. This list of tasks does not consider food preparation services, physical plant maintenance and repair, laundry, property room storage, and other more mundane but extremely important functions that add to the complexity of managing a jail.

In spite of the responsibilities jails have, the local jail is often one of the least understood of local government agencies. In spite of the complexities involved in managing jails, local jails often get no respect from executives and staff of other criminal justice agencies. Jail administrators have been content to accept the second class status of their work. The historic emphasis on the law enforcement function of the office of local sheriff has given jail administration a secondary priority (Poole and Pogrebin, 1988; Kerle, 1991). The inferior role of jail administration is also manifested in the passive role the jail system has traditionally played within the criminal justice system and with local political entities. This is especially made clear by the irony that local courts use jails as a place to store inmates during their judicial processing. On the other hand, state and federal courts have found jails to be subjecting inmates to "cruel and unusual punishment" when the jails have been overcrowded (Allen and Simonsen, 1998: 528), and jails have been subjected to an array of civil suits for conditions that were a result of inadequate funding by local governments. In other words, jails have been overutilized and underfunded and have been blamed and punished as scapegoats for these problems. Accepting this blame is in part the result of a jail administrator's inability to manage the external environment. As in the example at the beginning of the chapter, the struggle to deal with this paradox has been met by attempting to manage external pressures internally . The ability to manage external forces to the benefit of the jail starts with understanding the importance of and commitment to the jail's role. In addition, skills in dealing with the individuals and groups that impact, or could impact the jail, need to be developed and continuously honed.

This chapter discusses the importance for jail administrators of building bridges to the community. In addition, it provides information on building relationships with key actors in the criminal justice system and community that can impact the conditions and operations of a local jail. Specific information is provided on how to connect with and benefit from individuals and groups on both formal and informal levels. The chapter focuses on the jail administrator as the link between the jail and its community and his or her need to exhibit leadership in the community and in the jail. (As an elected official, the local sheriff is also linked to the political system but perhaps has an advantage over the jail administrator in building bridges to the community. Local sheriffs can play a liasion role on behalf of the jail.)

CHARACTERISTICS OF NETWORKS

Building formal and informal networks with key actors outside the jail system is critical to managing the external environment. A *network* is a group of individuals who interact on a regular basis to assist each other and are bound by common values and activities (Stojkovic, Kalinich, and Klofas, 1998). Networks form for social or professional purposes. Professionally based networks often become social in nature over a period of time. That is, the mutual aid and interactions between members in addition to their shared values and activities often tend to create friendships among the members. Members of networks assist each other on a number of tasks or problems in an ad hoc manner. As a result of the network members' continual exchange of assistance, they typically communicate effectively and efficiently with one another. Network members work in a well-established bond of mutual group trust and understanding toward a purpose from which they all benefit. The members may hold positions of some authority and assist each other in personal and professional development. The group's contribution to its own survival and prosperity is linked to the contribution the group makes to its larger organization. Networks interested in production, innovation, and the expediting of tasks are common in organizations. The focus of this chapter is on networks formed to enhance productivity.

Networks are particularly crucial in systems whose common process is shared by units or agencies that are not structurally linked together. The criminal justice system, of course, is a system that processes offenders from arrest to incarceration and release and is comprised of units that are not linked together by any formal mechanism. In fact, law enforcement and the judicial system work in different ways to protect the rights of individuals. Typically, each component of the system functions with little regard for the problems of the others, and no formal linking mechanism exists to require actors in one component to work in a cooperative manner with actors in other components.

Moreover, the local criminal justice system, unlike the state and federal system, is readily visible and vulnerable to the community and its political input. Most jails and their administrators are vulnerable to inputs from law enforcement and the judicial system and are easy marks for members of the community and local political leaders. Jail administrators, however, typically have no mechanism to reach back to actors in law enforcement, the judicial system, the political process, or the community. Administrators of local jails, therefore, need to build formal and informal networks with key actors in law enforcement, the courts, social service agencies, and the community.

The most important ingredient of a productive network is *actual or perceived exchange* (Stokjovic, Kalinich, and Klofas, 1998). That is, members will help other members expecting that they will receive assistance in return. The exchange is not necessarily quid pro quo; however, often a return of assistance is expected when necessary. For example, exchange of information on offenders networks probation and parole officers with law enforcement officers. This networking may lead law enforcement officers to enforce curfews on particular parolees at the request of parole officers.

The second ingredient of a good network is *shared values and beliefs* among members. Repeating our example, if parole and probation officers have philosophies and values that differ from those of law enforcement officers, they may not be able to cooperate. If parole officers have a strong treatment orientation and local police officers take a hard line against paroled offenders, it is not likely that the two groups will work well together.

Trust among members of a network is also an important ingredient. One author, working as a parole officer, had built a relationship of trust with local police by manifesting an understanding of their tasks and constraints and being open about information they were seeking. As a result of this trust, local police made a reasonable exchange by ignoring particular misdemeanors by parolees whom the parole officers identified as doing well. As the trust factor grew stronger, the police officers asked the author if they should pursue or drop charges.

The last element, especially important in informal networks, is *constant interaction and social exchanges between members*. In other words, it is critical to socialize with individuals outside our professions as well as work-specific colleagues.

BUILDING FORMAL NETWORKS

Formal networks come together readily in a crisis or when a number of individuals have a stake in a problem. For example, a county in the Midwest had a severe jail overcrowding problem. The jail had been built using an old linear design that decreases the ability of staff to supervise inmates. Several inmates had been brutalized rather severely by fellow inmates, leading to lawsuits and rather large civil judgments against the facility. To meet the crisis and provide better supervision, staff were assigned to double the corrections office complement. This approach resulted in dramatic increases of overtime pay to correctional officers. This increase in expenditures, in addition to the litigation, was brought to the attention of the public by the media. Because elections were on the horizon, judges, the prosecutor's office, and county commissioners had a stake in the jail problem. A formal network was established, consisting of the jail administrator, judge, chief probation officer, members of community corrections programs, the county government, media, other significant community members, and a consultant.

This network undertook to help pretrial detainees be released on bond more often and more easily. In addition, members made innovative changes. Judges, who typically spend two-thirds of their time on civil cases and one-third on criminal cases reallocated their efforts and spent two-thirds of their time on criminal cases and one-third on civil cases. This change attempted to reduce the total number of jail days that offenders spend awaiting disposition of their cases, thus reducing the jail population. The interaction between the jail administrator and probation department uncovered and corrected a delay in the investigation process. Presentence investigations were taking longer to complete than considered reasonable and were holding up the sentencing of current inmates. The problem resulted from the probation officers' practice of interviewing inmates in the cell areas. Such abusive language was directed at the probation officers during the interviews that only two officers were willing to conduct them. Hence, these inmate presentence investigations were slowed down and behind schedule. When the probation department identified this problem, the jail administrator provided an interview room. Additional probation officers were assigned to do the investigations, reducing production time dramatically and avoiding lengthy stays in jail for the inmates.

Perhaps the most interesting aspect of this situation is that a number of individuals were forced to learn about the complexity and needs of the local jail. In a micro sense, a county commissioner who did not understand the need to pay double time to additional staff on visitation day (Sunday) accepted the jail administrator's invitation to observe the visitation process. After watching, the commissioner fully understood the need to bring in the additional staff. For the longer term, the political and community leaders decided that a new jail was necessary. By being part of the network, they became part of the system and, through their experience, began to understand the problems of running a local jail. It is often through experience, rather than logic and dialogue, that individuals can overcome their biases. Therefore, getting the proper people actively involved through networking can benefit a jail administrator.

MEMBERS OF THE NETWORK

Local Probation Departments

The jail administrator is responsible for taking the initiative in networking. He or she can proactively develop a working relationship with probation and parole staff or their chief administrators. Proactive interaction with local probation departments is an immediate step in controlling the inmate population, at least at the margins. In addition to improving the jail facilities used by probation staff for conducting presentence investigations, jail administrators can work with probation departments, for example, in targeting individuals who are appropriate candidates for pretrial programming or alternative intermediate sanctions such as house arrest or community service (Center for Effective Public Policy, 1993). Such initiatives relieve jail crowding and move local criminal justice systems toward a sentencing continuum not totally dependent on incarceration (Tonry and Hamilton, 1995).

Developing or identifying shared values between probation and parole officers and jail staff is not difficult because they are all criminal justice professionals and have common interests in managing criminal defendants and offenders. Both groups also share the same goals—protecting the public and contributing in some way to the justice process. As such, they work within the same constraints, are subjected to similar codes of conduct and ethics, and often share similar frustrations. The issue is to give these groups of professionals an opportunity to work together, relate on a social and professional basis, and recognize the extent to which they share values.

Trust results from consistent and reliable interactions between the jail administrator and local probation and parole administrators and jail, probation, and parole staff. In addition, mutual understanding and respect for the duties of all parties involved can emerge over time, adding a significant ingredient to the development of mutual trust. Perhaps most important, an active, productive, and positive working relationship between jail and probation staff and administrators can assist the jail administrator in building a network relationship with judges and members of the prosecuting attorney's office.

Judges and Prosecutors

It is difficult to network directly with judges and members of the prosecutor's office. For the most part, judges and prosecutors perceive their offices as independent of and unrelated to the jail. Jail staff deliver inmates to the court for hearings. Judges have the authority to ensure that they do this in a timely and secure manner. Therefore, they have no incentive to enter into exchange relationships with the jail.

Similarly, members of the prosecutor's staff have no incentives to enter into an exchange relationship with a jail administrator. In fact, prosecutors may benefit from the plea bargaining process if pretrial detainees remain in custody and under poor conditions for a long period of time. Under such conditions, pretrial detainees are more likely to accept a plea bargain than their counterparts who are free on bond. Moreover, prosecutors are satisfying their political constituency and playing out their role by jailing large numbers of offenders. As a result, jail administrators must rely on the good will of judges and prosecutors to gain their assistance. However, the opportunity for jail administrators to build personal relationships with judges and prosecutors is severely limited. Social and professional status differences separate jail administrators from judges and prosecutors. However, jail administrators might exert influence with judges and prosecutors using the indirect avenues of influence offered by local probation officers, community leaders, and the local sheriff.

Judges are always anxious to keep their dockets on schedule, and jail administrators can contribute to a more efficient judicial process by assisting the probation department. For example, jail administrators could simply ask probation officers who have influence with the judges to develop methods to reduce the use of jails. Judges can do this by reducing sentences for misdemeanor offenders, reviewing bail bond decisions, scrutinizing requests by defense attorneys for continuances, and applying intermediate sanctions, ranging from intensive supervised probation to community service (Tonry and Hamilton, 1995). This is no guarantee that judges will take measures to reduce jail use. However, if they do not know that their local jail is being overused and are not asked to consider the problem by a credible source, there is little chance that they will take any action in solving the problem.

Community Leaders

Community leaders often have influence with judges and prosecutors, especially if they share membership in the same political party. Community leaders can also influence the political climate to the benefit of the jail system. Building jails, for example, needs the support of community political elites who, in turn, influence policymakers and the community at large.

Community leaders are often activists or members of politically elite groups and are usually known in the community at large. They frequently represent and lead community organizations such as church groups, unions, and prominent well-established business organizations. Often community leaders seek opportunities to take an active role in influencing change and improvement in government entities. The jail administrator must network to identify community leaders with interest in criminal justice issues. The next step is to make direct contact with these key individuals and recruit them as part of the network. The exchange in this relationship is symbolic and related to social status because it offers community leaders an opportunity to increase their influence base and stature in the community. The return in the exchange is the influence over aspects of the jail system that the jail administrator may have to give the leader(s) who opt to become part of the network.

The Media

Community leaders are not likely to become activists for institutions or causes that suffer negative reputations or are seemingly lost causes. Leaders, like the public in general, often get their information about the local jail from the media. Typically, the news media look for and publicize the negative side of criminal justice issues. Often, the news is based upon preconceived notions about the criminal justice system rather than first-hand knowledge. This creates reporting based upon incorrect inferences (Kappeler, Blumberg, and Potter, 2000: 4–7). Moreover, a well-managed jail does not provide exciting news; positive reports about the local jail are rare. It is important, therefore, for the jail administrator to bring key members of the media into the network to provide accurate and occasionally positive reporting.

It is possible for jail administrators to build a positive and productive relationship with members of the media that includes some form of exchange, shared values, and trust. The return from an exchange relationship with the media is accurate reporting of jail conditions and problems. Although airing problems publicly may seem a frightening prospect, the payoff includes public knowledge about the extent to which jail problems are a function of the operations and attitudes of agencies and political entities that affect the jail system. Such reporting can assist jail administrators in lobbying for assistance and cooperation from external agencies and political leaders. The cost in the exchange is opening the jail system to the media and providing reporters with hard facts about the good and the bad. For example, it is poor public health policy to allow inmates with infectious diseases to be released from jail untreated. In this case, lack of treatment can be reported in a public health context. Having the media frame inadequate medical treatment as a shared problem will facilitate the jail administrator's ability to get assistance from external sources in resolving the problem.

Shared values and trust can develop after a pattern of exchange has been established. The expression and content of shared values with media members or other civilians will be different from that with other fellow criminal justice practitioners. For example, the curt terminology criminal justice practitioners often use when referring to offenders will not likely be acceptable to civilians. However, the jail administrator and media member probably will share concerns for law and order, public safety, and good government. Trust will develop over time, but only if both parties to the exchange keep their commitment and avoid revaluing the currency of the exchange.

Defense Attorneys

Defense attorneys have a peripheral stake in the jail. Many of their clients are jail inmates, and they must use the jail facilities to work directly with their clients. Although defense attorneys have an almost absolute right to interview their clients privately, 24 hours a day, seven days a week, they must depend on the cooperation of the jail administrator and staff for the conditions of their meeting places (Inciardi, 1996: 370–74). Jail administrators can create a positive work environment for the attorneys and their clients by providing them a well-furnished and comfortable office. Having friendly, courteous, and helpful jail staff who deliver inmate clients to their attorneys in a timely manner is another positive step. Conversely, the jail staff can give the bare necessities, making attorneys' visits to the jail unpleasant or even difficult. However, jails may be forced to provide poor service to defense attorneys and their clients because of inadequate or antiquated physical conditions, overcrowding, and/or understaffing. This situation may place defense attorneys and their clients at a disadvantage in the plea bargaining process. As stated earlier, conditions in the jail can impact an inmate's willingness to accept a plea bargain offered by the prosecutor. However, comfortable and safe jail conditions can dramatically reduce the attractiveness of a plea bargain.

Ideally, defense attorneys who have stature within the local political culture and with key actors in the criminal justice system should be recruited as members of the jail administrator's network. An attorney who has stature within the local political arena and who is considered credible by governmental and criminal justice policymakers can have a great deal of influence on individuals and groups beyond the jail administrator's sphere of influence.

Community Mental Health

Numerous social service agencies share clients with the criminal justice system, especially the jail. An increasing number of jail inmates need mental health assistance. Research also suggests that the mental health of normal individuals often deteriorates as a result of their incarceration (Steadman et al., 1991). It is not the norm, however, for social service agencies to take an active role in working with inmates. For example, clients of community mental health agencies are still considered clients when they are in jail, but mental health workers usually do not follow up on them. Although parole and probation officers check local jails' daily booking sheets to identify any of their clients, mental health workers do not follow this routine.

Overall, the relationship between jail staff and social service professionals has not been productive and often has become adversarial in nature. Criminal justice and mental health agencies have a history of passing the responsibility for mentally ill criminal offenders to each other. Mental health agencies argue that offenders with mental health problems should be handled as criminals, while criminal justice agencies argue that offenders are ill and should be under the care and control of mental health agencies (Jerrell and Komisaruk, 1991). The adversarial relationship is understandable because mental health workers are reluctant to handle individuals caught in criminal activity, particularly of a violent nature. Conversely, criminal justice agencies, especially jails, typically are not equipped to treat and manage individuals suffering from mental illness.

The fact is that criminal justice and mental health agencies have a shared responsibility for mentally ill inmates. Working relationships and blending of the professional territories have developed in many areas. In Michigan, the State Department of Mental Health took the initiative in bringing jail and mental health staff together to work out cooperative approaches to manage and treat incarcerated mentally ill clients. Moreover, many large urban jails employ mental health staff or have in-house psychiatric services delivered by private firms working under contractual agreements. Networking with mental health agents and developing strategies to provide services to mentally ill inmates are possible.

Many jurisdictions lack adequate treatment for mentally ill inmates. In these cases, it is incumbent upon the jail administrator to reach out and include mental health professionals in his or her network. The exchange in the relationship between jails and mental health agencies is readily apparent. The jail benefits as mentally ill inmates who are provided with proper medication and a modicum of counseling become more manageable during

confinement. In the longer term, community mental health workers benefit by maintaining their clients' treatment program while they are incarcerated. If mentally ill clients are not treated while in custody, the progress
they made prior to incarceration may be eradicated. This gap in treatment
has been successfully bridged when jail administrators take the initiative
to build positive personal and professional relationships with mental health
professionals.

Political Leaders

Networking with local elected officials is a difficult task. As a rule, local
government officials give jails a low priority for funding (Mays and Thompson, 1991). Their primary role is to ration and allocate their governmental
unit's budget. In the budgeting process, they hear pleas and arguments
from all local governmental agencies for a bigger slice of the budgetary pie.
As elected officials, they are forced to deal with interest groups that argue
for more services in almost all areas. Moreover, it is important politically
to promote services that are readily visible to community members and
have an immediate and positive impact on the community. Expending
funds for jails is not popular among voters because of their attitude toward
offenders. They typically react negatively to increased funding for jails at
the expense of other services they view as more important. Hence, elected
governmental officials give a high funding priority to roads, parks, and
recreation, and even law enforcement, but keep a tight reign on funds allocated to the jail. The exchange in this relationship is the ability for the jail
to save money in the long run by receiving adequate funds or funding
increases in the short run to support a facility that is operating at a safe
and secure level.

    This exchange is difficult to sell to budget makers because all agen-
cies use this tactic to some degree. Moreover, it is difficult for elected
officials to believe they can convince voters of the long-term worth of a
short-term investment in their jail. However, the jail administrator has an
obligation to present the facts in an understandable manner and show a
clear link between conditions that must be improved and the potential
costs if conditions are not changed. For example, understaffing can lead to
environments prone to assaults among inmates and on officers, resulting
in expensive lawsuits. Also, physical plant problems may lead to escapes,
which, in turn, can cause embarrassment to the local officials as well as to
the jail (Mays and Thompson, 1991). Jail administrators need to demonstrate that they have made good faith and extensive efforts to manage
problems within their existing budget. Being manifestly frugal with funds
will bring jail administrators into the realm of shared values with elected
governmental officials.

Perhaps the best path to influencing local officials is through second-ary networking. Community leaders working within the jail administrator's network have the credibility and stature to influence active members of local political elites and elected governmental officials. Also, accurate media reporting of conditions within a jail can give officials public legitimacy to increase the size of the jail budget.

CREATING JAIL BOARDS: FORMALIZING THE NETWORK

In this section, the formation of jail boards is highlighted to illustrate a model that can be used to formalize existing networks. The first case study is an example of a committee formed out of crisis and the second is an example of proactive planning.

Genessee County

Genessee County,[1] which includes Flint, Michigan, formed a committee to deal with dramatic problems at the local jail. The committee was formed through the initiative of a member of the county board of commissioners, an elected official. The jail was an aging traditional linear-supervision facility built in the 1940s with an annex added in the late 1950s. It had its array of maintenance problems, and the structural changes brought about by the annex made the movement of inmates and corrections officers diffi-cult. During the late 1970s, the jail population expanded at a surprising pace that required double, triple, and often quadruple housing of inmates in cells constructed to house one inmate. This overcrowding added to the inability of officers to properly supervise and control inmates.

As a result of inadequate supervision of inmates and officers, inmate-on-inmate and inmate-on-officer, and officer-on-inmate assaults had in-creased dramatically. Incidents of inmate suicides and assaults on inmates led to costly lawsuits. In one particular incident, inmates severely and repeatedly subjected a handicapped and mentally challenged inmate to brutal and humiliating treatment. This activity went unnoticed by officers for a substantial period of time. The resulting lawsuit was expensive and received notoriety in the local media. Given the inmate's physical and men-tal condition, the public was outraged, and the jail and the county govern-ment suffered public embarrassment as well as the cost of the lawsuit. The

---

[1]Based on one author's direct experience with the jail system during the mid-1980s.

initial reaction was to increase supervision by assigning overtime to officers, causing overtime wages to skyrocket. In this situation, local governmental officials had no choice but to become actively involved in their jail.

The jail oversight committee was formed to develop solutions to reduce the jail population. Committee membership included a local elected official, the assistant county comptroller, defense attorneys, the local sheriff, members of the judiciary and prosecutor's staff, the local probation department administrator, community corrections advocates, a consultant, and community leaders from the private sector. Members of the media were not formal members; however, they were always informed of the meeting schedules and encouraged to attend. Forming the committee took considerable effort in spite of or perhaps because of the problems the jail faced. However, the commissioner who took the initiative and leadership role persisted and brought the group together to oversee and assist the jail.

The committee was able to facilitate substantial efforts in reducing jail use. The committee did not have any form of central authority over the criminal justice system, but it brought ideas to the table and, through its stature and influence, was able to support and legitimize the use of established methods to reduce the jail population. New programs were implemented, including the use of a vacant motel for housing minimum security inmates. Also, pretrial diversion programs were started, along with programs that facilitated the use of personal recognizance release for pretrial inmates. Presentence reports were expedited to move inmates from the jail to the state department of corrections more rapidly, and judges also altered their dockets. Although these efforts reduced the inmate population, the jail remained overcrowded and adequate supervision of inmates remained a problem.

To provide better inmate supervision, video and audio devices and other technological advances were installed in cellblocks. For example, officers were required to punch their time cards in a clock to verify that they made their cellblock rounds on schedule.

It became apparent that the jail's physical plant had deteriorated dramatically over the years. The almost tripling of the inmate population had stressed plumbing, food service operations, laundry facilities, and so on. Basic upkeep and repair in cells were almost impossible. The elevators operated capriciously, and locks began to malfunction. Members of the jail oversight committee and media representatives realized that a new jail was needed. Subsequently, collective efforts were made to plan and construct a new generation jail.

This case highlights the value of bringing a group of professional and community leaders together into a formal network. The members of the oversight committee were influential and credible. Moreover, as committee members took a responsible role in solving problems faced by the jail, they began to understand the jail's operations, limits, and needs. Overall, the committee made a good faith effort to continue to use the current facility.

Having failed in their venture to reduce jail use to a level manageable within the old facility, the committee members were convinced that building a new jail was inevitable.

King's County

The second case study of King County, Washington, provides an excellent example of taking a proactive approach to coordinate a county's justice policy, share information and ideas, and work together toward common goals. King County has a population of more than 1.6 million and is the twelfth largest county in the country. Its jail population is relatively low, however. The rationed use of jail space is the result of cooperation and coordination between key actors in the criminal justice system and community leaders. Moreover, the cooperative efforts have created a safe and efficient local criminal justice system.

Coleman (1998) summarizes the efforts and success of King County's cooperative venture. The county found the impetus for a cooperative system of criminal justice planning with the opening of the new direct supervision jail. This jail, with its large capacity, was filled and became overcrowded shortly after it was opened. This fact motivated the county executive to put together a panel of criminal justice administrators, local elected officials, and community leaders to address this problem. The original charge to the panel was to develop practical, legal, and financially feasible recommendations to reduce overcrowding and unnecessary utilization of the jail without endangering community safety. The group also had the responsibility to develop recommendations for long-term plans to allocate jail beds to the 32 municipalities served by the King County jail.

The first series of meetings focused on sharing information, especially statistical data concerning crime, arrest, adjudication, and conviction trends for each jurisdiction that would impact jail use. Each participating agency also had an opportunity to discuss how it planned to deal with future trends. The interchange of information and dialogue broke down interpersonal barriers and preconceived notions and fears and set the tone for the resulting collaborative efforts. The committee made more that 40 recommendations for managing jail use. It also recommended that the committee be made a permanent steering and planning unit for the King County criminal justice system.

Coleman (1998) reports that over the years, King County has designed and opened new jail facilities and, to control jail use, has developed diversion programs for mentally ill offenders, misdemeanor offenders addicted to drugs and alcohol, and other types of public nuisance offenders. At last report, 20 percent of the jail population is in alternative programs. In addition, the county executive charged the committee to develop programs for the transition of substance abuse offenders from the jail to the community.

While limiting jail usage, these programs have not reduced public safety and are considered an integral part of the county's public safety program. As Coleman (1998) reports, the King County jail system has never refused a misdemeanor booking or released an inmate early.

In this case study, involving key actors from the community, local government, and the criminal justice system can make a jail a rationally managed system that allocates jail space as a scarce resource without endangering public safety.

SUMMARY AND CONCLUSIONS

The management and administration of a local jail is a difficult job at best. The jail administrator must develop and maintain a network that supports the jail in performing its mission.

Jail administrators must take a proactive role in establishing and nurturing the networks and relationships with other system players in the jurisdiction to enhance the opportunities for the jail's success. Key to this process is the mutual understanding by members of the network of the issues, constraints, and problems that impact each of the elements of the network.

In the ideal situation, jails work with members of the system to arrive at mutually beneficial solutions to offender management issues while providing for public safety and supporting each agency or entity in the network. Examples from Flint, Michigan, and King County, Washington, provide models of forming these cooperative relationships that encourage an ongoing positive working environment for each agency in the network.

REFERENCES

Allen, H. E. and C. E. Simonsen. (1998). *Corrections in America,* 8th ed. Upper Saddle River, NJ: Prentice-Hall.

Carlson, P., and Garrett, J. S. (1999). *Prison and Jail Administration: Practice and Theory.* Gaithersburg, MD: Aspen Press.

Center for Effective Public Policy. (1993, October). *The Intermediate Sanctions Handbook: Experiences and Tools for Policymakers.* Washington, DC.

Coleman, R. (1998). "A Cooperative Corrections Arrangement: A Blueprint for Criminal Justice in the 21st Century." *Corrections Now,* 3(1).

Inciardi, J. A. (1996). *Criminal Justice,* 5th ed. Fort Worth, TX: Harcourt, Brace College Publishers.

Irwin, J. (1985). *The Jail: Managing the Underclass in American Society.* Berkeley: University of California Press.

Jerrell, J. and Komisaruk, R. (1991). "Public Policy Issues in the Delivery of Mental Health Services in a Jail Setting." In J. A. Thompson and G. L. Mays, *American Jails: Public Policy Issues,* 100–115. Chicago: Nelson-Hall Publishers.

Kalinich, D., and Klofas, J. (1988). *Sneaking Inmates down the Alley.* Springfield, IL: Charles C. Thomas.

Kappeler, V. E., Blumberg, M., and Potter, G. W. (2000). *The Mythology of Crime and Criminal Justice,* 3rd ed. Prospect Heights, IL: Waveland Press.

Kerle, K. (1991). "Introduction." In J. A. Thompson and G. L. Mays, *American Jails: Public Policy Issues,* ix–xv. Chicago: Nelson-Hall Publishers.

Kerle, K. (1999). "Short Term Institutions at the Local Level." In P. Carlson and J. S. Garrett, *Prison and Jail Administration: Practice and Theory.* Gaithersburg, MD: Aspen Press.

Mays, G. L. and Thompson, J. A. (1991). "The Political and Organizational Context of American Jails." In J. A. Thompson and G. L. Mays, *American Jails: Public Policy Issues.* Chicago: Nelson Hall Publishers: 3–21.

Poole, E. and Pogrebin, M. (1998). "The Work Orientations of Jail Personnel: A Comparison of Deputy Sheriffs and Career Line Officers." *Policy Studies Review,* 7(3).

Steadman, H. et al. (1991). "Estimating Mental Health Needs and Service Utilization Among Prison Inmates." *Bulletin of the American Academy of Psychiatry and the Law,* 19(3): 297–307.

Stojkovic, S., Kalinich, D., and Klofas, J. (1998). *Criminal Justice Organizations: Administration and Management,* 2nd ed. Belmont, CA: Wadsworth.

Tonry, M., and Hamilton, K. (eds.) (1995). *Intermediate Sanctions in Overcrowded Times.* Boston: Northeastern University Press.